JUNGIAN SYMBOLISM
IN ASTROLOGY

Cover design by Ricardo Sasia

Back cover photo by W. A. Andersen

JUNGIAN
SYMBOLISM
IN
ASTROLOGY

Letters From An Astrologer

Alice O. Howell

*This publication made possible with
the assistance of the Kern Foundation*

The Theosophical Publishing House
Wheaton, Ill. U.S.A.
Madras, India / London, England

A Quest original. Second Printing, November 1987

The Theosophical Publishing House
306 West Geneva Road
Wheaton, IL 60187

A publication of the Theosophical Publishing House, a department of the Theosophical Society in America.

Credits

Thanks to the following publishers for permission to reproduce quotations from their works:

Collected Works of C. G. Jung, trans. R.F.C. Hull, Vols. 9 and 20. Copyright (c) by Princeton University Press. Excerpts reprinted with permission of Princeton University Press.

The I Ching Book of Changes. The Richard Wilhelm translation rendered into English by Cary E. Baynes, Bollingen Series XIX. Copyright 1950, (c) 1967, (c) 1977 renewed by Princeton University Press. Excerpt reprinted with permission of Princeton University Press.

Library of Congress Cataloging in Publication Data

Howell, Alice O., 1922-
  Jungian symbolism in astrology.
  (A Quest book)
  Bibliography: p.
  1. Astrology.   2. Symbolism   3. Psychoanalysis.
4. Jung, C. G. (Carl Gustav), 1875-1961.   I. Title.
BF1711.H64   1987   133.5   86-40406
ISBN 0-8356-0618-X (pbk.)

Printed in the United States of America

Contents

Foreword by Sylvia Brinton Perera, vii

Acknowledgments, xi

Introduction: The Quest, xiii

 1 The meaning of a chart, 1

 2 Pitfalls for the novice, 10

 3 Astrology and science, 19

 4 On causality and synchronicity, 29

 5 Ego and Self, 37

 6 Symbols as bringing together, 44

 7 Consciousness and symbols, 53

 8 How a chart speaks, 58

 9 From glyph to image, 67

10 The Sun, 74

11 The Sun in India, 84

12 The Sun in the birthchart, 90

13 The Feminine, 95

14 The Moon, 104

15 More on the Moon, and we meet Saturn, 112

16 Sun and Moon as the Royal Pair, 117

17 Mercurial Mercury, 125

18 Grounded Mercury, 132

19 Venus, 136

20 Mars, 146

21 Some problems with Mars, 157

22 Reflections on karma, synastry, and Jupiter, 164

23 Saturn, 174

24 The balance of Jupiter and Saturn, 180

25 Uranus, 188

26 Neptune, 196

27 More on Neptune, and we meet Pluto, 204

28 Envoi, 212

Bibliography, 213

Foreword
Sylvia Brinton Perera

The relevance of astrology's symbolism to the psyche is age-old. The energies of life described in planetary pictures and the synchronicitous patterning of human lives in tune with those energies have been objects of wonder and study since the first questioners began drawing parallels between macrocosmic and microcosmic cycles. In our century the great student of psychology Carl G. Jung was interested in astrology as it connected to his alchemical researches. Many of his followers, among them his daughter, began to bring the study of astrology together with the clinical practice of Analytical Psychology. And at present a growing number of Jungian analysts, as well as other health practitioners, consult with professional astrologers or work themselves with their clients' horoscope charts.

For some years I participated in a case study group, one member of which was an astrologer; the rest of us were psychotherapists and analysts. We learned from experience how helpful the birthchart is to objectify the patterns of energy and the given life problems and gifts with which a person has to deal. We found also that knowledge of current transiting planets in aspect with those birth patterns is very significant for our working with clients (and ourselves). It helps to know that at inevitable passages in development Uranus energy, for example, is shaking up old structures to bring new challenges and insights. Or Saturn is returning to depress and restructure. We, in our own lives, can become conscious of the influx of those transpersonal forces symbolized in planetary images. We can know when and even how long a particular issue may be foremost to be worked with, as well as with what previous cycles the current one reverberates.

Without some knowledge of astrology in that case study group, we would not have been able to communicate with one another as we did. We had to begin by learning planetary symbolism before we could proceed, becoming acquainted with the signs, aspects, and all of the hundred or so factors which interrelate in any birthchart.

This book provides a rich introduction to the understanding of astrology, inviting and companioning the reader's approach to the depths which the planetary symbols reveal. Most importantly, Alice O. Howell has grounded her explanations of those symbols in examples from her personal life and from those of her clients during her many years as a professional astrologer. Thus she enables the reader to learn a style of bridging the transpersonal symbol to living human experiences. This is essential for the study of any symbol or symbol system or it remains an abstraction, a mere set of ungrounded word signs or "key words." Alice Howell shows how traditional understanding of the symbols can find root and current meaning when connected to personal experience of the energies that lie behind and come through the symbolic images themselves. She teaches us her particular way to meditate on the intersection of symbolic picture and living personal reality—to make astrology come alive.

Letters are an important way to share knowledge. Often, and perhaps especially for women, they enable (like private journals) the release of creativity from the perfectionist standards our inner judges set for us. The safety and intimacy of the personal bond woven by the shuttling back and forth of letters between friends makes a space on which a whole project may unfold. So these letters of Alice Howell's meditations on the symbolism of the planets became chapters in a book.

I was the original and fortunate recipient of these letters as Alice made her dream image a reality between us. I looked forward to each one and enjoyed getting to know my new friend as well as her views about the subject she explored. It is only another step to welcome you, a further reader, into the treasure house this book opens.

Acknowledgments

My heart opens in gratitude for all my teachers and their teachers, in turn, throughout the generations, the *catena aurae,* the Golden Chain. They form a lineage as potent, if not more so, than our physical parents. And every one of them suffered long on the Path to be there for us. May they be blessed, may we be worthy of them.

I also wish to express my deepest gratitude to the support early on from my friends, especially Brewster Beach, Sara Hopkins, Charles Newbery, Mary Lou Rude, James P. Samuels, Elaine Simard, and Rod Welles, and for the kind and wise words of Edward F. Edinger, Russell Lockhart, Nathan Schwartz-Salant, Edith Wallace, and Edward C. Whitmont. And, most particularly, thanks to my very dear, patient, and helpful husband Walter A. Andersen, and my friend and correspondent Sylvia Brinton Perera.

Introduction: The Quest

The format of this book came from a dream. I had long wanted to set down a few thoughts showing the connection between Carl Gustav Jung's archetypal processes in the psyche and the planetary ones in a person's chart, but I wished to avoid the formal approach of a text. The dream found me writing letters to a dear friend, who is also an analyst. So I called her to ask if I might attempt writing her and received a most enthusiastic response; over the months she encouraged me to believe in the dream. My dilemma was at first in writing of Jungian concepts, which she would know more about from clinical application than I. Such experience as I have comes from over forty years in the field of astrological rather than psychological analysis, and yet I began early on to see the connection.

I, like many others, got in touch with astrology at a critical juncture in my life. To many it comes as a last resort or at a moment that is just right. When this happens, the impact can be so powerful that it sounds like a great thunderclap crying AHA! Certainly, that's the way it came to me.

In my chart, I have the Sun in the Ninth House. The Ninth House has to do with interests in religion, philosophy, and travel, both literal and metaphoric. This may explain my early, if not somewhat precocious, hunger for God, which led me to astrology many years later. Perhaps having a clergyman for a grandfather helped too. Anyway, God must have been a household word. Perhaps I should share some of my experiences that culminated in the writing of this book.

For instance, when I was four and a half I went with my mother and nanny to spend the summer on Prince Edward Island, the birthplace of my grandfather Basil King. Even then I was wondering about God. I remember lying in the field on my back under the daisies, watching them criss-crossing each other as they nodded in the breeze. Above hung the great blue bell of the sky, and I was humming to myself. I remember a first intimation of something so right and so beautiful, it had to be what I was searching for.

From that fall on, due to my father's work, for the next eighteen years I traveled continuously with my parents and my nanny, living in hotels and attending various schools. We traveled through thirty-seven countries over the years. At one point when I was eight, I was dropped off at a boarding school in San Remo, Italy. My religious education began there, with catechism, church attendance three times on Sundays, and religion taught as literal fact. But by the time I was twelve I rebelled. We were in Portugal at the time. So I went to my mother and announced that no one in his or her right mind was going to convince me that some old snake hung on a tree and spoke English to Adam and Eve! Though Mother murmured it was more likely Hebrew, I firmly announced to her that from now on I was going to be an atheist. She sighed heavily and looked at me. "Well, dear, be a *good* one!"

My mother was wise and instead of trying to convert me suggested that, since Christianity was only one of several great religions, perhaps I might be interested in learning about some of the others. I was eager to begin. I'm glad I did. The exposure to a variety of symbols prepared the ground for my later work.

All along, you have to realize, we had been living constantly out of suitcases. I did not often have access to many books. I had cut my literary teeth on John Bunyan's *Pilgrim's Progress,* but very often I would lie on my mother's hotel bed reading what I called the "Bible Funny Papers." These were fascinating line drawings and reproductions in her Oxford edition of the King James version of the Bible. There were pictures of Egyptian gods and goddesses, hiero-glyphics, cuneiform, comparative alphabets, early Anglo-Saxon, Greek, and Hebrew parchments. For me they con-jured up something utterly magical and certainly rivaled the time spent with my mother's button box!

No doubt, this book had a further influence on me. At thirteen, I began a self-imposed study program that took me, chapter by chapter, through the Upanishads, the Dhammapada, the *Tao Teh Ching*, the Analects of Confu-cius, the *Life and Sayings of Gautama Buddha*, the Koran, the Zend-Avesta, Mary Baker Eddy's *Science and Health*, and for good measure, a repeat of the Old and New Testa-ment, all with arrogant and furious protestations in the margins. I plunged into Norse and Greek mythology, and spent my free time constructing a family tree of the gods that took up a 3x4 foot piece of wrapping paper and had lines of latitude and longitude for easy reference. In addi-tion, I continued, of course, to have formal Bible Studies and History in the upper grades of boarding school. I think I can truthfully say, without being immodest, that I knew more about the religions of the world than most young women of my age, which was then about twenty.

By the time the war had broken out and we had been forced to return to the States from Switzerland, I had moved on to St. Ignatius, William James, and Freud. But to tell the truth, I was still miserable. I knew an enormous number of facts but was not one step further along. I had still experienced nothing. Certainly, I had fallen in and out of love, been hurt and disappointed and heart-broken, but the love of my life, God, still eluded me.

Finally there came a crisis—I still call it "The Attack of the Visigoths." My parents and I were living then in a hotel on Washington Square in New York. In a history book that I had been reading, a remark was made about the Visigoths and the fact that they had left hardly any trace of them-selves in terms of art or literature. In fact, all they had done was to destroy what culture there was. An absolutely terri-ble thought occurred to me: supposing I had once been a *good* (naturally!) Visigoth maiden and had done all that my parents had expected of me, been virtuous and obedient. WHO THE HELL CARED!!

Though I smile about this today, it was no laughing matter at the time. In tears of despair, I set forth on a walk from Washington Square to Battery Park. Every time I passed a church, I wanted to rush in and seize the priest, force him into a chair, and scream at him, "Explain this!"

I got down to the Battery and walked all the way back, ending up at the Church of the Ascension on Fifth Avenue and 10th Street. It was already late at night, but it was open all night in those days. I sobbed in a back pew, angry at God, angry and bitter with myself for having wasted so many hours reading all those stupid books. I still wanted God with all my heart.

The very next day the phone rang and a friend of my father's was on the line suggesting that he take my father to meet a marvelous astrologer who might prove helpful to him. My father was in considerable distress, himself, at this time.

The astrologer was called Hermes and he lived on Prince Street in Greenwich Village. When my father returned from seeing him, he was visibly shaken and affected, and he absolutely insisted that my mother and I go to see him. He had made an appointment for us the very next morning. I protested, for I was to have a fitting for my wedding dress. (I was engaged at the time to a farmer whom I had met in Manitoba the previous summer, much to the concern of both my parents.)

My father's wishes prevailed, and so duly next day we were off to see this wizard. At the time, astrology was one thing I had not studied and knew nothing about. My acquaintance with it was limited to the short paragraphs describing the signs' characteristics in a five-year diary I had as a child. Consequently I took a rather scornful attitude toward it, and teased my father about being taken in by such superstitious nonsense intended only for ignorant nincompoops. My father grinned and said, "You'll see." In retrospect, I'm glad it happened that way. It has made me much more tolerant and understanding of many people's scepticism; in fact, I have great sympathy with them.

So there I was, heading down Macdougal Street somewhat impatiently, humoring my credulous parents. But I owed it to them, as my father was going through a severe reactive depression and had taken to drink and to dreadful outbursts of weeping. (He was a Pisces.) My mother was going through hell. This has not been the only time in my life when the most dreadful outer circumstances have led to the most wonderful consequences. "Wo aber Gefahr ist, wächst das Rettende auch," wrote Georg Friedrich Hölderlin. (Rescue grows close to danger.) At any rate, little did I know as I walked through the slums of Little Italy with my mother that morning that the course of my life would change entirely.

I confess that my intellectual arrogance and scepticism were always demanding proof. I am a Scorpio with the Moon in Virgo. I was not content just to believe, and I felt that the faith of my elders was either misplaced or hypocritical. Thus I suffered. I remember the last two lines of a poem that I wrote when I was fifteen. It was about Jesus.

> I do not believe, I cannot believe
> Yet I am a stone his tears fell upon.

Suddenly as we walked down Macdougal Street I recalled an incident that happened in Belgium the summer that I was thirteen. We were staying at a hotel in Nieuport-Bains. It was a big old-fashioned hotel that had a large open stairwell overlooking its lobby. It had again been a bleak time with no one my own age to talk to, but my father had given me a science book about atoms and molecules and the fairly recent new theory that all matter is energy. I remember sitting on my bed when a great AHA struck me: perhaps this underlying energy was God! As this thought dawned on me, it carried with it an enormous certainty. I began physically to tremble with excitement, my chest filled with gasping excitement; I was afraid and I was in awe. It came like a stunning revelation. I remember running out onto the landing and leaning over the bannister, wanting to share the idea with the world: *everything, everything is God!* At the same time, I realized that there was no one I could tell this to who would understand. They would just think I was a crazy child. I watched the *concierge* sorting some mail and then turned back to go to my room. I threw myself on the bed and wept.

Then another memory popped up from another time, even earlier, when I was ten and lying out in a field near the Swiss school I was attending. With me was a classmate whose name was Dorothy. The sky was thickening with stars, and we were solemnly discussing our future. "What do you want to do when you grow up?" she asked me. "I want to unite science and religion," I replied modestly. As silly as that sounds coming from a child, I even now remember saying it, so the seeds of my agnosticism were already there, sprouting those unanswerable questions that were to continue plaguing me. I promptly began writing a book entitled *The World as it is and the World as it ought to be,* alas, now lost to posterity! Its first line was, "A fish has no neck nor any voice at all." Pity, that.

Did these memories presage the understanding that was to come? Anyway, after a hot walk my mother and I arrived at Prince Street and stood before a narrow three-story building. It looked dilapidated. When we walked in, the place smelled of clorox and roses. The stairs were painted white, and an Italian woman was on all fours scrubbing them clean. She made way for us to climb to the top floor and to the door, which was promptly opened by Hermes himself.

And there he stood, a tall, handsome, imposing blond man with strange and penetrating blue eyes. (A Leo with Libra rising, Aug. 14, 1908.) He wore a black suit, a white shirt, and a tie. His office was taken up mainly by a large flat-topped desk. Behind him were shelves filled with books, many by then already familiar to me. This was reassuring, at least we had the same tastes. Quickly glancing at the two of us, he decided to do my mother's chart first, so I was ushered into another small room at the front of the house. He closed the door and left me to observe the first home I had ever visited in New York City.

I waited for over an hour. When Hermes finally summoned me from my reflections, I discovered that my mother had left, so I had no way of reading her face to see how things had gone. Also now, as he told me with a grin, we had unlimited time.

Hermes drew up my chart on a piece of plain paper using a compass and a ruler, while I thought about the Masonic emblem. He did it swiftly and silently. Then he reached for some small books of reference, his Ephemerides, which contained the positions of all the planets on my birthday, November 13, 1922. Then he asked me the time of my birth, which was 12:45 p.m., and the place where I was born. I told him it was 1 Berkeley Street, Cambridge, Massachusetts, at the home of my grandfather Basil King. He smiled and told me that he now had all the information he needed. He pulled out a Table of Houses, did some more calculations, glancing up quickly every now and then with a gleam in his eye. By then I was both nervous and greatly intrigued.

I realize now that all this is part of the process. This was a *rite d'entree* for him, and he was using the time to get an intuitive sense of how conscious I was of what was going on. On my side, curiosity was replacing my skepticism. How could those incomprehensible squiggles on that piece of paper represent me? Before I could say anything, he leaned back in his chair, put his big fingers together and tapped them a few times, and began his interpretation.

Needless to say, he was an extraordinary astrologer and, as I was to discover later, an exceptional man. Certainly, I was fortunate to have fallen into his hands. He knew better than to start by flattering me with generalities and went straight to the point of my deepest quest and the barrier of my intellectual arrogance. The more he talked, the more devastated I became. All the pride of a twenty-one year old convinced that no one could be capable of understanding her vanished into thin air. He penetrated my soul deftly, humorously, and not in the least unkindly. In fact, his eyes sparkled, almost as if he had been waiting for me to show up all his life. As for my upcoming marriage, he dismissed it with a wave of the hand, indicating that such a marriage would be a total disaster, especially for the man himself, and that I had fulfilled my function of initiating him into the world of the feminine of which he knew nothing.

The fact that my fiancé had already left on the bus to come east made no impression on Hermes. It simply was not right and therefore would not happen. A calamity could be averted to everyone's benefit, providing I woke up in time. The more Hermes talked, the more insightful he became, and the more I began to wonder and question the basic premise of astrology. What was there on that simple piece of paper that gave him access to my deepest and innermost being? It was not just the personal implications of what he was saying but the spiritual implications that were blowing my mind. What he was implying was that something is connecting the furthest reaches of the solar system with my innermost being, and everyone else's, and that though there is ever an enormous amount of suffering in life, it has a purpose and a time and possible solution. I felt humiliated and exalted at one and the same time.

We stopped for tea, which he served in some exquisite bone china cups, and I kept up my barrage of questions. Was this, indeed, the proof that I had been searching for? At that time I had totally forgotten about the order of the universe, so overwhelmed was I with my own disorder. He asked me how I supposed I had been led by destiny to his door on this very day, when Uranus was squaring its own place, to encounter the very thing that could, if studied and applied, begin to prove to me that some answers did exist, had always existed, and were only kept from me by my own limitations. (As Heraclitus sighed, "How many things are lost through disbelief!") The air around us pulsated and intensified, and it seemed to me as if during these few hours he was genuinely devoting himself to saving me from my own foolishness. Something was ringing true, and convincing me that my prayer had been heard.

Hours flew by, the windows darkened, and we talked on. He had removed his jacket and tie, and his hair fell out of place, giving him a boyish look. He was utterly charming as well as wise, and I began to realize that I had never known such a person could even exist, so different was he from all the men I had met. Finally, he stood up and announced that he would walk me back to the hotel, but made me promise that I would return on Thursday.

Two days and nights went by, and I sweated things out. When I arrived at Prince Street on Thursday, he had a client. Again I was led into the other room. After what seemed an eternity, Hermes came in. He set the table and lit a candle and invited me to sit down before he said gently, "Tell, me, what have you decided?" I told him that I had decided not to get married. I still remember looking up at his face through my tears.

As if it wasn't enough to find a man like Hermes, four days after we met, I met his teacher. This was an older man, one whom I refer to only as M. Not that I wish to make a mystery of it, but it was his wish to remain totally anonymous, and though he is no longer in this world, I feel obliged to honor this.

He invited me to his "lab" to have a conversation. This was on the second floor of the building on Prince Street where Hermes lived. It was simply furnished but had an extraordinary feeling to it. The minute you entered you began to shimmer inside. My first impression was of a noble-looking, most dignified white-haired man. I had no clue as to who he was or what he was. I remember his looking into the palm of my hand and then deep into my eyes and smiling a smile so rare that he made me feel as if I were some long-lost daughter returned to him at last. Strength and love and severity were all somehow mixed in him. I could not get him out of my mind. He turned my life around in every sense.

M was not an astrologer but more a spiritual mentor, yet he encouraged me to further my studies of astrology. So it was in response to this that I began to study with Marc Edmund Jones, the winter and spring of 1944-45. This was a great privilege.

The classes were held on West 57th Street in New York and consisted of a small group of students. I remember that

I was by far the youngest in the group. I was very shy and so sat at the back of the class, taking copious notes. My impression of Jones was that he certainly was one of those who lived astrology and saw its vast potential to shed light on the meaning of life. He was a serious, gifted, and thorough teacher. His lessons were mimeographed, and I treasure to this day my collection of them.

With the agonies of the Visigoth maiden over, as well as the crisis of the wedding (the farmer soon met and married another), I put my energies enthusiastically into this new direction. My lessons with Marc Edmund Jones gave me the foundation for endless and fruitful conversations with Hermes, and I began to learn almost by osmosis. A romance blossomed, and then died out, but he opened new vistas for me that still profoundly affect my life. I will always be grateful to him.

I became quite interested in alchemy about that time and copied a dictionary of alchemical symbols which I found in a reserved section of the New York Public Library. I decided to conduct an experiment in which I would build up a layer of lead, tin, iron, copper, silver, and gold. So I ransacked the city to find a small sheet of each. This took me to some strange places, indeed. But when it came to pure gold, I decided to pan for it in my bathtub, having bought a bag of earth containing gold dust. I actually did find the bits of gold, but the cost of the plumbing bill ran higher than the gold. At that time, and at that age, I was game for almost anything. This exploration of alchemy became meaningful much later when I encountered Jungian psychology. My search for God had somehow led me to astrology, but it was many years before Jung entered my life.

I had heard of Jung already in 1939 when we were in Switzerland during the early days of World War II. A friend of my mother's was in analysis with him, and his name came up at a luncheon in St. Gallen. The famous psychiatrist sounded so interesting that the name stuck in my memory. It is tantalizing to me to realize when I read his works today that I spent much of my childhood within a two-hour drive from him in a German-speaking Swiss school. In *Memories, Dreams, and Reflections,* Jung describes going along a path in a field when he was eleven and walking out of a mist into knowing who he was. I know exactly the kind of path it must have been, how the grass smelt, and how the clouds swung over the mountains.

I had to wait years to be ready for Jung, and it took another crisis—one of the worst—to force me to reach out to his work on a shelf in the East Meadow Public Library.

I should pause to give homage to this library—it was the source of over twenty years study for me. My husband worked mostly at night. With the children in bed, I turned quite naturally to my favorite occupation of reading, but I did not just read. I studied, and I took notes. I did this because I really enjoyed it and not because I was cramming for exams or good reports. These years plus the previous twenty gave me a good foundation for the schoolteaching I was subsequently called to do. I read histories, biographies, classics, plays, novels, trash, poetry, psychology, education, and, of course, religion. Reading provided an oasis for me in a neighborhood where only two people out of sixty-five had been to college. It was a new experience to have neighbors, all of them naturally proficient at housekeeping. These were my years immured in walls of peanut butter, so to speak, in a tiny development house with four children and with a craftsman husband so introverted that we never once went out to dinner in seventeen years!

The crisis I mentioned had to do with my husband's frustration and his thwarted career. He began to suffer outbursts of rage and abnormal behavior which bordered on the psychotic. We lived literally from hand to mouth and sometimes on the charity of friends and relations, so the seeking of professional help was out of the question. I knew something was terribly wrong, so I went to my friend the library, headed for the psychology section, and came home, at last, with my first volume of Jung. Ironically, when I gave a lecture to a Grand Rounds in Psychiatry at the East Meadow Hospital, some fifteen years later, I passed that little house on the way. How little we know what lies in store for us!

In *The Gospel According to Thomas* are the following words: "Jesus said, 'If you bring forth what is within you, what you bring forth will save you. If you do not bring forth what is within you, what you do not bring forth will destroy you.' " Coming to Jung's work at this juncture in my life brought this home. It was not unlike finding a savior in the Tenth Ring of the Inferno. While it did not solve my husband's problems, it opened a way of redemption for me.

I spent hours and hours reading and studying and absorbing Jung's thought, always with an intense sense of personal excitement and exultation. What he said made sense, and on so many different levels. And, of course, I kept seeing the parallels to the premises and foundations of astrology. Shock after shock of recognition floated up off the pages. One of the biggest came when I stumbled onto the fact that Jung respected astrology and had even conducted some statistical experiments with it. Today, I sincerely believe that if Jung had not chosen to put alchemy first in his studies, he might have hastened the understanding of the new purpose and function of astrology. But as it is, he was a man far ahead of his time, and we should appreciate his enormous integrity and courage in taking a public stand on behalf of a discipline considered by his peers to be superstitious nonsense. Every serious astrologer stands in his debt, as does every analyst.

I believe that Jung's tolerance was based on his conviction that, if the collective unconscious had brought forth astrology (and alchemy) down through the centuries, it must have arisen from the human psyche, and thus it deserves serious attention. This kind of tolerance was what was sadly lacking in the clergy of Galileo's time and in the consortium of scientists who attacked astrology not so long ago.

The second major shock was more personal. It came from the frontispiece of *The Secret of the Golden Flower*. This is a picture of a Tibetan *tanka* or wall hanging used for meditation, one belonging to Jung himself. Its twin was hanging in my bedroom right there on Long Island! Mine was identical in every respect, with the exception of the arrangement

of the *dorjes*, the lightning bolts, in the center. My tanka
had been given to me by a friend of my mother's, who had
purchased it in Peking, before World War I. I had always
loved Tibetan tankas, and I even remember cutting some
out of *Life Magazine* when I was fifteen and mounting
them on oil cloth to hang on my wall at boarding school.
The frontispiece truly excited me and made me feel somehow deeply connected to Jung. I resolved to write him, to
send him a photo of my tanka, and to thank him for all the
help I had received through his books. Alas, I lacked the
courage and vacillated too long. He died. Now I sometimes
feel that my life is the letter that I am writing to him. As to
the tanka, I still have it. When I went to Dharamsala in
northern India, the seat of the exiled Tibetan government, I
took a photo of it with me. There I was told that mine was
a meditation on the active path of knowledge, and that
Jung's was on the passive path of knowledge.

Finally, after leaving my marriage of twenty-six years, I
encountered the marvelous book *Ego and Archetype* by Edward F. Edinger. This book affected me so profoundly that
I *did* write the author. He responded, which helped and encouraged me immensely. But it took twenty years from the
time I first began to read Jung to the moment I actually
met another Jungian in the flesh.

I do not want to give the impression that I read all of
Jung and grasped all he had to say. Every time I pick up his
work, I see more and more of what I missed the last time.
As with astrology, Jung has to be lived. We read only who
we are at any given moment. But the impact of this man's
work upon my own life and thought has been radical, to say
the least, as I know it has been for so many others. Step by
step, I began to climb up out of my largely self-imposed
darkness. So enclosed had my life been that my alchemical
process during those years could be described as *in cementio*.

Aside from my personal growth, what emerged for me in
reading Jung was the deep connection between his
psychology and astrology and the implications of a wholly
new approach to the understanding of the individual
horoscope. Jung likened the individual psyche to "the king-

dom of heaven which is within," which Christ spoke of. Jung also perceived that every psyche contains archetypal contents in common with all others and he saw myths as dealing with these at a collective level. Then, after many years of careful study, he put forth his monumental concept of the collective unconscious.

Today there is a growing number of psychotherapists interested and proficient in astrology, as well as a growing number of astrologers seriously studying Jung. This is indeed heartening. Though it has been pioneering work for a relative few over the last fifty years, someday it may be a perfectly natural procedure for a therapist to consult the chart of a patient. This practice, by its very nature, could guarantee that Jung's concern with the spiritual dimension of growth would be included in therapy. He felt that therapy involved more, much more, than just restoring a person to mental health. He said flat out that he never saw a person truly healed without a religious experience. Nor should astrology be restricted only to psychology; it could serve all the helping professions, including pastoral counseling.

Why and how astrology connects to the spiritual dimension is the underlying thrust of this book. It is my prayer that these letters may bring anyone reading them a sense of the enormous value of this symbolic language of archetypal processes. One does not have to become either an astrologer or a therapist per se to use this universal key to the wonder of leading what Jung called a symbolic life. It is the power of the symbol to connect the individual to the universal and the known to the open-ended mystery of the human psyche and to the unknown cosmos itself.

1
The meaning of a chart

Dear friend,

Thank you for your invitation to put down a few personal reflections and memories on the subject of astrology. I am so happy that you are interested in seeing the potential of astrology to serve psychotherapy!

Astrology has a fascinating history, and it has been evolving as we evolve. Now it is beginning to emerge as a potentially valuable adjunct to psychotherapy. Just as an X-ray can reveal a fractured bone, so the chart can function as an X-ray for the psyche. Neither can heal per se, but both can show the direction to understanding the nature of a problem and the way to healing and growth. It is for this reason that I am so delighted that you as an analyst and a psychotherapist are venturing forth, along with others, with an open mind.

Jung's courageous viewpoint was that if such disciplines as astrology and alchemy emerged from the collective psyche, they are worth another look, and, as you know, he became fascinated with both, recognizing their validity when viewed as symbolic languages of psychological processes. Though he spent more time on alchemy in his public writings, he also spent time on statistical experiments involving astrology, and he actually consulted his patients' charts when he deemed it appropriate. His daughter Gret Baumann-Jung is a lifelong and distinguished astrologer in Switzerland.

The acceptance of astrology has been slow. There are still a great deal of negative associations, ignorance, and the like surrounding just the word. Yet I have been invited to lecture at the Grand Rounds of three hospitals to groups of psychiatrists in London, in California, and in New York. And I have taught several psychiatrists, psychologists, and analysts, and many refer their patients to me. This is true of a growing number of analysts and astrologers. We now have an Association for Astrology and Psychology founded in New York City by a psychiatrist, Dr. Bernard Rosenblum. So you are not alone in your exploration.

I'll look forward to your questions and will answer them as well as I can. Let me start right off with your first: *What does a birthchart or horoscope mean to you?*

A chart, to me, yields a description of how a person is likely to process experience. As Carl Jung wrote, "In the end, all reality is psychic reality." In view of this, astrology does not (in the case of an individual horoscope) describe the actuality of a situation but rather how each person would tend to respond to it. This is the reason that an astrologer can describe the father or mother of the client, for instance, because the description will fit the client's perception of that person.

For example, suppose that you have two brothers and a sister and that the four of you had the same parents, grew up in the same home, and attended the same schools. Would you not agree that, despite this, each of you is different? Further, suppose that today someone asked each of you to write a personal description of your father, your mother, your home and schooling. Would you not agree that each of these would turn out to be different? Imagine then that these descriptions were given to your parents to read. Might not each be quite stunned and exclaim, "But that's not the way I really am!"

This little exercise can be extended to every part of our experience, helping us to realize that we are all projecting a reality of our own onto the outer world, in fact, co-creating a microcosmic universe of experience or that "kingdom of heaven" within, which is unique despite the fact that it is shared with others.

This is the paradox the pre-Socratic philosopher Heraclitus

described when he wrote, "With our eyes open we share the same world, but with our eyes closed each of us enters his own world." I always begin my classes by having everyone stand in a circle holding hands while I quote this. From the astrological point of view, this demonstrates most effectively, both physically and geometrically, that though each of us shares the same circle, no two occupy the same position on that circle; thus each processes the experience from a different perspective. From Jung's point of view of individuation, you can see that the perspective of each in the circle adds to the collective experience of the whole, and that our individual experience and consciousness enrich the collective unconscious.

Whenever possible, I try to demonstrate principles of astrology using the whole body. Astrology involves the total person and is never to be learned only with the head. So this simple exercise becomes profoundly symbolic.

The natal chart of a person demonstrates this paradox as well. *Every* chart has the same ingredients: Sun, Moon, planets, etc., but no two are alike. As Martin Buber remarked, "God never repeats Himself."

I hear your next question: *What of twins born the same instant?* Well, there are consanguinous twins and astrological twins. The same holds true for both: though they may have almost identical charts, the contents of the life which they have to process will differ, so the final outcome will too. Some valuable studies have been made in this area. There is a striking account of synchronicities in the lives of some astrological twins in the book *The Case for Astrology* by John Anthony West and Jan Gerhard Toonder.

What we see is who we are. Who we are determines what we see. This also implies some significant limitations. There will always be projection involved in our perceptions. We cannot see things as they really are, as Immanuel Kant discovered and explained when he wrote about "das Ding an sich" (the thing in itself) in his *Critique of Pure Reason.* I remember a fascinating conversation I had with an eight-year-old on the subject of color. How could she be sure that the color blue was blue and not red? Maybe what I called blue was really red to her. I put forth the evidence of the spectrum and that each color has certain measurable frequencies, and I talked of the structure of the human eye, but she remained sceptical, and I can see why. Short of climbing into each other's heads, we can never really know. What Kant was saying, as I understand it, was that we can never really know this stone in front of us; we can only know our version of this stone. Jung extended this to one's image of God and always tried to refer to God as the *imago dei* or the image-of-God-as-it-seems-to-me, since the god that can be known is not God. More recently, theoretical physicists are maintaining that the observer and the observed mutually affect each other. This raises an interesting theological aside: Does humanity affect God? Is it a two-way street? Both Jung and Edward F. Edinger have written eloquently on this point.

Philosophically, the chart tells us that all we can really know is modified by ourselves. So, "Know thyself!" Yet that, too, can be tricky since the minute we try to do this, we split ourselves into subject and object. The poor ego gets tied up in knots and tautologies. What we *can* do, however, is to experience life, which is different from thinking about it. Experience is unitive, thinking by its very nature is fragmenting. What the chart does is describe the ways in which we are likely to experience, and because this can be quite accurate, it can help us become more *conscious* of how we tend to see things. The next step, obviously, once we are more conscious, is to realize that we don't have to do it only this way, but have free will and free choice. We can use our newly-won understanding to guide us to new growth. In other words, from a psychological point of view, much of what the chart points to is our habitual or unconscious way of reacting to things. Analysis would bring this out over a period of time, but I am sure you can see that the chart can be a most immediate and helpful diagnostic tool both for the analyst and the analysand, to say nothing of those interested in getting to know themselves better. In that way, the chart becomes a guide to self-acceptance and self-realization. Not all pain can be avoided, but much can be mitigated when we confront our problems within the psyche. It is only when we remain unconscious of our problems or stubbornly refuse to deal with them that we are forced to confront them in our outer lives as events.

So often we sigh and wish that circumstances were different. If only they were, then we could change! Jung reverses this by stating that if we change our consciousness, the circumstances will take care of themselves. This means, of course, taking responsibility for our consciousness and giving up the constant projecting of blame onto others or upon the outer environment. I know this to be true because I have experienced it both ways. Just when you are convinced that nothing you do within yourself can make a difference, but you do it anyway to the best of your consciousness, then the miracles occur. They do. They really do. One has to trust the process, which I suppose is another way of defining faith.

You might want an example. Take someone with Saturn in the Seventh House. (If this makes no sense yet, don't worry, it will.) Such a person, either man or woman, will more than likely expect and introject negative criticism from others. From childhood such a person would be likely to build up a defense mechanism and an instinctive ability to "psych out" other people—parents, siblings, other children, relatives, or strangers—to anticipate criticism and protect the ego. Later in life, the person may have difficulties in relationships and feel lonely and suspicious. The skill of psyching out others may go too far, even lead to perceiving criticism when it isn't there.

Perhaps some with Saturn in the Seventh House would seek professional help, or perhaps some ego-surrender would be demanded by life through a crisis. Either way, if the person is able to become conscious of this attitude of introjecting criticism and become able to sacrifice the use of the process of Saturn in ego-defense, a breakthrough can occur. And the best surprise is that the *skill* of psyching out others remains, but now it can be put to use in serving others rather than shutting them out. A person with Saturn in the Seventh House can develop extraordinary sensitivity in

5

perceiving other people's pain and needs. In responding to these, he or she will begin to find a new self-worth and an ability to love and reach out to others.

I can't resist interpolating a true story about a woman who had remarried ten years after an unhappy marriage of almost thirty years had ended in divorce. She married a widower who had had a very happy marriage but lost his wife to an illness. The new marriage was a blissful one and naturally entailed the merging of household goods. In time, the wife got a job which required her leaving her husband alone one night a week. This meant he had to cook his own supper on that night.

Several weeks went by, and each night when the wife returned from work, she observed that her husband had not touched any of her utensils, nary a dish nor a pot nor even the silverware. The wife began to wonder if he didn't like her things. The following week she began to wonder if this was her husband's private little ritual to remember happy times with his first wife. The next step, of course, would be to become jealous and resentful. Fortunately, this woman had been in analysis and knew her own capacity for negative introjections. All she had to do was ask. "How come, dear, every night I go to work, you never use any of my things, only yours?" The husband beamed and gave her a big hug. "Why, I use my things, dear heart, because yours are so beautiful, and I am afraid of my own clumsiness in the kitchen. I'm so afraid I might break something!" A little self-knowledge, confessed the woman, saved the night.

As you can see, I approach the birthchart mainly from a psychological point of view, because we are the sum of our reality at any given time. Whether we believe in astrology or not, the chart still operates. What a pity to ignore or reject such a gift from the universe. It is, *in potentia*, a treasure map to the individuation process or greater awareness of the Self, and I am using Self in Jung's definition of the word as meaning the center and totality of the psyche. The chart will impel us unconsciously, as do our complexes, until we become more conscious. Thank goodness

6

that a new generation is arising in this New Age that is more comfortable with and receptive to such a guide.

One more remark, before I close. To me the chart is a *temenos*, a sacred precinct, a holy place, because it describes most certainly a place where God dwells in us as a Divine Guest. "God lives in you as You," as Swami Muktananda used to say. The Christ Within, the Atman, the Self, these are all terms pointing to an unfathomable mystery, which is what the psyche remains. Be humble, then, and in awe when you look at a chart, yours or anyone else's. It is a map to the kingdom of heaven which is within and a symbolic depiction of limitless potential. No astrologer can define another person; our task is always to point, no more, no less.

I am appalled sometimes at the damage that can be done by astrologers who have no understanding of psychology and who are free with "predictions" and sow seeds of doubt and fear in their clients. Fortunately, their number is few, and real efforts are being made by reputable astrologers to form self-regulating associations with a true sense of ethics and insight.

Very often, too often, astrologers as well as therapists are apt to fall into their own jargon and speak of their clients and patients in a patronizing way. People become "cases," and the professional falls into what Martin Buber called an "I-It" attitude rather than one of "I-Thou." This is all too human and deplorable and the bane of many professions, including teaching. We tend to forget that God dwells in the client as well as in us, even though, let's face it, sometimes that's mighty hard to believe!

Now computers are in the act—how Aquarian can we get? They are absolutely marvelous, but they are not human—yet. As Arthur Koestler remarked, "Computers don't bleed." A computer can set up a chart more quickly and more accurately than can a human being, but a computer can never tell at what level of consciousness a chart is being lived. Nor can an astrologer or a therapist do more than attempt such an evaluation. A map is not the territory,

7

and you can't eat a menu. As Jung said of psychology, it is as good as the awareness of the psychologist. We are all limited by our own amount of experience and consciousness. What matters is not what we know but *who we are* at any given moment. This is hard to remember in a society that places such a high premium on what we know and so little on the knower.

Forgive me for starting out with such a philosophical letter when perhaps what you had in mind was the nuts and bolts of the subject, but the premise of astrology is a tremendous prerequisite and may require even more attention.

M, my teacher, made a few remarks to me when I was twenty-one and starting out eagerly to become an astrologer, over forty-three years ago. This is what he said:

1) Do not assume that astrology is just a subject in which you have a certain number of facts to remember and understand. It is not like that at all. The number of facts is inverse to the infinite number of variations in which they appear.

2) Know that astrological study involves a spiritual dimension, since it mediates between inner and outer worlds, and that its practice is for guidance and healing. Know also that there will be tests along the way when you will be sorely tempted to use it for personal advantage or for the manipulation of others. The misuse of astrology is a form of "black magic" (we might say a psychological crime today) and this is one of the reasons that the Church once turned against it.

3) Know that as you learn, you will be required to apply what you have learned and to share this wisely. So be quite certain this is something that you wish to commit yourself to because it will change your life and the way you approach life and the very mystery of Spirit itself. It has to be lived to be understood.

To you, as a Jungian analyst, this can come as no surprise, but for me these seemed very solemn and heavy admonitions at the time. I saw them as a form of Hippocratic Oath, and my teacher made me think about them quite a while before he would take me on. Looking back, I see how very important those warnings were. Once a woman desperately in love, I almost fell into the temptation, of misusing what I knew, and only those wise words protected me, much to my eventual benefit. The warning applies, I think, to all the healing professions, and points to their ever-present Shadow, as Guggenbühl-Craig has discussed in his *Power and the Helping Professions*.

I'm sitting out in our gazebo as I write, looking over the lawn in the late afternoon sunshine, and the leaves on the trees are all waving encouragement. I am so grateful to you for your letter of inquiry—it both forces me and enables me to bring together some of the odd bits and pieces of reflections I have gathered over the years about a subject which, I suppose, I really have lived.

I wish you nothing but the best as you undertake this new study. But please remember that I cannot teach anyone how to become an astrologer. I can only encourage you to become an astrologer in your own way. That is the only right way. Keep sending questions!

Love to you,

2
Pitfalls for the novice

Dear friend,

So your next question is: *What are some of the pitfalls for the beginning astrologer?* That is indeed a good question. Naturally, there are quite a few pitfalls, and they range from the psychological to the practical. Let me start with the former and end with the latter.

As you know, I had to establish for myself that absolutely and without a doubt a cosmic and divine order does exist. (How foolish this sounds, but "the ocean is not worried by the drop's philosophy!") I had come to the sad conclusion that there was no answer to such questioning. After I met my teacher Hermes, I knew, because I had experienced a glimmer of it, that there *is* an answer. I may never know that answer. It is sufficient for me today to know that an answer exists. On this I stake my life. At the ego level, no one can know the fullness of that Self which dwells in the Unconscious. To know it truly exists may well be sufficient.

I resolved solemnly to study astrology. That was the beginning. Also, after I got to know my teacher, I solemnly vowed to "go on the Path." These were intense days of spiritual excitement and stress, as you can imagine. Within a week I fell into at least two pits.

Most of us assume that when a person truly decides to go on the Path there will be rejoicing in the celestial regions. Perhaps a few trumpets will sound and a red carpet will be rolled out to welcome us. That I was inflated would be an understatement. I was filled with a renewal of spirit, a zeal,

10

a joy, a determination to accomplish everything all at once to make up for lost time. My experience of going on the Path, was, by hindsight, pretty funny. I found out that the Path begins with a pile of you-know-what. I can honestly say that the external difficulties which beset me from that day forward continued apace for the next thirty years. This is neither the time nor the place for an autobiography, so all I can say is that Jung was right about alchemy: we all start out with the *massa confusa* or the confrontation of previous mistakes. Some would say the mistakes of lifetimes. Anyway, I have no regrets. I consider myself so blessed in having been given the opportunity early in this life to get going, but it is, as you very well know yourself, a difficult process. Our complexes, as Jung says, have to be drunk to the last dregs.

The biggest pitfall for me, astrologically, was fear. During those first numinous days with my teacher, I had experienced certainty at one level. Soon I was beset by doubts on another. As I said, we live our everyday lives mainly with our ego. So I would look at my chart, or those of others when I got to be that proficient, and be filled with fear. I would see the potential for catastrophe, and I would doubt my ability to know what to say and how to say it to others. I came to know that transits (aspects to the natal chart formed by the planets on a daily basis) always work out. What I did not know, and could not know, was at what level they would be experienced. The same process that governs a serious accident operates when you drop a plate. The texts of those days were still almost medieval in their approach. Things were labeled bad or good, malefic or benefic. The assumption was entirely one of "stellar influence" with emphasis on predictions. So I had no sense that many aspects can be addressed inwardly in the psyche and thus need not necessarily be "acted out" in outer life, that, mercifully, we often have options. Nobody had told me this; I had to find it out the hard way.

In those days the bug-a-boo was Saturn. Here he comes, watch out! Poor Saturn, what blame is heaped upon his shoulders. But I still had not learned that the *archetype* of

Saturn has to do with the acquiring of wisdom, so I trembled along with everyone else.

So for me the first astrological pitfall was this fear and trembling, this negativity. The very certainty that astrology works, paradoxically, led straight to a limbo of doubts and speculations. I really think that every astrologer goes through this at the outset. We forget that the very fact that it works should lead us to trust the process, even when we don't understand it. This may sound like cold comfort, but it means that someone is running the store. Our misfortunes are not haphazard. At some level, they will lead to greater understanding. This is tantamount to saying that we know there is a Self, that Divine Guest, even though we feel at times cut off.

A good analogy is the experience of the absence of the Sun at night, and the certainty that we will see it again the next morning. And during the night, we always have the testament of the Moon, which is reflecting the Sun, however indirectly. Even clouds can cover the Sun and render it invisible. But I was far from seeing the solar system as a paradigm for the psyche. A little knowledge was proving to be a scary thing.

If pitfall number one was fear, pitfall number two was discrimination, or the lack of it. It took me many years of practice to learn that what the astrologer or therapist says is not necessarily what the client or patient hears. I knew nothing then, really, about projection, nor had I even the basic understanding that we always process experience according to our own psyche. Then I began to hear clients repeat something to me that I had patently never said. It began to dawn on me what a tremendous gap there can be in these areas of communication. Slowly, through the years, I learned from teaching children in school what I call the "Hum-dee-dum-dum Process."

I learned from my young students, confirming what I knew as a child myself, that true education proceeds only by fortuitous attacks of insight. I learned that it is virtually impossible for one person directly to teach another. Most of what we call education is merely instruction, the building in of rules or matters of rote. The very word *education* comes from the Latin words *ex-ducare*, to lead forth, and for that there has to be a "third," something extraneous. At best, the teacher can offer that something. I used to tell the children, "Hum-dee-dum-dum, there's something on the table." Hint, hint! Eager and astute students would pick up the point and realize it creatively by meeting the material with something pre-existent in themselves. Then followed the "Aha! I get it!" or that attack of insight which is a teacher's delight. I would make this an actual game in the classroom, and the students learned quickly to start looking for the clues when I would draw a deep breath and whisper mysteriously, "Hum-dee-dum-dum."

This is a familiar process to an analyst, and it can work wonders for an astrologer, since the chart itself, that magical piece of paper, is the tangible and visible third. It is a symbolic diagram lying between two people, which enables and gives permission to one to be who one is. It fairly sparkles with potentials for attacks of insight. It is a true invitation to growth, unfolding, and self-acceptance when skillfully presented, but never a *definition*. That would be instruction. It never works that way.

Free will consists in agreeing to become who one is. It comes through surrendering to the realization that we are created; we are yet another mask through which that Urge-to-Life we call Spirit is looking for consciousness. As the saying goes, "Every day is a gift from God. What we do with it is our gift to God." That would seem to be *our* creation.

So pitfall number two warns of our need for right discrimination in what we say and warns us not to say too much or too little. It points to the value of meeting clients at the level of their need and of trusting their capacity to hear what they need to hear, not what we think they should hear. I do not wish to scare would-be astrologers, simply to warn them of the damage that they can do if ignorant of this process. I imagine the same warning would apply to your analytic trainees. My teacher used to add the caution

13

that we become spiritually responsible for everything we say to a student or client. No wonder we need to pray for guidance!

For me, another of the hard pitfalls was the baffling realization that you cannot really study astrology. Studying from a book is the equivalent of studying how to cook without ever going into a kitchen. And, believe it or not, I tried that, too! In my early years of never living in a home, I would compensate by buying cookbooks. I would spend hours imagining cooking the recipes. I even cut out recipes from Swiss and French magazines, confident that I would get to try them. Yet when I was sixteen I was asked to boil some water on a stove, and I was afraid to leave the pot because I had read that things boil over.

This handicap about learning astrology kept tripping me up. I would forget that it had to be lived. I had always been a highly competent student and loved to study. Yet I realized every time I picked up an astrology text that the task was nigh hopeless—a matter of memorizing what seemed a great number of facts, the combination of which changed with every chart. At the very beginning, I had no teacher other than myself. The man I fondly call my teacher was a spiritual teacher, not an astrology teacher. Though I continued to have many interesting conversations with Hermes, he did not give me formal instruction. Eventually, I had the good fortune to study with Marc Edmund Jones.

These struggles alone may have paid off. There are very few mistakes I did not make, and this has helped me in teaching astrology in later years. There can be no "dumb" questions in any of my classes, no matter how foolish the student feels in asking. Each question gives another opportunity for an attack of insight. In fact, I profit from my experience in cooking (I have since learned how to boil water!) and use it as an example at the outset.

"Take two cups of flour, an egg, half a cup of sugar, some baking soda and vanilla....What am I on the way to making?" The answer will be a cake or some cookies. "How do you know that I am not making beef stew?" I ask, and they will take that, quite naturally, as an idiotic question, but I will persist. "Where is the flour? The eggs? Do you see any here?" No, of course not. We've done it all in our heads because we know about this from experience. However, if we were told to slice a gzompet very thinly and describe its aroma, we all would be in trouble. Thus it is with astrology: it has to be linked to what one already knows. And the splendid thing about this approach is that, of course, we all know quite a bit about many things. The psychotherapist, such as yourself, is already halfway there, being familiar with the concept of the psyche. The Jungian has even a greater advantage, being familiar with archetypes and archetypal processes. Since astrology has the capacity to connect almost anything with everything, it does not matter so much how one finds one's way in. Whether it's cooking, a business, medicine, botany, chemistry, or family life, the underlying processes will be the same. It is just a matter of recognizing them for what they are.

These archetypal processes have been around since the beginning of creation. Prehistoric people, and later people within history, began to recognize them and give them names and personifications. They became gods and goddesses, as we shall see.

In actuality, the basic "facts" of astrology are remarkably few, at least compared to many other disciplines. You certainly have to master the glyphs (symbols) of the planets and signs for these are the astrological alphabet. And you have to master the five variables: horoscope, planets, signs, aspects, and houses. These, indeed, have to be memorized and understood. This can be accomplished in about thirteen weeks by the average student. But mastering these basics will not make you an astrologer. The awful catch is that it is not what you know but who you are that counts! The same, of course, is true of any analyst. All of you, all of your experiences (the more, the better) go into who you are and how ready you are to practice your profession. It seems that all such knowledge enables us to communicate more widely with clients or patients, to hear them at their level, and to speak to them in their field. But, as Jung pointed out, we are all limited by the range of our experience, and one cannot take a patient where one has not been oneself. This could be downright discouraging. But for the astrologer there is some consolation in the wealth of images arising from the chart itself, and for the analyst, the wealth of images that come from a patient's dreams. These present, at least, the material that can be worked on. I confess I did a lot of praying when I started out, and I still do, both before and after seeing clients. Nowadays, some might argue that we are all drawing on insights gathered in former lives. This may be so, but we cannot yet really prove it. Remarks like that belong to the realm of esoteric astrology, and I hesitate to inject them here, when even accepting astrology itself is difficult for many people.

Another terrible pitfall for me was on the practical level, with the mathematics of setting up a chart. I struggled for three weeks, often in tears of frustration at my own stupidity. In those days we used logarithms. There were no computers. I do realize that for many this practice comes more easily. I had good days and days when my brain turned rapidly to cement. Having someone to guide me would certainly have helped, but I was obstinate and determined, and finally, using a number of different texts, managed to reason out what was going on. Nowadays, an astrologer does not even have to do the mathematics; one can send away to a computer service, which will be far more accurate, or even purchase one's own minicomputer.

I have noticed an interesting thing about astrologers. There are those who spend an enormous amount of time on preparation of the actual chart. It can be a beautiful production with colored lines and so forth. Or it can be a marvel of mathematical accuracy. Often, though not always, this is the greater strength of that astrologer and the gift of interpretation comes in second. For others, like Hermes, a few chicken scratches will do. You have to find the method that works best for you. I am certain that it has to do with one's typology in the Jungian sense. The sensation and thinking types will take great pains to be methodical, the feeling type will wait for the client, and the intuitive type, such as myself, will try to avoid doing the

16

chart ahead of time because the images will come prematurely and the client won't be there.

I, myself, now that I am capable of it (and I wasn't for quite a while) prefer, like Hermes, to do the chart in the presence of the person, for the following reasons:

1) The client *sees* what is going on and realizes that at least part of the operation of setting up a chart involves visible paraphernalia: books, tables of numbers based on the positions of actual bodies in the heavens. These are tangibles, and they comfort any client who is fearful of magic and mumbo-jumbo. Some astrologers may get a power kick out of mumbo-jumbo, but not I. Analytical astrology takes no part in that. There is enough mystery in the psyche as it is.

2) The client becomes part of the process and is participating actively by being present. This, in my opinion, obviates some of the fear attendant to coming into the presence of someone who is about to sit in judgment and thus seems automatically superior.

3) This gives the intuitive astrologer time to "sense" the attitude of the client—nervous, sceptical, depressed, curious? I pick up quite a bit in the earliest moments when the client comes in, as I am sure you do. One also gains a hunch as to what level the chart may be being lived. I have learned to be instinctively observant.

I remember, for instance, a woman who introduced herself as a psychologist. I was struck by her clothes, for absolutely nothing matched. They appeared to have come from the jumble sales or a thrift shop. She looked like a waif dressed in hand-me-downs. It was not surprising to see that the archetype of the orphan emerged from her chart, and, indeed, this was unconsciously the sad image that she had of herself—a neglected child. She was surprisingly unconscious of this, but being a trained therapist recognized it instantly when I presented the image. A few days later I received a letter telling me that she had gone to Bergdorf Goodman's and bought herself an entire ensemble, all co-ordinated and matching. And she felt just great.

4) Casting the chart gives clients time to relax and feel

more comfortable with the astrologer and the environment. Sometimes they will get up and look at books or watch intently, or even question what I am doing. Very often Aquarians will get more interested in the procedures than in their own psyches!

5) Finally, the moment enters into it. The famous astrologer Evangeline Adams would often not only draw up a birthchart but a chart for the moment her client entered her study.

In the beginning, naturally, you will have to prepare ahead of time. In fact, since you are dealing with patients whom you see on an on-going basis, you can do the chart at your leisure and with a much greater advantage, since you know them. I generally have to deal with people I have never met before. When the chart proves accurate, as my own chart did with Hermes, there is an additional shock factor. The client is flabbergasted, and I confess, even after all these years, so am I. Every time.

Well, here's to the pitfalls, God bless 'em. They end up being our best teachers!

Yours fondly,

3
Astrology and science

Dear friend,

Your next astrological question is really a tough one: *Why do you suppose so many scientists are unable to accept astrology?*

A friend of mine, Bill Davis of NASA, once gave me a clue. I asked him a question, and he replied, "Which hat do you want me to put on, my scientist hat or my metaphysical hat?" When I asked him what he meant by that, he replied that science, by its own definition, has to deal within limits with data that can be proved or disproved. It is always uncomfortable with the intangible. Bill is an unusual scientist in that, along with a growing number of others, he is open-minded to learning more about the intangible unknown. This kind of scientist I call the New Age scientist, and such are not as threatened by the emerging challenge of the Age of Aquarius, which has to do with *invisible* energy. It is important to note here that the symbol of Aquarius is the Water-bearer. He is shown pouring zig-zags out of a large urn. However, Aquarius is not a water sign, it is an air sign, and those zig-zags are not water but the "waves of life," which are prana or energy (or Spirit).

The time may come soon when science catches up, within its own terms, to astrology. Science, after all, grew out of astrology, to begin with, over 4,000 years ago.

The whole problem lies with the nature of astrology, which is to mediate between outer and inner worlds and to show that, in essence, they are really one. This is where

Jung's theory of synchronicity works. Science is still having difficulty with that; science is concerned with the objective world, and so even psychology has had quite a time establishing itself as a science. Science belongs properly to the ego's world of consciousness. Scientists need to know that.

Jung's greatest struggle, in many ways, was with his peers, his scientific colleagues. Despite the fact that he analyzed 64,000 dreams before publishing some of his findings, despite his personal emphasis on the importance of the empirical and pragmatic approach to all he discovered, he was accused of being woolly and mystical and, even today, is ignored by many psychologists. My own son, a psychiatrist, was exposed during his medical training to only about five pages of Jung at Stanford, one of the top universities in the country. This is a truly sad situation. It presages a widening split between old and new approaches to science itself, something already happening in many fields. The work of Fritjof Capra, Karl Pribram, Rupert Sheldrake, David Bohm, and others will hopefully be seen, by hindsight, as tremendous pioneering work at the beginning of our aeon. So the limitation of science by its own definition has to be one of the reasons astrology continues to be problematical for it.

One of the serious reproaches that I have against scientists is that they have not been scientific *enough*. Several years ago, in fact, a group of them got together and issued a public manifesto denouncing astrology (in *The Humanist* magazine, September 1975). Yet, one could ask how scientific any one of them had been. Who among them had studied and applied astrology for a year, five years, a decade? There are those of us who have studied and practiced astrology for over forty years. Granted that this is an *ad hominem* argument, but either we are frauds or we know something from direct experience that they do not. Some scientists have studied the matter and have come away convinced there is something there. I am thinking of Michel Gauquelin. His work, while enormously helpful, still is statistical and therefore seems to lean more to a causal view than a synchronistic one; thus the psychological level is left out, to say nothing of the spiritual implications, but perhaps this was an attempt to meet science on its own ground.

The Christian definition of a sacrament could be applied in a very profound sense to astrology: a sacrament is an outward and visible sign of an inward and spiritual grace. I would like to paraphrase this and say: the universe is an outward and visible sign of an inward and spiritual force. But that does not sound very scientific, I admit. A nuclear bomb is more scientific than a nuclear heart.

There are two areas, specific ones, where scientists arguing from their perspective are quite right and quite wrong at the same time. This is not the paradox that it seems: it is the dilemma of levels. An example is Freud's and Jung's differing opinions concerning libido. Freud insisted that sex is at the bottom of everything. Jung argued that there is more to life than just sex. (I am greatly oversimplifying.) If one looks at this in the context of the chakra system, which apparently was unfamiliar to both at the time of the argument in 1911, one can see that Freud was right, since the kundalini starts at the root chakra and the area of physical sexual activity. But Jung was also quite right because sex as a *process* involves the union of all opposites, and these operate all the way up the system, at level after level, right up to the union of Shiva and Shakti in the balancing of the two currents of ida and pingala in the crown chakra. I owe this insight to Swami Rama and Dr. Rudolf Ballantine in their book *Yoga and Psychotherapy*. In it they even hold that Adler was the psychologist of the third chakra with his theory of the power principle. So, here we have a perfect example of the dilemma of levels.

In astrology, one of the first examples of this kind of dilemma of levels is the matter of the Precession of the Equinoxes. If you will bear with me for a short technical explanation, I can clear this up.

Most scientists do not realize that for astrologers there are *two* zodiacs:

The first is called the Sidereal Zodiac (*sidus*, Latin for *star*). This zodiac is made up of visible and fixed stars, and

we generally refer to it as "the Zodiac of the Twelve Constellations." And these twelve constellations are given the
names Aries, Taurus, and so forth. You can go out at night
and look up in the sky and see parts of them. These constellations are of varying width, and they form a mighty belt
around the heavens when seen from the Earth. (This zodiac
is used mostly by Eastern astrologers).

The second zodiac is called the Tropical Zodiac and is
formed by the apparent path of the Sun, or the ecliptic.
This zodiac is conceptual, therefore invisible, and is neatly
divided into 360 degrees with twelve signs of 30 degrees
each, *also* called Aries, Taurus, and so on, through Pisces.
(We could call the constellation Taurus and the sign Taurus'
[prime].)

So what we have here is a wheel within a wheel, not unlike what Ezekiel described in the Old Testament. The outer
one is visible and fixed, and the inner one is invisible and
turns clockwise at the rate of 1 degree every seventy-two
years, because of that astronomical phenomenon called *the
Precession of the Equinoxes*.

In layman's language, this phenomenon, which was discovered by Hipparchus in the second century B.C., amounts
to the fact that the moment of spring, determined by the
Sun appearing to cross the celestial equator or hula-hoop of
the earth, falls short every year by a fraction of a degree, or
1 degree every seventy-two years, due to a wobble in the
earth's axis. If you can imagine using the two points of the
Sun and Earth to draw a line way out into space at that instant of spring, the result would be that the point of that
line (the Point of the Vernal Equinox) would fall like the
point of an hour hand on a clock onto a constellation com-
posed of fixed and visible stars.

The constellation hosting the Point of the Vernal Equinox
gives its name to the age in question, so when you hear that
we are entering a New Age of Aquarius this means the point
of that "hour hand" has left the last visible star of the
previous constellation of Pisces and is traveling through an
interface of space towards the first visible star in the constellation of Aquarius. Each of these ages lasts roughly 2,200

years, and it takes approximately 26,000 years to complete a full cycle or Platonic Year. The wobble in the Earth's axis is caused by gravitational pulls from the Sun, Moon, and other planets. It also accounts for the reason that the Earth's axis points very slowly to different pole stars.

All of this is frightfully complicated, I grant you, but this celestial movement is agreed to by scientists. You can read up on it in any good encyclopedia. They do not argue with the Precession of the Equinoxes. What many of them cannot seem to grasp is *why* the astrologer insists that Mars is in Scorpio, when for them it is in Libra. They do not realize that the astrologer is using the Tropical and not the Sidereal Zodiac. Then they add insult to injury and say that the astrologers are all off because the Point of the Vernal Equinox (zero degrees of Aries) has shifted from lining up with Aries (the constellation) for over 2,000 years. What they don't realize is that's the way it's supposed to be! Astrology itself probably was conceived of during the Age of Gemini, maybe about 6,000 years ago. The discrepancy is part of the "program."

In the very beginning, even Jung had difficulty with this and assumed that since the whole thing was a kind of human projection anyway, it didn't matter. Now we understand a little more, and we see the entire matter is a marvelously slow moving clock that seems to describe the evolution of even the Collective Unconscious, since each of these ages has an uncanny way of bringing forth a new spiritual movement or religion that by an odd synchronicity or coincidence uses in its mythos and symbols the very characteristics and symbols of the astrological constellation that it reflects. But that will be another letter. It is sufficient to say that we are four and a half ages past the beginning of recorded history, so that anyone with the patience to combine ancient and modern history with psychology and an understanding of Jung's concept of the Collective Unconscious can see that the patterns are truly there. Later Jung wrote extensively on the Age of Pisces in his book *Aion*.

The Tropical Zodiac is geocentric, and the scientist points out that the solar system is heliocentric. Astrology is anthropocentric. We live on the Earth, not the sun. And if we see the solar system as a paradigm for the psyche, this Tropical Zodiac reflects a psychic truth. The life that we live between our birth and our death is a kind of illusion, or what the Hindus call *maya*, or what Shakespeare called "the stuff that dreams are made on." But while we are here, they seem mighty real. We are being asked a great deal: to extend our consciousness prior to our birth and past our death, at least to accept the hypothesis, for only in so doing can we begin to grasp what the sages meant by the concept of *maya*.

The closest analogy I can come up with is that of a movie or of television. Both have a kind of undeniable reality. But in another sense, this reality is not real, it is an illusion. Perhaps there is a way in which our daily lives also have a kind of reality but are not really Real. What Jung says is that all reality in the end is psychic reality. As for Shakespeare, he put it best:

> Our revels now are ended. These our actors,
> As I foretold you, were all spirits and
> Are melted into air, into thin air;
> And, like the baseless fabric of this vision,
> The cloud-capped towers, the gorgeous palaces,
> The solemn temples, the great globe itself,
> Yea, all which it inherit, shall dissolve;
> And, like this insubstantial pageant faded,
> Leave not a rack behind. We are such stuff
> As dreams are made on, and our little life
> Is rounded with a sleep.
>
> *The Tempest* IV, i, 148

We get a hint of this when we sleep or fall unconscious. Our sense of the outer world ceases. We are in another place, within ourselves. All our outer identities cease, and yet in dreams we know we exist. And mysteriously someone is watching the life and the dream and questioning and experiencing its meaning. It is a very subtle thing, as you well know.

So when the astrologer puts the Earth at the center of the

chart, or more specifically a particular spot on Earth, he or she is following the logic that wherever we happen to be as individuals, there is our center and our focus in the great scheme of things. Historians have discovered that the ancient Egyptians knew that the Sun is the center of the solar system. Certainly the ancient Greeks knew that the Earth is round because Eratosthenes measured its circumference and was within twenty-seven miles of measuring it correctly!

In a sense, "the medium is the message." Since we live on Earth, we are forced to see the Sun "up there" and "out there" in the heavens and to feel separated from the source of life, God, whose symbol from the most ancient times has been the circle or mandala of the Sun. This is the ego's point of view, and as such makes good sense. Now astrology is pointing to an age in which the task will be also to discover that Sun within ourselves and in each other.

This manner of thinking is symbolic and therefore not scientific. Science is more interested in facts; astrology accepts facts but bridges through symbols to the importance of their meaning. We should remember what Galileo said: "Facts which at first seem improbable will, even on scant explanation, drop the cloak which has hidden them and stand forth in simple and naked beauty."

No scientist has ever disproved astrology. When they set out to prove it wrong, they end up proving it right—but only partly so. The statistical approach is helpful but never really conclusive. It is like pulling a daisy apart to prove that it is a daisy. No, one has to approach the matter of astrology in a holistic manner, and then it yields up its insights on many, many levels. One rises up or descends the caduceus of symbols. Another way of putting it is to suggest that more scientists look into it wearing, like Bill Davis, their scientific hat, but realizing to go further they will have to change hats.

Of all the scientists, the theoretical physicists have the edge. They truly understand the problem, at least. When I listened to David Bohm lecture on his theory of the implicate and explicate universe, he, too, was venturing into the same world Jung did. I saw that it is the ego that ex-

25

periences the explicate universe and the Self that experiences the implicate. The Hindus put this into mythological terms as the breathing out and breathing in of Brahman. The East has never repudiated astrology, perhaps because they have tended more to an introverted view of the universe from the beginning.

All I am hoping is that someday scientists will see that astrology offers a description of *how* the "whats" of the so-called manifest world get to be the way they are. Astrology is a most beautiful symbolic language of processes which function on both the physical and the psychic level. For me, this is the best definition I have. As I have said before, astrology itself is in a state of evolution because we ourselves are evolving. We have come a long way already.

Originally, back in the days of ancient Sumer and Egypt astrology united science and religion. As I have mentioned, when astrology was rejected by both, both suffered, since it furnished the proof of the latter and the import of the former. Possibly the Church feared its misuse or the potential power it gave to the laity. And though such scientists as Newton and Tycho Brahe were proficient astrologers in their day, eventually that art/science became suspect as being too mystical. (You probably have heard the anecdote about Herschel mocking Newton for his interest in astrology. Newton drew himself up and retorted, "Sir, you have not studied the matter. I have!")

The same fate awaited alchemy; both astronomy and chemistry separated themselves from their mystical mothers, and while alchemy fell into oblivion, astrology fell into the streets. Its reputation dropped to an all-time low, and it was relegated to the world of magic, witchcraft, and gypsy fortune-tellers. Even today in some of the popular pulp astrology magazines, the connection remains all too apparent, and serious astrologers have had to put out their own journals cleared of the kind of advertising that gives astrology such a bad image.

Yet even during the last two centuries, astrology continued to be studied quietly by a few. It surfaced at last during the late 1800s with the coming forth of the supporting work of such people as Anna Bonus Kingsford, Helena Blavatsky and the Theosophists, Rudolf Steiner, and later Edgar Cayce. But the great forward thrust for astrology came with the new approach of such great astrologers as Alan Leo, Dane Rudhyar, Grant Lewi, and Marc Edmund Jones. But I truly think that Carl Gustav Jung was the first to see the psychological value latent in the subject. It was Jung's work that led to Dane Rudhyar's classic *The Astrology of Personality* in the 1930s, a serious and dignified study. Today, at last, we are seeing much distinguished work in the field with the contributions of Liz Greene, Steven Arroyo, and others.

As I have said before, the separation of science and religion resulted in religion losing its external proof and science its sense of the sacred. This we have to take seriously. Orthodox religion is suffering a tremendous decline, while segments of it are currently experiencing a return to literalism. For all the sincerity of proponents of the latter, it can lead to an idolatry of its views, banishing the value of symbolic thinking, so essential to the individual's spiritual growth. Symbols are what mediate between levels of consciousness. We should honor them.

The good news is that we cannot kill an archetype but only destroy its personifications. God, or the *imago Dei*, is the name we give to the central process of creativity itself. God is not dead, but alive and well in the Unconscious within us and in the universe we perceive to be outside of us. We are witnessing all around the world a new approach to religious experience. As Jung pointed out, even if all the religions of the world were wiped out entirely, by the time a new generation was ten years old, it would have begun to recreate another. So profound and central to our deepest values is the mystery of ultimate meaning.

Jung studied alchemy and astrology on the grounds that they came out of the collective psyche and thus were automatically worthy of study and research. Jung ended up giving more time to the processes of alchemy because he saw in them compelling parallels to the process of individuation. But his interest in astrology gave impetus to a new way of perceiving it. It became more introverted. Medieval astrology was completely extraverted, and dealt with planetary influence, fate, and predestination. In this century it provides the basis for a deeper understanding of individuals and how we approach our lives. Today, an analytical astrologer would not be likely to predict, "You will wear yellow socks on Tuesday." He would be more likely to note that the color of one's socks is important to the client.

Certainly, I am being facetious, but, seriously, there is a link between character and destiny. Fate is simply that part of our lives which has to be acted out in the outer world, because we have remained unconscious or refused to be conscious of that something in ourselves which precipitated it in the first place.

This is especially true at the collective level. Life seems to be precariously balanced between our capacity to be detached and to be involved. The great miracle remains that a chart for each of us is available for the asking, and that with its exploration we can become more self-aware and self-accepting. The same is true of any psychological analysis that provides, besides healing, an opening to further growth and healthy self-expression.

To conclude, science has a lot to learn about and from astrology, and astrologers can benefit enormously from science. Today we have a growing number of astrologers who are profoundly versed in science and applied technology. Their knowledge and work is staggering. I am thinking in particular of Robert Hand and Neil Michelsen, and the late John Addey in England. The useful and time-saving devices of computer programs are already highly sophisticated. Planetary aspects are taken into consideration in radio and TV reception; studies are being made in the fields of meteorology, biology, and medicine. It is all happening very slowly but surely, and it is *not* a matter of regression.

To repeat, "How much is lost to mankind through disbelief!" Science and theology both need to keep an open mind.

My very best to you, always,

4
On causality and synchronicity

Dear friend,

Your question: *Do you believe the stars cause things to happen to us?* is a very basic one, perhaps it's the one science has the hardest time dealing with.

Personally, I do not believe the stars are the cause. This was the medieval view. Predictions, which are largely based on transits (the relationship of the planets on any given date to the planets in the natal chart), are to me analogous to a weather report. And you know how accurate they are! Certainly, there can be a psychological weather report, and if "rain" is in the forecast, it is wise to take a raincoat along, or it would be safe to predict you will get wet. That there is an ongoing connection between the planets and our psyches is evident and indisputable. It is as clear as it is that there is a connection between our psyches and our bodies, and as mysterious.

This is where Jung's theory of synchronicity is so helpful, because it is an acausal definition of time. Jung wrote that whatever is born or done at any particular moment of time has the quality of that moment of time. And he wrote this:

> The causalism that underlines our scientific picture of the world breaks everything down into individual processes which it punctiliously tries to isolate from all other parallel processes. This tendency is absolutely necessary if we are to gain a reliable knowledge of the world, but philosophically it has the disadvantage of breaking up, or obscuring, the universal interrelationship of events so that a recognition of the

29

greater relationship, i.e., the unity of the world, becomes more and more difficult. Everything that happens, however, happens in the same "one world" and is part of it. For this reason events must have an *a priori* aspect of unity.

We are not the way we are *because* of our charts; we are not forced to be who we are. We simply start out coinciding with the chart that describes us. Of the numerous specific synchronicities arising out of a chart, I can cite the example of a woman in her late thirties who came to see me. The image emerging from her chart, as I looked at it, was one of a wistful little girl who had not had much opportunity to play, but probably had spent much time with folded arms looking longingly out the window and wishing that life were different. The archetypal motif suggested by her Saturn in Gemini was the poor little princess in the tower wishing that the handsome prince would come someday to rescue her. The woman's eyes widened as I described this, and then I went on to suggest that, in Jungian terms, waiting for an outer prince might not have worked, and that her task might be to find her own strength within her animus or the inner masculine aspect of her psyche. At the end of the session, I asked her what she did for a living. The response came with a great burst of excitement. She was a toy designer. She had, in fact, designed a series of dolls which were archetypal characters in fairy tales. When it came to designing the princess doll, she had placed her in a box built like a tower, and the doll with folded arms was gazing wistfully out the plastic window! Thus the impact of the image arising out of her chart was especially powerful. She readily admitted her identification with it.

Parenthetically, I found this another example of a person whose job is a meaningful metaphor for what they need to learn themselves. This happens very frequently. Sometimes it's downright funny, as in the case of the man whose birth sign was Taurus (banks, money, security) with Pisces (peacefulness) rising who worked for the Pacific Security Bank! Such are some of the serendipities of the astrologer's life.

None of this, of course, answers the question of *why* we are the way we are. Any answer to that, at this point, would have to remain purely speculative. In esoteric astrology, they would say that we earned our chart karmically or that we picked our chart in order to learn certain lessons, but we really have no way of knowing. It is enough for us to take in the staggering thought that if A is the Mars out there in the heavens and A' is the Mars in my chart, both, in essence, are one and the same Mars. And both would seem to be subject to a prime mover we can call X. A therefore does not influence A'; they are intrinsically one and the same, one the reflection of the other. This is a great paradox, but human perceptions function through duality, in this case inner and outer or subject and object, which makes the matter more difficult.

It is as if each of us lives in a separate bubble submerged in an ocean. Inside the bubble is water and outside the bubble is water, but our separate reality is limited to the water within our own bubble. However, when something affects the water outside, it simultaneously affects the water inside all the bubbles. But in our own bubbles we feel isolated and different from everything outside our own sphere. The underlying unity remains elusive at the experiential level.

One has to see astrology as a symbolic language, uniting that outer and inner, and as a language of correspondences. A symbol mediates between levels of consciousness, and this astrology does with ease. It is, as astrologer-philosopher Dane Rudhyar put it, "an algebra of life." It has the capacity to convert "things" through symbols into processes, and a symbol is the best way to describe something that is in a constant state of flux.

This is a most profound thought. It leads us to an appreciative acceptance of what Jung called archetypes or primordial images. The closest we can come to dealing with universal processes is to personify them and make them into gods, which is to acknowledge with reverence the level of their reality.

Astrology helps us to decode the gods back into the archetypal processes that they represent, and still represent, in the outer world of nature and events, and in the inner world of meaning in the psyche. Symbols are images; we read them

31

with the right brain. The chart shows nothing but glyphs or symbols, so images arise quite spontaneously when we look at one. Thus we should not be surprised that a synchronicity exists and that the images are, indeed, valid. The truth of this is something I have experienced over and over again firsthand. It works.

To the astrologer, or at least to what I call the analytical astrologer, the chart virtually represents a living map to that kingdom which lies within. This is not a new thought. Origen, the early Christian theologian, as early as the third century A.D., wrote the following words: ". . . understand that thou thyself art even another little world, and hast within thee the sun and the moon, and also the stars."

He also wrote (in one of his commentaries on *The Book of Wisdom*) something that permeates astrological thinking, the relationship and correspondence between outer visible manifestation and inner psychological meaning.

> For when that writer of divine Wisdom had enumerated all things one by one, he says finally that he has received knowledge of things hidden and things manifest. And he doubtless shows by this that each of the manifest things is to be related to one of those that are hidden; that is to say, all things visible have some invisible likeness and pattern. Since, then, it is impossible for a man living in the flesh to know anything of matters hidden and invisible unless he has apprehended some image and likeness thereto from among things visible, I think that He who made all things in wisdom so created all the species of visible things upon earth, that He placed in them some teaching and knowledge of things invisible and heavenly, whereby the human mind might mount to spiritual understanding and seek the grounds of things in heaven [psyche]; so that taught by God's wisdom it might say: "The things that are hid and that are manifest have I learned."

These symbols are hidden for us, not only in nature, but in religions, in geometry, in colors, and also in the etymologies of languages, for words and the unconscious ways they are used are full of secrets, as well. Later you will see how the Mother Goddess and the Moon have hidden links of meaning with a cup, a womb, a chalice, conception, the receptivity of the ego in the psyche, and how all of these are connected with each other.

Another who held similar views was Jung's compatriot Paracelsus who lived in the fifteenth century. Jung, in fact, gave two important lectures on Paracelsus, from which I would like to quote a few of the old physician's words. You really should read these lectures, if you haven't already, as they are full of good wisdom. Paracelsus wrote:

> From the external we learn to know the internal.
> There is in man a firmament as in heaven, but not of one piece; there are two. For the hand that divided light from darkness, and the hand that made heaven and earth, has done likewise in the microcosm below, having taken from above and enclosed within man's skin everything that heaven contains. For that reason the external heaven is a guide to the heaven within. . . .
> For heaven is man and man is heaven and all men are one heaven, and heaven is only one man.

Jung also refers to Paracelsus, no doubt familiar with *The Emerald Tablet*, the classic authority of medieval alchemy, and quotes the famous lines: "What is below is like that which is above. What is above is like what is below. Thus is the miracle of the One accomplished."

There are times when I wish we could read "as above, so below," in a horizontal sense: as without, so within. The polarity of above and below plays too much into the concept of a heaven and God literally up in the sky, and we below on earth. I intuit that without/within suggests a unity no less meaningful and easier for us to understand in terms of outer events and inner meaning. Jung also suggested that we tend to think that we could be different if only our outer circumstances were favorable, but that quite the reverse is true. Only when we change our consciousness do the outer events begin to follow suit. I hope you understand what I am implying. Paracelsus uses the outer to diagnose the inner, not to excuse it.

Paracelsus did not limit the "planets" to existing only in mankind. He perceived them in all of nature, in minerals, plants, on every level of creation, tangible and intangible.

As materialists, growing up with a materialistic viewpoint, we tend to take this literally and dismiss it as so much poppycock, but if we see what he was trying to say in symbolic terms, then we can understand these "planets" to be symbolic of universal processes. A process can function both in the outer and the inner, and indeed reveal them to be essentially one.

It is as if these levels of creative manifestation are like octaves in music. Though they represent energy at different vibratory levels, nevertheless, they resonate with each other at every level. This idea was put forward by the great Greek geometer, Pythagoras, who related the planets to the musical scale. Almost two thousand years later, an English astronomer, William Bode, discovered what is now known as Bode's Law, which demonstrates that the mathematical proportion between planets from the Sun out to Saturn (and including the belt of asteroids) is precisely that of the notes on a guitar string!

Astrology describes a law of correspondence between the visible exterior world and the invisible interior world of the psyche. The New Physics and the mystics imply that the reason behind this is that they are really one. Yet for purposes of evolution, in terms of consciousness, it would seem important that we continue to perceive them as two—outer and inner, subject and object. In any case, both viewpoints—ONE and TWO—are equally valid and necessary. Jung's contribution is enormously significant in this respect: the world of the ego (as he defines it, the center of consciousness) is that of the Two. It must be the ego that perceives the world of space/time and matter, of masculine/feminine, all the way from the genitals to the highest levels of the tension of opposites and the worlds of paradox.

If we are to find the world of the Self (as he defines it, the center and totality of the psyche), then we will have to see it through the Third Eye. ("Let thine eye be single," said Jesus.) And what we will see then will be the Oneness. We are told over and over that the only way to know God is to "know thyself." God, as Nicolas of Cusa said, is that circle whose circumference is nowhere and whose center is everywhere. Perhaps if we were able to open that great Eye within, we would be privileged to see "that kingdom of heaven which is spread upon the earth, but men do not see," as stated in *The Gospel according to Thomas*.

The Self must live in that holy place called a *temenos* and in that time called by Jung *illud tempus* or "Once upon a time," which are the place and time of synchronicity. If we all have a Self which is alive and well in the Unconscious, it follows that there is nothing to get. We have it all, as the sages tell us. It's just darned inconvenient that the ego doesn't know that! So we have to struggle along as best we can, making it more and more difficult for ourselves.

The exciting task ahead in the New Age of Aquarius is to discover God, not "out there," but in the Spirit's true home, the kingdom of heaven within the psyche. Jesus even told his disciples: "Ye are gods," and he told us to seek first the kingdom of heaven, and all else would be added unto us. Perhaps we could paraphrase this, psychologically speaking, as seeking first to find the Self within the psyche, and then the gifts of meaning would be given us.

Here, of course, we have to remember that for Jung the Self was the equivalent of the Christ Within, or the Atman, or what perhaps is meant by some as the Transpersonal Self. In any case, the concept is a spiritual one and not a selfish or completely personal one. I find these definitions very risky and tricky; they are almost always subject to misunderstanding, which is why a glyph or symbol is much safer and more truly understood. The symbol for God Manifest in us is that of the circle with a dot in the center. This is also the symbol for the Sun and the metal gold, as you shall discover later.

In conclusion, this basic idea of the two ways of perception, the One and the Two, is not necessarily a dualistic approach or Manichean. It simply implies that All is One, but that the One needs the Two for the purpose of forming and sustaining manifestation, and that when the opposites meet, a Third appears. The Manichean heresy was the idea that only two opposing forces of good and evil, light and darkness, were out there, and the One was not emphasized (a misunderstanding on the part of Christians, according to the scholar Henri Corbin).

You can see that these deep metaphysical concepts underlie many Eastern religions. They have been so dreadfully misunderstood in the past because Christians took the Eastern gods literally, as well as the Greek and Celtic deities. They didn't see that the gods were personifications of those universal processes flowing out of the One. Brahman, for instance, is the Ground of Being or God Unmanifest, who in manifesting becomes Brahma the Creator, Vishnu the Preserver, and Siva the Destroyer. The breath we breathe in is creative, the circulation of oxygen in the blood preserves life, and when we exhale we die a little, only to be reborn with the next breath. In birth we take on a body, in life we preserve our body, in death we leave it behind.

It broke my heart to enter the caves at Elephanta, outside of Bombay, to see the serene, majestic, and powerfully dignified sculptures of these gods smashed by ignorant though well-meaning Christian invaders. This iconoclasm is still lurking everywhere, and the demon is literalism. It is when we take things literally that we kill the power of symbols to lead us from level to level of understanding.

I write you sometimes with a true sense of urgency. The need for tolerance and respect for differing views is so great. I will never forget hearing Joseph Campbell remark that it is erroneous to assume that all wars are fought for economic reasons. They are fought, he said, because of differing mythologies and worldviews. Unless we see the processes that unify these at the very deepest level, we will continue to find fault and mutually to project our collective Shadows on each other, as we have done for thousands of years. This makes the study of a language of symbols profoundly significant. It might lead us to new understanding and to peace.

Closing now, and with love,

5
Ego and Self

Dear friend,

With what changes in perception do you think Jung helps astrology?

I do not think that Jung intended deliberately to change our views of astrology. Most of his thoughts on the matter appear in his letters or in his private conversations with friends or students and reported by them. It is his psychology in itself that offers new insights, and the discovery in his own life of a way to describe psychologically something the mystics have always averred: the existence of the Self and its distinction from the ego. Today, we are beginning to realize that we are not our egos, we have egos. This discovery came to Jung in his childhood, and here is the section from the chapter "School Years" in *Memories, Dreams, and Reflections* in which he tells of it:

> Somewhere deep in the background I always knew that I was two persons. One was the son of my parents, who went to school and was less intelligent, attentive, hard-working, decent, and clean than many other boys. The other was grown-up—old, in fact—skeptical, mistrustful, remote from the world of men, but close to nature, the earth, the sun, the moon, the weather, all living creatures, and above all close to the night, to dreams, and to whatever "God" worked directly in him. I put "God" in quotation marks here. For nature seemed, like myself, to have been set aside by God [by his teachers?] as non-divine, although created by Him as an expression of Himself. Nothing could persuade me that "in

the image of God" applied only to man. In fact, it seemed to me that the high mountains, the rivers, the lakes, trees, flowers, and animals far better exemplified the essence of God than men with their ridiculous clothes, their meanness, vanity, mendacity, and abhorrent egotism—all qualities with which I was only too familiar from myself, that is, from personality No. 1, the schoolboy of 1890. Besides his world there existed another realm, like a temple in which everyone who entered became transformed and suddenly overpowered by a vision of the whole cosmos, so that he could only marvel and admire, forgetful of himself. Here lived the "Other" who knew God as a hidden, personal, and at the same time suprapersonal secret. Here nothing separated man from God; indeed, it was as though the human mind looked down upon creation simultaneously with God.

What I am here unfolding, sentence by sentence, is something I was then not conscious of in any articulate way, though I sensed it with an overpowering premonition and intensity of feeling. At such times I *knew* that I was worthy of myself, that I was my true self. As soon as I was alone, I could pass over into this state. I therefore sought the peace and solitude of this "Other," personality No. 2.

The play and counterplay between personalities No. 1 and No. 2, which has run through my whole life, has nothing to do with a "split" or dissociation in the ordinary medical sense. On the contrary, *it is played out in every individual* [italics mine]. In my life, No. 2 has been of prime importance, and I have always tried to make room for anything that wanted to come to me from within. He is a typical figure, but he is perceived only by the very few. Most people's conscious understanding is not sufficient to realize that he is also what they are.

So we could say that Jung's personality No. 2, which he went on later to define as the Self, was the part of him that apprehended the One, and that his personality No. 1, the ego, perceived the objective world which arises through the process of duality, the Two.

As I mentioned before, David Bohm, a British theoretical physicist, confirms this in another field with his concept of implicate and explicate order. Fritjof Capra does much the same in his book *The Tao of Physics*. I have heard Karl Pribram, a neurologist, explain some of his studies of the brain, showing how our organs of apperception—eyes, ears, nervous systems, and the brain itself—function in stereo, yet yield a holographic view of our environment. Pribram's work is highly complex and difficult to follow, but indirectly it addresses a question that Jung raised, which I have always loved: how, Jung wondered, did the sofa in his living room get into his head? Stanislav Grof, to mention another, confirms Jung's discovery of the Collective Unconscious in his studies in Czechoslovakia with patients and LSD. It is as if many disciplines have gone up another step in perception, and so it is not surprising that astrology has too.

Here are some astrological perceptions to entertain:

1) The solar system may be a paradigm or model for the psyche or the "kingdom of heaven within." It, too, has a living center of light reflected by the planets and their satellites and held together by a force field of gravity. We ourselves are subsumed within it.

Should this be so, in principle, and not forgetting to think in terms of processes (!), this would presuppose an acausal connection between outer and inner at the level of the One, the *unus mundus*, though at the same time this is experienced as a duality by the ego. Certainly, the ego perceives the physical reality of the solar system. But at the metaphysical level, the level of the Self, it could be something else.

Jung's theory of synchronicity suggests that there is an acausal connection between inner psychic states and meaningful outer physical events which we occasionally experience and call coincidence. This happens in another kind of time, one in which meaning and event coincide. Thus the planet Saturn, out there in the physical heaven, might not be "influencing" us so much as resonating with the Saturn within each of us. Saturn and Saturn. Something like the one Moon in the sky at night, reflecting in ten thousand puddles simultaneously. There is only one Saturn, but each of us has a different one in his or her chart.

This is not just philosophical speculation; I can give you any number of actual examples. For instance, one of the biggest experiences of synchronicity for me occurred a few years ago in Shelburne, Vermont. I was co-leading a work-shop for Burlington College with my dear friend, Robert Bly, the poet. I was asked by someone to explain the symbolic meaning of some of the planetary glyphs, which are all made up of variations of a circle, a dot, a crescent, and a cross. Accordingly, I drew first a circle, then placed a dot in the center, then drew a vertical line, explaining it, and finally a horizontal line. Afterwards the group of some forty people got out their picnic lunches, and we all sat on the bank of the lake. It was a glorious day. Suddenly, someone called out and pointed up to the sun. There was a complete rainbow-like circle around it, and this larger circle had the sun for its dot. Within the circle, the sky seemed darker. Below the circle hung a vertical strip of white cloud, and as we watched, a plane came along and drew a horizontal cloud-jet across it to make a cross. Virtually everything that had been on the blackboard inside was now drawn on the blueboard of the sky. I still get goose bumps when I think of it.

2) If the solar system is a paradigm for the psyche, then we perceive this paradigm as paradox. There is, for us, only one solar system. Yet there are no two charts exactly alike, which goes for the billions of individuals that have ever existed, exist, or shall exist. Still the ingredients or archetypal components of every single chart are one and the same. Their unity and diversity are simultaneously true.

3) The paradigm of the cosmos is beauteous. The word *cosmos* means "beauty," as in *cosmetics*. The solar system moves in celestial harmony, weaving an ordered dance. It ever offers an order to what we often perceive within us as continual chaos. We are more than often anxious, neurotic, confused, depressed, or just plain bored, usually because we have been cut off from our sense of wonder. And yet all we have to do is lift our eyes to see something that can be depended on. As the psalmist sang, "The heavens declare the glory of God."

Chaos is what you see at the wrong end of any kaleidoscope (kaleidoscope: beauty-picture-seeing). Instant order is achieved by looking through the other end. Inside the tube are two reflecting mirrors which seen by one eye make for order and meaning.

4) The chart, then, which is drawn up with the three necessary co-ordinates of latitude, longitude, and time of birth on a given day of a given year, *is a diagram of meaning and purpose set in space/time.* Those three co-ordinates give us the three-dimensional cube so important in the Kabbalah. The cube in Hermetic wisdom represents matter. If you unfold a cube you would get the symbolic proportions of a Christian cross.

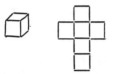

So the co-ordinates of a chart also suggest the incarnation and crucifixion of spirit held in matter, and perhaps psychologically imply the suffering and passion that each of us undergoes in feeling separate and alone.

In any case, the chart represents a specific moment in a specific place that gets up and walks about on two legs for a lifetime of unfoldment. As Jung stated, every moment in time partakes of the entire nature of that moment, so our potential to encompass the All in One must be there. It is indisputable that no one else in the universe has had your particular set of experiences, memories, and affects. When each of us is born, a microcosm is born unique unto itself, totally *sui generis.* So when it is declared in the Old Testament, that God made man in his own image, rather than reading anthropomorphically that God looks like a man or a man like God (which is literalism), we could perceive instead that the Creator has given us the power of the *process* of co-creating, since we create our own world of experience. Just as in a hologram in which every piece contains and can reproduce the whole, just as in a body where each cell contains the coded DNA/RNA that renders it unique, so we turn every experience into our own particular version of it, according to the template of our chart.

Should this be true, it would then follow that only by

41

knowing and fulfilling ourselves, can we approach the knowing of the whole or the One. This is the only "Way." Both Christ and Krishna have maintained that they represent the "only way." We tend to take this literally, too, and say to ourselves that they can't both be right. And yet in terms of "process" they are both pointing to the same way, or verb, of reaching. What Paul called salvation, or today we might call *Christ-* or *Krishna-consciousness*, is what I believe Jung was referring to as the process of individuation. No matter what we call it, we have to assume that for human beings there is only one "process" or "way" to reach that level of consciousness, and this process takes place within us.

Many today are paying attention to the theory and practice of raising the kundalini force within the spine, the so-called "serpent power" which we associate with yoga and the East, though the symbolism is in the West, as well. There are plenty of serpents and magic rods in the Bible. There are references to serpent worship at Delphi, in the Orphic mysteries, not to mention St. Patrick chasing the snake worshippers out of Ireland. (There never were any snakes there, in the first place.) If we look at these references symbolically rather than literally, they yield quite different insights.

The symbol of the chart, as a circle, is also a serpent: the ouroboros, or the cosmic snake swallowing its own tail. I do hope you can see how astrology can be valuable in making these connections. Forgive me if I repeat myself, but it can help us to look with new eyes at those things we tend to take literally. Then we may see them as hiding symbolic processes, which can lead us to deeper and deeper understanding and appreciation and wonder.

Astrology per se is a language; it is a language of universal processes. It shows correspondences between levels of creation and levels of consciousness. As a language of symbols, it mediates between levels of consciousness. As above, so below—as within, so without—as without, so within. This gives astrology a function quite apart from its importance in chart interpretation and makes the subject priceless to anyone seeking a key to understanding. Certainly alchemy and the Tarot and the *I Ching* share this distinction, to say nothing of the *Kabbalah;* they can each shed light on the others. But astrology holds its unique position because of its connection to the physical planetary system. It connects outer with inner space, sense with meaning.

Astrology makes possible the concept of a spirituous earth, because you cannot seriously study the subject without experiencing a direct panentheism, the experience of the sacred in the commonplace. And why should we not begin with those things that are simple? As the wise rabbi answered the one who asked him why he thought it was so difficult to find God, "Perhaps we do not stoop low enough."

I wanted to share something else from *The Gospel according to Thomas,* so I just went into my study to find it. The book fell open at the page. When things like that happen, it always gives me a good feeling. The quotation is:

> Jesus said: I am the Light that is above them All, I am the All, the All came forth from Me and the All attained to Me. Cleave a (piece of wood), I am there; lift the stone and you will find Me there.

Summarizing, it can be said that just as the solar system has a sun orbited by a number of planets, so does the psyche have a Self which is reflected and transformed by a number of universal archetypal components. This gives us a kind of equation: a god = an archetype = a universal process = a planet.

I am so glad that these letters are proving helpful. They certainly are to me.

Always fondly yours,

6
Symbols as bringing together

Dear friend,

You ask: *How do you interpret symbols?*

The word *symbol* comes from the Greek *sym-bolos*, which means to throw together or bring together. It has a very interesting antonym, *dia-bolos*, which means to throw apart or separate. And *diabolos*, of course, is the origin of our English word *devil*, cognate to the French *diable* and the German *Teufel*. So the process we must associate with this archetype is that of separating or even denying the symbolic, which would be to kill the power of the symbol to mediate between levels of consciousness. This results in literalism and fallacious concretist thinking, probably one of the greatest evils and dangers in our time. It is at the root of all fundamentalist thinking and dogmatic inflexibility. Millions of people throughout history have been killed for this very reason, from the days of the Old Testament right on up to the present. It can happen whenever the symbolic potential of religious dogma has been denied. Instantly, the diabolos effect takes over, and one group will claim to have the only truth and deny any other version; though symbolically understood, both might be attempting to express the same thing.

The greatest potential for this kind of misunderstanding comes at the interface of the great ages. There the new dispensation sets up its own *dramatis personae*, with new names and outer trappings, and proceeds to wipe out the religious symbols (and the devotees) of the previous age. The ancient Hebrews did it to the Canaanites; the early Christians did it to the pagan Greeks, Celts, and Norsemen; the Moslems to the Christians, and vice versa. Think only of the Romans and Christians, Christians vs. Christians, Moslems and Hindus, the Crusades, the Inquisition, the Cathars, the Protestant/Catholic Wars in England and Europe. Think of Lebanon and Northern Ireland today.

The one ray of hope is that the nature of Aquarius, ruler of the New Age, is basically tolerant and potentially capable of understanding symbolic thinking, even of expressing gratitude for ancient wisdom instead of destroying it. But we are not there yet.

There is a difference between a symbol and an emblem or a sign. The latter two point to things known. A symbol points to the unknown and guides us to its knowing, to deeper understanding. For example, you can take the delicate matter of the doctrine of the Virgin Birth. For the Christian, this means the miraculous birth of Jesus. I am not about to dispute whether or not Jesus was literally born to a woman without a human father. Literally, it might or might not be true. This is a matter of belief. The early Christian fathers speculated about the mechanics of this. I recommend Marina Warner's book *Alone of all her Sex* which raises questions like: Was Mary intact? Was she perforated? Did she conceive through her ear? (But they missed a point which occurred to me as I put a fresh white filter into my coffee maker: even at the physical level, in a sense every birth is a virgin birth because the womb relines itself every month!)

We are rarely taught that there were other virgin births. I had to find out for myself that Gautama Buddha's mother, though married to a king, conceived by the holy spirit through a vision of a white elephant; that Krishna had a virgin mother, Devaki; that Cuchullain, the Celtic hero, and Adonis, Attis, Osiris, Dionysus, Zoroaster, Herakles, and many others, be they solar heroes or human saviors, had virgin births. One of my favorites is the virgin birth of the Chinese philosopher Lao Tzu. His mother conceived him by a falling star! Since there are so many, it seems as if the motif of Virgin Birth is telling us something extremely important in terms of an archetypal process; perhaps that saviors and solar heroes come to us through mortal mothers and immortal fathers, or God. Then we must ask ourselves, why is this so important?

There are two ways to react to this. We can get angry and say this threatens Christian dogma, or we can acknowledge that this is a symbolically beautiful way of expressing a truth in the realm of the psyche. It is, perhaps, the closest way the collective can come to describing the rebirth of the Divine Child in us: the undiscovered Self. Any such inner conception will by its very nature be a virgin birth and of a spiritual Father. For the Spirit to incarnate in any of us, we have to have a body or a vessel or a grail. This is the feminine principle or the Mother Goddess (process), and it gives life form. We need to honor this in a new way.

Earliest men, archeologists maintain, did not understand their own role in the reproductive process. The issuing forth of a child from the cave of the vagina must have been an unfathomable mystery (it still is), as was, and is, death. Reverently the bodies of the dead were bound in the fetal position, covered with red ochre, and placed in the tomb-cave. Astrologically, Cancer is the mother womb, and Capricorn the grave, and this was during the prehistoric Age of Cancer.

The mystery is still with us, though at a different level. Meister Eckhart, the German mystic, points to it in his words: "What good is it to me if this eternal birth of the divine Son takes place unceasingly but does not take place within me?...What good is it to me for God to give birth to his son, if I do not give birth to him in my time and my culture?" And he told us that the sign of this new birth would be to find God in all things.

If we could see this as a psychological truth perceived and projected with beauty and reverence upon all these savior births, then we could share appreciatively with other religions and find some wisdom in ancient cultures. All too often, we insist that only our particular savior is the right one. Yet each of these saviors came as a model or paradigm to his people at an appropriate time and place to repeat the divine pattern for our own inner rebirth. But we are not taught this. It might help, if we were.

So, it is part of that process of dia-bolos to cause separations and arguments; by using sym-bolos we can heal the split and see the wisdom hidden in the process.

In astrology, it is Mercury or Hermes (or Thoth, he goes by many names) who is the personification of the process of uniting or dividing opposites. The god Hermes carries a marvelous symbol for symbolism itself: the caduceus, that staff with two twining serpents, topped with wings. This, too, is a universal symbol, going back to the Assyrians, Egyptians, Indians, and others.

I like to demonstrate the *process* of its capacity to unite and to divide with a simple zipper. When the zipper tab goes down, the fabric divides (dia-bolos) and when it goes up, it unites (sym-bolos). Mercury "zips" about as a god with his magic winged sandals and becomes invisible with his winged helmet (as are our thoughts, also ruled by Mercury). I shall never forget sharing this image with a group of Episcopal clergymen at a seminar. They were particularly taken with the idea, and during the afternoon when a number of them fell into an argument on semantics, one of them cried out, "I think the Bishop's zipper just came down!" Things sorted themselves out rather quickly after that.

I think by now you can see the ease with which processes function on the highest and the humblest of levels. The helpful thing is to look for the process in a humble place and learn to recognize it at a sacred level. This is a gift of astrology: it uncovers our eyes. It rewards us, now and then, with synchronicities.

One night ten years ago I was studying and reading about the Holy Grail. The next morning I got up and was almost blinded by a radiant goblet of light. I had left a wine glass

47

in the sink under the tap. Overnight, drop by drop, it had filled to its fullness and was catching the rays of the rising sun. The beauty of that silent yet radiant communion is still with me. I waited in a state out of time. Then I drank with the angels.

Dia-bolos as a process is neither good nor bad; it just is a process of separation. The morality issue came in with the story of Adam and Eve in the Garden of Eden. The concept of "sin" is historically rather recent, given the millennia that mankind has been around.

The other side of dia-bolos is Lucifer, the Light-bearer. That story of the Fallen Angel has to do with the pride of consciousness carried by the ego. Consciousness depends on duality, as has been wonderfully explained by Jung and by Edinger in their commentaries on the story of Adam and Eve. The apple, after all, hung on the Tree of the Knowledge of Good and Evil, and once eaten, the paradise of innocence was lost, because with consciousness come the twin shadows of guilt and pride. Yet without the apple (and the serpent force) we would not have become conscious. So perhaps we may conclude that it was a good thing, the *felix culpa*. This is what is indicated in the lovely medieval English carol "Adam lay y-bounden."

> Adam lay y-bounden, bounden in a bond
> Four thousand winter, thought he not too long
> And all was for an apple, an apple that he took
> as clerkes finden written in their book.
> Ne had the apple taken been
> Ne had never our Lady abeen heavene queen
> Blessed be the time that apple taken was
> Therefore we moun singen Deo gratias!

Perhaps the lesson ahead in our New Age is to learn to use consciousness more humbly, remembering where it came from, and to allow our egos to become handmaidens to the Self. It is only when we deny or forget the existence of the Self (Christ Within) and identify with our ego alone, that we must fall like Lucifer.

While we are on the subject of Adam and Eve, I can't resist asking if you have ever cut an apple sideways? If you do, you will discover the most beautiful pentagram in the middle of each. And this symbol upright

is the symbol in esoteric geometry for "man" and mind, and when reversed

is the symbol for the devil and black magic, which is the use of a universal (divine) process for individual (selfish) ends. The pentagram or pentacle is the emblem of, guess who? If you guessed Mercury, you were right. The pentagram is also a symbol and has a geometric relationship to the Golden Mean, the Golden Rectangle, the Parthenon, the Fibonacci Series of numbers, and the logarithmic curve of growth found in spiralling shells, sunflowers, pine cones, spiral galaxies: the geometry of being.

I hope I have been able to convey our terrible loss when we take things exclusively at the level of literalism. It is our loss because we fail to allow the symbol to guide us deeper. Mercury was the "messenger of the gods," the great communicator between heaven and earth, between psyche and soma (body and soul), always connecting, enabling us to become more conscious, if we will. Today, his archetype is relegated to delivering telegrams and flowers and hiding his caduceus on doctors' license plates, but at least he is not totally forgotten. Nameless and invisible, his process remains our caring psychopomp and guide, even down into our own Hades. No wonder Jung set him in the midst of the Bollingen Stone, and no wonder the alchemists valued him above all in the alchemical process of turning lead to gold or grief to wisdom.

So, though dia-bolos belongs to the world of Two, the process as sym-bolos can lead us back to One. We need duality for both evolution and involution, both aspects of manifestation.

Goethe put some wonderful wisdom into the mouth of Mephistopheles. When Faust asks, "Who are you?" Mephistopheles replies, "Part of that force which ever would do evil, yet ever creates good.... I am that spirit which ever denies."

Another area where symbolism operates is in connecting astronomical events with collective rituals. Christianity, as well as other solar religions, is based on agriculture and the dance of the earth about the Sun, played out at the cosmic level in the heavens. From Earth's perspective, the Sun makes four major stations, a veritable grand "sign of the cross" in the heavens at its apparent ingress into the four cardinal signs, Aries, Cancer, Libra, and Capricorn. This movement marks the solstices and equinoxes.

The motif of the period of Christmas is the rebirth of the Light or the Son of God. It coincides with the winter solstice, the point where the Sun appears to pause and change direction, moving northwards and again bringing back more light and warmth. This is still good news in the darkest of times.

The Sun enters the tenth astrological month, Capricorn. This occurs nine months after the Sun entered the first sign, Aries. After these months of gestation, Jesus is born, as were Mithra and Attis. Spirit is given form, which is incarnation, (Latin, in the flesh). So the "word is made flesh" and comes to dwell among us. The moment of the winter solstice is the very darkest we can experience, and so the rebirth of the light is both literal and symbolic; it must always have been a moment of immense joy.

The next three months or signs mark periods of intense hidden preparation for the "resurrection" of new life at Easter (the ingress of the Sun into the first sign of Aries). What is true for the Earth in terms of new vegetation in the spring is played out spiritually in the message of the new life coming to us after our death in the grave of Capricorn, where death and rebirth coincide.

The Sun remains in ascendancy until Midsummer's Eve around June 21, when the Sun enters the sign of Cancer, the Great Mother. This is the time the Sun rises above the heelstone at Stonehenge and falls through the chink of stained glass window of St. Apollinaire at Chartres at high noon, as Louis Charpentier points out in his book *The Mysteries of Chartres*. (This magnificent cathedral is dedicated to Our Lady.) Historically this was the time the "king must die," and so from that day on, for six months, the feminine takes prominence. The feasts of harvest and thanksgiving are celebrated in the "fall" of the Sun; it appears to move into its physical decline, yet also its spiritual gestation. This concept could lie behind the celebration of Rosh Hashanah, the New Year for the Jews and the beginning of the Christian year with the First Sunday in Advent (Latin for coming). Christmas was chosen by the early Church fathers to replace the pagan Saturnalia, formerly celebrated at the winter solstice.

The "crucifixion" takes place in the heavens as well, as the Sun (or the Earth) makes these stations. At the same time, the little year of the month is doing the same. Every month the Moon is new, then quartered, waxes to the full, then wanes. I remember the guide at Stonehenge pointed out to me that the lunations, i.e. new moons, form the sign of the cross every year, occurring at 90 degrees from each other during the seasons. The Sun takes twelve months, and the Moon has thirteen lunations in the average year. So the static constancy of the Sun is thrown into new gear by the Moon. The cycle of lunations is called the "Saros cycle of fifty-seven years"; it was known to the builders of the Aubrey holes around Stonehenge which, according to *Stonehenge Decoded* by Gerald S. Hawkins, marked how many years it would take before a new moon would occur on the same date of a given month or sign.

The astronomical sophistication of prehistoric people defies comprehension, but investigations going on over the last thirty years by distinguished scientists are forcing us to reconsider our assumptions about the ignorance of our pre-historic forebears. R.I.L.K.O. (Research into Lost Knowledge Organization), based in London, is to archeology what Capra and Bohm are to physics. Distinguished researchers such as Dr. Alexander Thom, Keith Critchlow, and John Michell are publishing valuable contributions to this field.

It seems that in our New Age, assumptions in almost every field of scholarly and scientific endeavor are requiring open-minded review and reinterpretation This applies to history as much as to physics, medicine, and psychology.

Well, time has raced by again. I will close for now and look forward, as always, to hearing from you!

Love,

7
Consciousness and symbols

Dear friend,

You ask: *"How does an individual relate to symbols?"*

I think Jung devoted his *Collected Works* to answering that question. My understanding is that there are two inter-related ways: through leading a symbolic life, and through consciousness.

Jung wrote eloquently of our need for the former:

> We have no symbolic life. Where do we live symbolically?
> Nowhere, except where we participate in the ritual of life.
> But who, among many, are really participating in the ritual
> of life? Very few....
>
> Have you got a corner somewhere in your house where
> you perform the rites, as you can see in India? Even the very
> simple houses have at least a curtained corner where the
> members of the household can lead a symbolic life, where
> they can make their new vows or meditation. We don't have
> it. We have no such corner....
>
> Only the symbolic life can express the need of the soul—
> the daily need of the soul, mind you! And because people
> have no such thing, they can never step out of this mill—this
> awful, grinding, banal life in which they are "nothing
> but"...and that is the reason why people are neurotic...
> Life is too rational, there is no symbolic existence in which I
> am something else, in which I am fulfilling my role, as one
> of the actors in the divine drama of life.

Elsewhere Jung makes the comment, "When the intellect does not serve the symbolic life, it is the devil. It makes you neurotic." This is the dia-bolos effect of identification with the ego. Yet we need our egos; they are the instruments of consciousness. So we are caught in the painful bind of a paradox. This is where the symbol can step in to heal. By using consciousness, we can become conscious of our need to lead another life *within* this one. How? By inviting the Divine Guest or the Self to participate in the meal we eat, the friend we greet, or the taxi ride we take. The Divine Guest is far more democratic than we think. He or she must be bored to tears being left out of all the fun stuff or the real stuff of life and consulted only on the Sabbath or in times of pain and crisis. The choice is ours—we can either invite this sharing or shut it out. As Jung remarked, "God is not interested in theology." Or as Dadaji, a Hindu anti-guru guru, told me, "God does not expect us to understand him; it is quite enough if we remember him!"

The Sufis tell us that a symbol is a theophany of the Absolute in the relative. They tell us we cannot invent symbols, only allow them to transform us. The ego lives a quantitative life; the symbol connects us to the qualitative life and has the capacity to imbue the simplest thing with meaning.

Perhaps the problem lies with the way consciousness operates. In order for the mind to come to grips with the flow of reality, it seems to have to stop the film for a second to realize what is going on, and while we are looking at a frame, life flows on. It is a no-win situation, probably one of the reasons it says in the Upanishads "The mind is the slayer of the Real." Which reminds me of the best definition of reality I ever heard: reality is that which is really going on while you're busy thinking it's something else.

We take consciousness so much for granted and even throw it away with mind-bending drugs and drink. We seem unmindful of what both Teilhard de Chardin and Jung were telling us: our collective consciousness may be the divine purpose of the human species in the evolutionary scheme of things through which, according to Teilhard, the Earth's aura, the noösphere, may be formed, which could eventually spiritualize the earth itself. What a task! What a vision!

As humankind has evolved, so has greater consciousness. Joseph Campbell in his series *The Masks of God*, Erich Neumann in his *Origins and History of Consciousness*, and Julian Jaynes in *The Origins of Consciousness in the Breakdown of the Bicameral Mind* are three others who have written much on the subject.

Astrologically speaking, consciousness took a leap forward during the Age of Gemini (Gemini rules the bicameral brain) during the period roughly from 6500 to 4000 B.C.

Edward C. Whitmont has pointed out that the Age of the Great Mother, the just-past Age of Cancer, has left us with many artifacts of the Mother Goddess being alone. This was the age of a kind of *participation mystique*, instinctive and collective, with little or no emphasis on the importance of the individual. Neumann likens it to that of human infancy when a baby is still closely fused with its mother. With the dawning of self-consciousness, the Goddess is depicted holding a child or a bird (both symbols of consciousness and both ruled by Gemini). Astrologically speaking, during the Age of Gemini, a shift probably took place from the dim awareness of processes themselves to the *naming* of the processes as archetypal gods to be worshipped ritually. And so as time went on the outer personifications became reified and concretized as idols. However, the idols then lost their *mana* or divine power and became objects of ridicule. The gods of one age become the devils of the next, or if that is not their fate, they end up more safely in fairy tales or, today, in comic strips. A surge of iconoclasm usually arises with each shift of astrological ages, and the objects or "things" of veneration are smashed to pieces for archeologists to dig up centuries later.

So the warning we need to heed when the dia-bolos process is at work pertains not to the personification of archetypal processes per se but to the mistake of forgetting that that is what we are doing, and perhaps have to do. A menu is not sinful; it is useful and describes the meal. What is ludicrous is to deny the experience of eating the meal entirely while we argue the meaning of the words on the menu, which, alas, is how many theologians come across today. Ramakrishna used to repeat the Oriental proverb, "We are all like two little birds in a tree. One of them eats the fruit and the other one watches."

Consciousness, so far, floats like a paper boat on the vast ocean of the Unconscious. Individuation calls for us to go fishing. A symbol is what we fish with. Half the symbol is known and above the surface in the conscious mind, and the other half is hidden in the unknown. It takes silence, patience, and attention to catch an insight, though occasionally one will leap directly into our basket. The important thing is to fish for oneself, not walk around looking at other people's fish. Astrology has taught me a bit about the nature of these fish: they swim up as images, not as words. The ones closest to the boat are personal ones, but if you drop the symbol deep enough into the depths of your own dreaming, you'll find that's where the deep and universal ones hide.

Now we are ready to approach the sigils or glyphs of astrology. You will see that they are a kind of shorthand of wisdom. They need to be memorized at first, always remembering they are pointing inwardly to processes in ourselves that will enable us better to understand those outside ourselves.

I never cease to marvel at the limitless wisdom these glyphs connect us with. They have slipped from age to age transcending nationalities, words, languages, and boundaries of time or space. They wait for us to see them, as Paracelsus says, "by that inner light which God has hid in nature and in our hearts from the beginning."

THE PLANETS	THE SIGNS
☉ : Sun	1. ♈ : Aries
☽ : Moon	2. ♉ : Taurus
☿ : Mercury	3. ♊ : Gemini
♀ : Venus	4. ♋ : Cancer

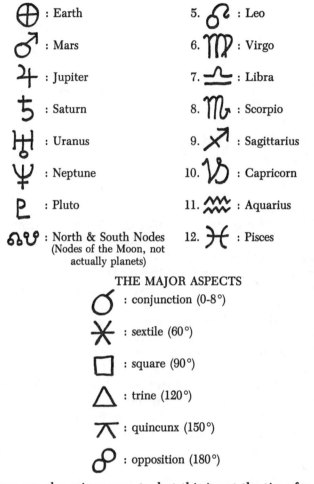

⊕ : Earth

♂ : Mars

♃ : Jupiter

♄ : Saturn

♅ : Uranus

♆ : Neptune

♇ : Pluto

☊☋ : North & South Nodes
(Nodes of the Moon, not
actually planets)

5. ♌ : Leo

6. ♍ : Virgo

7. ♎ : Libra

8. ♏ : Scorpio

9. ♐ : Sagittarius

10. ♑ : Capricorn

11. ♒ : Aquarius

12. ♓ : Pisces

THE MAJOR ASPECTS

☌ : conjunction (0-8°)

⚹ : sextile (60°)

□ : square (90°)

△ : trine (120°)

⚻ : quincunx (150°)

☍ : opposition (180°)

There are also minor aspects, but this is not the time for them. I hope you'll try contemplating some of these sigils to see what they say to you.

Good luck and enjoy!

8
How a chart speaks

My dear friend,

I am delighted that you don't mind the curious admixture of my letters, the bit of personal along with the philosophical. It's a feminine approach, a sort of homely one, to be sure, but it has always helped me to keep grounded.

Whenever I don't understand something in astrology, I go back to the Natural Zodiac (with 0 degrees on the cusp of the First House), which is a paradigm, or I go to the human body. Every planet and sign is involved in the human body, and if you want to understand a process or function of one of them, see what it rules in the body and how it contributes to the whole. We carry everything we need to know right along with us all the time, but the more we seek to know, the more we convince ourselves (or others convince us) that we are separated (dia-bolos) from what we are seeking. My teacher used to say that to me forty years ago, and, naturally, I resisted it completely.

Your next question is:

How does a chart "speak" to the astrologer?

Well, a psychopharmacologist once gave me a big hint. I asked him a question about brain function, and he explained to me that if you see "NEW YORK THRUWAY" on a sign, you will read that with the left brain, but if you see a sign with an arrow on it or a deer—in short, a picture—you read this with the right brain.

The Natural Zodiac

St. Columba
by Kathryn Smith

This gave me an astrological insight. Everything placed on a chart is, and definitely should be, a symbol. No words. The astrologer thus reads it with the right brain, so images come up. This has always happened for me, but it took many years before I came to trust the images and to share them directly with the client. When I finally found the courage to do so, the synchronicities began happening, because more often than not the image was one already familiar to the person.

I remember an early case of this. I was doing the chart of a woman who was a Gemini, with Jupiter and the Moon in Leo in the Ninth House. I think she had Sagittarius rising, and I remember that she had Venus in Cancer in the Eighth. All her "feminine" or yin planets, as well as all her masculine planets, were in masculine signs except this Venus, and Gemini is an androgynous sign as the Twins are both yin and yang. (If you read this with little comprehension at this point, don't worry. Just let the words slide through. Someday, it will make sense.)

The woman was most attractive, with a boyish Amazon quality. She had lost her mother when very young, had grown up with a father and brothers, married and had four sons, and was now divorced. Two images floated up for me. One had to do with the lost little girl or the lost femininity (Venus).

I asked her if she disliked pretty little girls or "Southern belle" type women. She laughed and admitted I was right on. Later, she spoke of a recurring dream of a baby or a little girl drowning in a pond or a lake (the Unconscious). She had never connected it to her own lost or neglected femininity.

Next I took up the Jupiter and Moon in Leo in the Ninth. The archetype that arose for me was the Emperor, and since the Ninth House rules history, what came up next was the Roman Empire. I decided for once to trust the image, but tentatively. I inquired if she were interested in history. Indeed she was. My next question was about Roman history. Her mouth dropped open, and she began to blush and look extremely embarrassed. I waited for an explanation. Finally she blurted out something she had never confessed to anyone but considered to be a perversion. One of her sexual fantasies was that of gladiators torturing, brutalizing, and mutilating little girls in a Roman arena. This both fascinated and horrified her. I waited until she was through and then asked her if she could not see this might be less a perversion than an unconscious metaphor for the way the masculine side of her psyche was brutalizing and almost eliminating her pleasure in being feminine. Her relief and recognition were clearly apparent.

At the end, she thanked me profusely and told me that only the other day she had noticed her body was growing a little softer (she was an ardent jogger, sportswoman, and camper). "You know, Alice," she said, "for the first time I wasn't all that upset. I even patted my ovary and said, 'Isn't he cute!" Sensing my astonishment, she looked up and grinned. "Woops! I did it again! I mean, isn't *she* cute!"

When the insight comes out of the person's own chart and Unconscious with that much clarity, the impact and the release is positively cathartic. It was a great lesson to me in trusting the image, however unlikely that image might appear.

This, in turn, reminds me of another client, another Amazon, brilliant, getting her second doctorate in law. She was an ardent feminist, a Lesbian, a statuesque goddess. Her passion was to protect younger and less self-confident women from masculine aggression. I smiled and told her that there was a goddess who personified that kind of energy and purpose, and that her name was Artemis. It was her turn to smile. "I started an Artemis Club in college—now I know why it had to be called 'Artemis'!"

Another example where an image from a chart provided a dramatic release was that of a middle-aged woman. She was a Capricorn with Scorpio rising, a dusky black-haired lady with large dark eyes and a kind of smoldering energy. The image which emerged, not surprisingly, was that of a gypsy.

I began by asking her if she liked music. She did. Gypsy music and dancing? How did I know? Well, it was all there, along with an interest in subtle power, intrigue, and the occult. We had a lively and interesting session. Then, at the end, the woman grew serious and sad. She had a recurring problem. She had even sought help in therapy, but it remained something over which she had no control. She was a kleptomaniac. She pinched things in stores, things she really had no need for and could afford to buy. There was a long pause. Finally, she looked up and, with a hollow whisper, said, "My God! That's what gypsies do!" The unconscious identification with the gypsy in her was so strong that it was taking over the "throne" of her psyche and running things against her conscious will. I only hoped the image was justified, and that through becoming more conscious of the gypsy, she could learn to keep her in check.

This brings up a most interesting question that years ago would have been unthinkable to mention. It is the question of reincarnation. Was this woman, in fact, once a gypsy? As an astrologer, I have no way of answering. To tell her outright she was once a gypsy would be overstepping the line by far for me. I stick with the image, and if it speaks to the client in a meaningful way, I am content to see it as metaphor and to use the expression, "It is almost *as if* you have a kind of gypsy in you."

However, I should mention that an analyst friend of Jung's, Erlo van Waveren, has written a book called *Pilgrimage to Rebirth*. In it he not only discusses recall of his own former lives, but seriously suggests that these lives live on in us as subpersonalities, sometimes as complexes in conflict. It would seem sometimes as if this could be the case. Nowadays, many are taking a serious look at past-life regressions.

I remember the first time this came up in a session. The client, a man, was a Leo with Jupiter and Venus in Cancer in the Ninth and four planets in Virgo in the Eleventh. The image clearly was of one who desires only to feed the world and be of service to his fellowman. The image was not of just a monk, but of a hospice and monastery all rolled into one individual! When I began tentatively by saying, "It is as if there is a monk in you," he laughed heartily and told me he had had a life regression and knew perfectly well he had been a monk for several lifetimes. In this life, he had indeed tried to feed others by starting a food program for orphaned children in Korea, and, at the time of our meeting he had about seventeen people living in his own house—he wasn't even sure of all their names. He was a marvelous soul; his only problem seemed to be that his wife had left him. Perhaps, I ventured, he had assumed too much and volunteered her services without consulting her. Such was the case.

Not surprisingly, I have done the charts for quite a few "monks" and "nuns." I believe I've already mentioned that their spiritual quest continues, yet these men and women have difficulty in relating easily to the opposite sex and in accepting the material world. It is as if they got $A+$ in renouncing sex and the world in one life and they came back with the message they must embrace all that they once rejected and find it, too, to be sacred. This comes hard. Issues of money, sex, and authority arise.

The "nun" sometimes needs to overcome anger and resentment against men, as if these women resent being spiritually directed against their better judgment. I remember one such woman who now worked in a unisex barbershop and who took pleasure in her Delilah-like power to stand behind a man and cut off his hair and to have the choice of either speaking to him or not. It seemed to give her a kind of grim satisfaction. Another was a nurse who smoldered with resentment against the male doctors and their way of handling patients. In each case, the archetypal image emerged from the chart. You begin to see the "signatures" of such attitudes and how they affect the way the person "processes the experience." Many of these people were already in analysis, and astrological sessions yielded a wealth of material to be worked on with ongoing therapy. This is why it is so very helpful for therapists to avail themselves of astrology and to study it, as you are doing.

Fortunately, an increasing number of analysts are now sending their patients to qualified astrologers, and by qualified I mean those who have some working knowledge and understanding of psychology. When I receive such a patient, the synchronicity then works in the other direction.

A man who was a minister and a Scorpio, with Saturn in Gemini, came to see me. His chart showed all the potential to be happily in touch with his own sensuality and with his wife, if he could only get over the puritanical repression he felt was necessary for his own salvation. He even had difficulty giving himself permission to laugh at anything, let alone at himself. Finally, I burst out, "But you could be so happy were it not for this old Cotton Mather in you!" That did it. He started to laugh, in spite of himself. His analyst had been calling him Cotton Mather for the last six months!

When I know that a person is in a Jungian analysis, I find it is often appropriate to look for a character in a myth or fairy tale which can objectify the problem faced by the patient. I am a great believer in the efficacy of this, and I will even use examples from my own life, if necessary, to help the patient turn the problem around, see it objectively, and apply the new insight. Anyway, another man came to see me, who since has become a friend. He was an Aquarian with Jupiter in Sagittarius rising and the Moon in Gemini in the Seventh, both squared by Saturn and Mars in Pisces in the Fourth House. His persona was naturally one of extraordinary enthusiasm; he almost blew me out of my chair with happy confidence and curiosity about his chart.

I described his persona, while he beamed at me, and then I worked my way tactfully to the "but" which had to do with the enormous emphasis he placed on success and the hidden fear of failure. I cast about in my mind for an example from mythology and could find nothing at the time. But the image in the chart suggested a classic character in a modern American play. I asked him if he were familiar with *Death of a Salesman* by Arthur Miller. My client sat still, shocked. Only a few days previously, his analyst had been reading him Willy Loman's letter to his son.

When these things happen, I get goose bumps, and the patient experiences in psychological stereo. Not only has the image come up in analysis, it has arisen independently from his own chart. The impact is doubly powerful all around. Needless to say, in not a single one of the instances cited had I met the person before. More often than not, I never see the person again, though this has begun to change now that I am more settled and people know where they can reach me for an update or further counseling. In the case of the Aquarian, I did have the pleasure of meeting him again. The last time I saw him, he thanked me for the insights of the chart, because he was in a temporary financial crisis and looking potential failure in the face. It was all right, he knew he would survive psychologically. He did financially, too.

Sometimes people accuse me of just being psychic. But I am only trusting the images arising out of the chart. I can always point to where the image came from, as you will experience yourself. Certainly, I am intuitive, and years of practice have helped. Like a computer, my mind scans the various options of examples suggested by aspects or sign placements of planets. Everything the astrologer has ever experienced, directly or vicariously, may come into play. Nothing in one's life can be wasted. In the end, your self is all you have to give.

You may pick up the fact that I am leaning more in the direction of believing in reincarnation. Are you familiar with the work of Dr. Ian Stevenson of the University of Virginia? Or Morris Netherton? I understand Jung himself kept an open mind on the subject. I know from Erlo van Waveren that Jung came to the conclusion that reincarnation was likely, and had ideas of who he himself might have been.

Stan Grof has written about the LSD experiments in Czechoslovakia. He found that over time people under LSD would deal with the personal content of the Unconscious first, and then they would break through to what appeared to be a recall of a former life; finally they would come to a level of the transpersonal or Collective Unconscious. So the work would seem to be a kind of objective proof of Jung's theory.

I met Stan on several occasions and was invited by him and his wife Christina to attend his workshop at Esalen in which he was using music and hyperventilation as a substitute for LSD. About a dozen psychiatrists and psychotherapists from South America were in attendance and a sprinkling of others. With this technique, it took only minutes for them to "go under" and to experience all manner of emotional contents.

I have two striking memories of the workshop. One is of a psychiatrist from Argentina, a man, suddenly re-experiencing being below deck on a medieval galley, chained, and drowning as the ship went down in a battle. The other is of an American woman of Russian Jewish heritage, who on the last day began to give a sermon in a deep man's voice, in a language unknown to us (and to her, it turned out later). However, one man in the group could understand it—it was Ladino, the Sephardic equivalent of Yiddish, but with a Spanish base. What she (or rather "he") was reiterating was, "I am suffering, and I have suffered. We are suffering, and we have suffered." It was a powerful experience. What made it even more so for me was that I had done this woman's chart the day before and pointed out that she tended to feel "persecuted."

I came away from Esalen with the conviction that Jung was right when he said we know practically nothing about the human psyche. Perhaps we have potential access to all of history built into the very cells of our psychosomatic being. If so, then we must thank the ego for protecting us from more than we can bear at any given moment. It is like a ladle that spills over if too much is served. Perhaps drugs interfere with that delicate balance, so that we get swamped with more than we can assimilate. I would be very grateful for your opinion.

Ever yours,

9
From glyph to image

Dear friend,

It was so good to see you the other day, and it makes me very happy to know my letters are proving helpful. Your last question addresses the next step to take in astrology:

How does one get from the glyph to the image?

The answer to this is difficult to put into words but simple to put into practice, because you cannot learn astrology with your head alone; you have to learn it with your whole being: body, soul, and spirit.

I think now we should discuss the planets as archetypal processes in the psyche, beginning with the Sun. So I will share with you how I came to experience the Sun, and I ask you to think back to your childhood, as well. Have you ever noticed that almost all small children will spontaneously put the Sun in their drawings? It's uncanny.

When I was living back then in Greenwich Village I hungered for ritual. Sometimes I attended services at the Church of the Ascension. More often I turned to my own altar, which I had set up with a little ziggurat-type pyramid of seven metals, and I would conduct the Communion Service right down to the breaking of the bread and drinking the wine. The "dear Lord," as Grandpa used to refer to him, must have smiled at my oblivion of the essential nature of communion, which means sharing with others. Yet I was sincere and came to know and deeply appreciate the lovely wording of the service. To this day, I use the opening sentence as my mantra, ever finding greater depth of meaning to the thought: "Almighty God, unto whom all hearts are open and from whom no secrets are hid, cleanse the thoughts of our hearts with the inspiration of Thy Holy Spirit that we may more worthily love Thee and magnify Thy Holy Name."

One spring Sunday, I had just concluded the "service" and decided, since it was so balmy, to do my *lectura divina* on the fire escape. So I climbed out the window with my book and a comfy pillow and began to read. Suddenly, without warning, I experienced a moment of satori, an attack of insight so powerful, I almost get dizzy remembering it. It was the realization: THE SUN SHINES!!!

It doesn't have to, it just does. Out of a void, a nothing contained in a nothing, came this great blazing affirmation, this great *yes!* before a no can sound, shouting "HERE I AM!" (yah-weh—I am). For me, it was an experience beyond words of the process of Creation. I AM THAT I AM. TAT TVAM ASI. I thought my heart would burst. It felt like a cup filled with light and love. Tears brimmed in my eyes at the grace of it, the wonder of it. I realized, as never before, I had eaten the Sun in the bread and drunk the Sun in the wine, and in offering myself "a living sacrifice" to God, I had only given Spirit back to Spirit. It was all One. So not in a church, but on a fire escape in New York City, came my first lesson about the process of the Sun.

The way I felt that day is best expressed by Yeats in his poem "Vacillation":

> My fiftieth year had come and gone
> I sat, a solitary man,
> In a crowded London shop
> An open book and empty cup
> On the marble table-top.
>
> While on the shop and street I gazed
> My body of a sudden blazed;
> And twenty minutes more or less
> It seemed, so great my happiness,
> That I was blessèd and could bless.

68

What can I tell you? Only that we carry this Sun, each of us, in our breast. As Dadaji put it, "God is making love to you twenty-four hours a day in your heart-beat."

It is curious that in order to speak of the image conveyed by the glyph of the Sun, which is

you really have to resort to the indirect approach of the poet. It is the poetic which creates the poet in you or me and brings the image to a level where it can unite with our own inner experience. There it takes root, like sperm, in the inner lining of the receptive heart. Whisper these words to yourself:

> The heavens declare the glory of God; and the firmament sheweth his handiwork.
> Day unto day uttereth speech, and night unto night sheweth knowledge.
> There is no speech nor language where their voice is not heard.
> Their line is gone out through all the earth, and their words to the end of the world. In them hath he set a tabernacle for the sun,
> Which is as a bridegroom coming out of his chamber, and rejoiceth as a strong man to run his course.
> His going forth is from the end of the heavens, and his circuit unto the ends of it: and there is nothing hid from the heat thereof.
>
> Psalm 19

There are so many beautiful images in this, and I find myself often being reminded of it. For instance, every time my husband comes out of the bath, freshly combed and pink-cheeked, having shaved and showered, he walks to the bureau in our bedroom for his clean underwear. His body is straight and firm for all his years, and there is a resplendent quality in him that reminds me of the "Sun coming forth as a bridegroom from his chamber." As this simple daily act often coincides with the actual sun rising (we rise early), the image is doubly reinforced. It is a source of secret delight, a

joyous allusion and a daily reaffirmation of love and gratitude. It helps me to remember that the Sun in a woman's
chart rules her husband.

The experience of the Sun, at least for me, cannot be
separated from the experience of life and of love, the kind of
love that suffuses one with joy and gratitude for the simple
beatitude of being. Sometimes it feels like a big locomotive
light in the middle of one's chest.

I often wonder at the punning in the words *light, life,
love, laughter.* They all begin for us with the sound "el,"
and of course *el* means Lord in Hebrew. And B-aal,
etymologically, means the Son (sun) of the Lord and is
cognate with our word *ball.* A ball is a perfect sphere or
three-dimensional circle. The Sun is associated, astrologically, with fire, heat, light, and life, and in the body with
the heart. Sun : solar system = heart : body. You can see
how the symbolism of the glyph hints at the essence and
totality of "being," the very process of fire.

What is so unique about this element of fire? Why is it
present on the altars of so many religions?

1) It defies gravity, reaching to return to its source.

2) It consumes.

3) It is hot, both comforting and terrifying.

4) Most significantly, unlike the other three elements of
earth, air, and water, *it can be shared without being
diminished.* Like love, the more you give away, the more
there is. (This observation can be helpful in counseling those
who suffer sibling rivalry and doubt the parents' ability to
have enough love to go around.) This can be demonstrated.
You can prove that one candle can light an infinite number
of candle flames, providing they in turn light others.
Similarly, one seed can generate an indefinite number of
others, providing the new ones go on generating more. The
maple tree I see standing in the snow outside is connected
back through time with generations and generations of
maples, just as we are with all past humanity. The Sufi
mystic Shabistari wrote:

> Each creature that goes before you has a soul,
> And from that soul is bound a cord to you.

Therefore are they all subject to your dominion,
For that the soul of each one is hidden in you.
You are the kernel of the world in the midst thereof.
Know yourself that you are the world's soul.

If with such a poet's eye and a poet's hand you were to
touch a tree of yours, all trees in creation would shimmer at
your touch; and when our hands touch in friendship, the
very Net of Indra sparkles. This is "the instruction of the
heart and the enlighten ing of the eye."

It is so simple, so direct. No wonder it is considered a
mystery. One has to be a child to see it, and we have to be
"reborn" into such simplicity, which requires the feminine.
Certainly, we are not taught to see with the heart, and yet
the instinct is there. Ask anyone quickly to identify himself,
and he will point to his heart not to his head.

But the intellectualizing masculine continues to prevail.
Only consider the following which I picked out of *The New
Yorker Magazine* not long ago:

COROLLARIES WE NEVER GOT AROUND TO READING

From "Prolegomenon to a Theory of Religion," by Gerald
James Larson, in the *Journal of the American Academy of
Religion*

[3.1] *The Definition.* Within the context of these considera-
tions, let me now proceed to suggest a definition of Religion
and to offer as well two corollary definitions that grow out
of the basic definition. I suggest the following: *Religion* is a
"complete system of human communication" (or a "form of
life") showing in primarily "commissive," "behabitive," and
"exercitive" modes how a community comports itself when it
encounters an "untranscendable negation of...possibilities."
The two related corollaries' definitions are...

An extreme case of the academic approach, but delicious for
all that!

Astrology connects unexpected things through its symbolism. The songwriter writing, "Baby, baby, won't you
light my fire!" is referring in essence, to the same process
that David did in his Psalm, though we might not ordinarily
associate the two. We would be more likely to think of the
Egyptian "Hymn to Ra" or the Vedic "Hymn to the Sun."

Once I had an interesting dream: I am walking down a hotel corridor. In front of me is a man whose head is a sun, a ball of fire. Briskly, he opens first a door on the left and then a door on the right and so on down the line. Each room is dark, but the minute he sticks his head in, he exclaims almost irritably, "I can't see anything dark in here!" and again, "I can't see anything dark in here!"

I awoke laughing, it seemed so silly. And then I realized that here was something an omnipotent Solar God could not know without us, and that is the nature of darkness. Perhaps this is the secret of the Black Madonna. The goddess knows something the god can not know without her. It is she who can bring forth both sons *and* daughters, masculine *and* feminine, light *and* darkness. It is she who is the Mother of All Living.

Consider the traditional collects for Christmastide, the time of the annual rebirth of the Sun Child:

> O God, who hast caused this holy night to shine with the illumination of the true Light: Grant us, we beseech Thee, that as we have known the mystery of that Light upon earth, so may we also perfectly enjoy him in heaven.

and

> Almighty God, who hast poured upon us the new light of thine incarnate Word: grant us that that same light, enkindled in our hearts, may shine forth in our lives.

The reading on Christmas Day quotes the beautiful words of the Gospel of John, filled again with symbolism of Light.

> In the beginning was the Word, and the Word was with God, and the Word was God.
> The same was in the beginning with God.
> All things were made by him; and without him was not any thing made that was made.
> In him was life; and the life was the light of men.
> And the light shineth in darkness and the darkness comprehended it not.
> There was a man sent from God, whose name was John.
> The same came for a witness, to bear witness of the Light that all men through him might believe.

He was not that Light, but was sent to bear
witness of that Light.

*That was the true Light which lighteth every
man that cometh into the world.*

Gospel of John I:1-7

I have tried to introduce a number of images which
cluster around and amplify the solar process associated with
the Life-Light-Love aspect of the ongoing creating Spirit.
Naturally, such a process was from the beginning divine and
is no less divine for being in us.

Here again we can miss the point by taking these images
literally, seeing God only as Father, and Christ only as his
"only begotten Son." How else could one express and imply
the love existing between God and this extension of himself
which we all are except in terms of a family? But the real
implication in terms of *process* is that this divine Light-Life
is in each of us but we don't "comprehend" it, we are not
conscious of it. Yet we live and love by this Light and stand
to see it in each other. For Hindus it is called Atman; for
Christian mystics, the Christ Within; for Sufis, the Divine
Guest; and for Jung, it is safe to say, the Self.

So I assign you, dearest friend, on your birthday to find a
quiet spot and therein to meditate with body, mind, and
soul on this mystery of Spirit, which clothed itself so
beautifully when it incarnated in you. Feel it beating in
your heart, know the many ways it passes through you physically, mentally, and emotionally leading you always to
greater understanding and deeper awe at the wonder and
mystery of being.

"God dwells in you as You."

With much love,

10
The Sun

Dear friend,

> Good morning, Life—and all
> Things glad and beautiful.
> My pockets nothing hold,
> But he that owns the gold,
> The Sun, is my great friend—
> His spending has no end.

This stanza from a poem by W. H. Davies expresses something significant from our point of view: the Sun never takes
back its rays, its spending has no end. And so should we
learn to love. It is the Sun's *agape*, the love spoken of by the
avatars.

The Moon, our satellite, and all the other planets merely
reflect and modify the light of this powerhouse of constant
shining, and, for this reason, I cannot agree with some
astrologers that the Sun shows the ego in the chart. If you
think of the process of the ego, it is to reflect and distribute
the light of the Self. Jung even made the simile himself in
the Zarathustra Seminars.

Astronomically, the Sun, when seen from the Earth, gen-
erates both the sidereal and the tropical zodiacs, to say
nothing of holding the swinging of the planets in orbits. The
solar system is the invisible body of the Sun. So, for me, the
Sun is the generator of each psyche, acting as the scintilla of
Spirit manifest in each of us during a lifetime. As Jung
pointed out, the Self is the center and totality of the psyche,

and also an ongoing and unfathomable mystery dwelling in the Unconscious. Identifying the ego with this inner Sun would seem to be quite an inflation. Yet I cannot tell you that the Sun in the chart is the Self, either, only that it is a focus from which all but the houses derive. One would assume that the entire chart and its unfolding through life would reflect the Self.

The twelve houses are determined by the Earth (except in a heliocentric chart), and that is as it should be, since the houses deal with the psyche's relationship to outer, objective life. The planets' positions in the houses are determined by the three co-ordinates of birthtime, latitude and longitude: these yield the basic crucifix of the midheaven axis with the horizon. The houses show where in life the application and manifestation of the psyche will be acted out, and how the outer events of life will be processed as experience.

In the glyph for the Sun ☉, look at the circle. You can see its whole area quite easily, can you not? So it should be easy to measure. Yet simple as this seems, it cannot be done. Why? Because the formula for measuring the area of a circle is πr^2, and we know now this never is resolved. Harvard has published a compilation of π worked out by a computer to an incomprehensible extent, and it still defies final definition. The parallel to the psyche is there: the chart as a mandala is by implication infinite. No one can either define or limit another, one can only help the unfolding. Our own potential is limitless.

The point in the middle of the circle is called by the Hindus the *bindu*, and in Hebrew it is termed the *yod*. A point has no dimension. Again we are reminded of Nicolas of Cusa's definition of God as a circle whose center is everywhere and whose circumference is nowhere.

The circle without a dot ○ is the equivalent of Brahman or "the Ground of Being" or the Void (zero) out of which all creation comes; it is Spirit Unmanifest. The circle with the dot is Spirit Manifest, specific. This symbol, therefore, is pointing to the process of ongoing *creating*. Both religious and astrological symbolism try to show that Unity becomes manifest multiplicity by the union of polarities through trinities.

75

As a scientific aside, there are two remarkable volumes of photographs by a Swiss scientist, Hans Jenny. He was a contemporary of Jung's and lived in Zurich. The titles are KYMATIK/CYMATICS. These photos are pictures of the impact sound has upon matter. Fern spores, sand, even oil and water are placed on a metal plate, and then a measurable pitch is sounded. Instantly, the material moves into a geometric pattern in response to the sound, a repeatable pattern. These patterns are of the greatest beauty and intricacy. The vowel *O*, for example, gathers the material into a perfect circle which bulges up as if it were trying to make a sphere. (Perhaps the sound *OM* creates a circle around us at the auric level?) A fragment of an orchestral piece by Bach produces a webbed fabric. I find these figures highly significant and wish architects could study them, because they must contain structural resonances that would be both sound (sic!) and resonate with human consciousness. There is even a picture showing a twelvefold pattern, a natural horoscope. Jenny's theory is that forms in nature may have been the result of sound.

What is relevant here is the number of patterns which are divisible by three. It really seems as if the One in becoming Two makes Three out of Four, to paraphrase Maria Prophetissima. Jung was fascinated all his life with the question of Three and Four. Astrology simplifies this, as you will see. The three modalities (cardinal, mutable, and fixed signs), like the gunas, describe the three ways, the "how." The four elements (fire, earth, air, and water) describe the "what" that is to be processed. Jenny's work would seem to bear this out, and since Saturn rules both matter and sound and the whole process of manifestation, there may well be some connection.

Let's continue with solar symbolism in the round dance of the year, since we are approaching New Year's Day.

The Sun is naturally associated with the number twelve.

Take a sphere, any sphere, a Christmas ornament or a ping-pong ball. Ask yourself how many other spheres of the exact same diameter could you place around it, so that each one would touch the other *and* the center one? The answer is readily demonstrated: it is twelve. So the "Twelve Days of Christmas" are forming a baby year straddling the Old and the New. The celebration for a rebirth of the Christ Sun has a midpoint at New Year's and a climax at Epiphany, the "showing forth" to the gentiles, i.e., the Three Kings. [These seem to be eponymous replicas of the three sons of Noah: Ham, Shem, and Japheth, who represented the three then-known races of the world: the Hamites (blacks), the Shemites (Semites), and the Japhethites (Caucasians).]

On New Year's Eve, the Sun Ball is placed amidst the twelve.

Jung has pointed out that the ball has always been traditionally associated with New Year's and that jugglers would perform in churches and cathedrals on that day. Is it just coincidence that a ball descends in Times Square to mark the New Year, to say nothing of millions of Americans glued to their TV sets watching the ritual playing of football in "bowls" all over the country?

These rituals also involve a secular re-enactment of crowning a "virgin" with roses and garlands and making her a "queen" for the day. The floats and pageantry are a modern repetition of the old Saturnalia, and the games bring out the contest between opposing forces for the Solar Ball. You really cannot kill an archetype; he just puts on a Rams or a Bears or a Dolphins uniform! The marvel is that so many of us participate so unconsciously in these rites without realizing what they are.

Another motif, of course, is that of the Old Year, personified by Saturn (who else!), ruler of Capricorn, with a long white beard and a sickle, giving way to the New Year (Mercury) as a newborn baby. Beneath the more obvious message lies another one about time (Chronos, Saturn's Greek name). Time is at once old and new. Hidden within eternity is the freshness of now; hidden in the now is the mystery of eternity. This paradox is with us always and is implicit in the circle with twelve spokes, the chakra or wheel of Surya, the Hindu God of the Sun. The wheel of time, the wheel of fortune, the cyclical nature of time are all generated by the "apparent" motion of the Sun.

77

In Europe it is a tradition at New Year's to touch a chimney sweep or a baby pig for good luck. In Switzerland even today people eat little pink marzipan candy pigs on New Year's and children watch nervously for the coming of the Schwarzer Peter with St. Nikolaus on December 6. Black Peter is the one to whom the naughty ones are delivered or from whom they receive a lump of coal for their misdeeds. Saturn is also the Black Man. The chimney sweeps go from party to party on New Year's Eve bringing luck. The tradition extends to Celtic Scotland where on Hogmanay (January 1) a black-haired man is desired as "first-footer" or the first to set foot in the house on that day. These playful games are re-enacting something almost lost to consciousness.

I am not sure about the little pig—it may go back to the Eleusinian Mysteries, when on the second day of the feast, people projected their sins onto little pigs and then washed them off in the sea at Kantharos. There must have been a lot of squealing! Perhaps you have some further insight from your own studies. The pig was sacred to the Mother Goddess and is ruled by Cancer in astrology.

Let us look again at the wheel of the circle:

We can see that the center unites every point on the circumference. The ego travels "round and around in circles" trying to make sense of life. But if we "seek first the kingdom of heaven, then all else will be added to us." To do this means to med-itate (Latin—*meditare*), the root of which means literally to go to the center. Translated into Jungian terms—to form an ego-Self axis.

The geometric symbol of the Sun yields a wealth of insights. Add to these Jung's definition of the mandala as a symbol of the Self, and that the ubiquitous symbol for God, going back to early man, has been the circle or solar disc, and you begin to see how astrology can provide a key to decoding all kinds of things.

So far, much of this symbolism of the Sun seems exclusively masculine, but we must remember that in several cultures, the German, for instance, the Sun is considered feminine. We are aiming, according to St. John, for the Woman clothed with the Sun, perhaps the "spirituous earth." Without the feminine, all that solar energy could take no *form* or bring forth life manifest. So you cannot have a "Christ" or a Krishna or a you or a me without a mother, nor a green earth without an atmosphere giving us moisture and distributing light; without a Moon or without a night as well as a day.

Become a collector of "dodechisms," twelves, because this number is archetypal and represents a totality that is solar. Here are a few to get started:

12 acupuncture meridians in the body

12 pairs of cranial nerves (24)

12 tissue salts

12 hours on a watch (24 hours in a day)

12 meridians on the globe

12 months in a year

12 inches to a foot

12 people on a jury

12 Signs of the Zodiac

12 Constellations

12 sons of Jacob

12 running springs in Helim

12 rivers flowing from the spring Hvergelmir (Norse)

12 loaves in Sanctuary

12 stones in Hebrew breastplate (Old Testament)

12 stones on Hebrew altar (Old Testament)

12 oxen bearing brazen sea at Temple of Solomon

12 stars in bride's crown (New Testament)

12 foundations of Jerusalem

12 disciples/apostles

12 aeons

12 Labors of Gilgamesh

12 Labors of Hercules

12 Olympian gods

12 dii maiores (Roman)

12 Buddhic nidanas: states of emergence

12 saviors *(Pistis Sophia)*

12 Knights of King Arthur

12 deities on Ra's solar boat

12 gates of the Ming-t'ang

12 fruits on the Tree of Life

12 dynamic aspect of 4x3 (female & male) for Dogons and Bambaras of Mali

12 spaces between knots on Druid's Knot

12 total of sides on two dice

12 Merry Men about the Oak King

12 Sacred Chinese Ornaments

12 Norse gods

12 episodes of Moses' life

12 exploits of Odysseus

12 Meistersingers

12 Paladins of Charlemagne

12 Tablets of Roman Law

12 Stations of Christ's Passion

12 sides to the dodecahedron (which adds the 5 to the 12)

This gives you some idea of the deep significance of this number and its association with the Creative power.

Remember those two helpful hints I mentioned before: 1) *When in doubt go back to the body;* 2)*When in doubt, go back to the Natural Zodiac.* What, in the body, creates and sustains life and is our physical Sun? If you answered the heart, you are right. The heart, and the spine of thirty-three (sic) vertebrae, and the right eye in a man and the left in a woman. The other eye, of course, is ruled by the Moon.

In Hatha Yoga and the chakra system, *Ha* means Sun and *Tha* means Moon, and the ida and pingala spiraling up the spine through the wheels or chakras represent the feminine and masculine energies raising the spinal "serpent of power," the Kundalini force, up the shushumna or central subtle cord in the spine itself. This process, aided and abetted by breath (Mercury), results in an inner *coniunctio* of Sun and Moon and the begetting of consciousness, the reborn child within. It is superfluous to note that physical death occurs with the final cessation of the heartbeat.

Not long ago I was doing the chart of a Virgo woman who was suffering terribly from a negative inflation or inferiority complex. I was staying at the home of a Jungian trainee at the time and working in her basement. I should add that the lady was also in analysis, because I find synchronicities seem to occur more often than not when Jung is involved. Anyway, I was chiding her for not accepting that she had a Divine Guest within her like anyone else, a Self. She looked doubtful. Then I quoted Dadaji, "God is making love in your heartbeat twenty-four hours a day." There was a moment of silence, and then a pump kicked on behind the wall next to us, and throughout the session it continued a steady "heartbeat." Needless to say, it made an impression on us and we both "took heart." It pumped for the rest of the session and could be heard on the tape.

The Sun is the "star" in the chart, since the Sun itself is the active principle in the solar system, and the Moon and the planets reflect it. However it is frequently not perceived by the individual as the most important part of the psyche.

Very often the "throne" of the psyche has been usurped by another, and the Sun, or rightful heir, is "in exile" as in the many legends and fairy tales of this motif. The question then for the analyst is to find out who the usurper is: the Shadow? the Ego? the Animus?

The astrologer can often point to the guilty archetype in the chart, because the client experiences it so much more strongly than any other. If you put your thumb up to your eye, you can blot out the Sun: the world becomes all thumb. In the same way, a very strongly placed Uranus or Saturn or Mars can almost eclipse the sense of who one really is. The chart can be such a help here, because the client can be reminded that no matter how powerfully Saturn appears to be inhibiting him or her, the truth is that the Sun is a star and Saturn only a reflecting planet.

I owe this insight of the myth of the usurped throne again to a client. She was born in Europe during the war and had a terrible childhood, totally lacking in nurturing. She was an Aquarian, and the chart pointed to the fact that no matter what advice I gave her, she would not follow it. Indeed, she had been in Freudian analysis for over eight years and had been dismissed by three psychiatrists, for lack of co-operation.

She was delightful, curly-headed, impish and yet dreadfully unhappy. She knew neither how to give nor to receive love. I asked if she knew any stories that begin with, "Once upon a time there was a kingdom, and the kingdom was a wasteland, because the true ruler had been cast out as a baby, and a wicked uncle or queen was sitting unrightfully on the throne." She nodded her head. I threw in a dragon for good measure, and she smiled. Then I pointed to the chart and said, "This is the story of your own psyche. Someone is usurping your throne and the real You is in exile. And what's more, the chart shows me the usurper."

She looked up at me and grinned defiantly. I drew a deep breath and shouted, "It's a brat!" Well, that did it! She burst out laughing and clapped her hands like a child caught in disguise. I was right. None of those psychiatrists had discovered the brat, she said (I wonder). Now she was

81

willing to listen and to realize how this unloved tyrant was running her life and causing her more misery than she knew how to deal with. Again, as with that other client, she confessed what she assumed to be a perversion. It seemed she was unable to achieve sexual satisfaction without fantasizing that a child was watching her lovemaking. When we viewed this as a metaphor for the brat having to give permission even to this, her relief was evident. The task now was clear: to bring the brat to her Jungian analysis, to find ways of loving and redeeming it and moving it off the throne, where it was patently miserable and causing her untold grief besides.

So I find these powerful tales of usurped thrones very useful in counseling and in examining my own life. Thrones are for rightful rulers, and in the kingdom of the psyche, this has to be the cathedral of the Self.

So we can deduce that the Sun is also a symbol of authority. And, in line with our definition of the chart as being a description of the way we process experience, that authority is most often projected onto the experience of the father and the psychological formation of the father imago. By extension, a negative projection or introjection leads to a negative relationship to any authority: teacher, boss, government, and the ultimate authority of God. Everything gets mixed up with fear, anger, resentment, suspicion, and rejection, or with the loss or absence of "the good father."

Father complexes always involve the Sun in some aspect to Saturn in the chart. It will, however, affect men and women differently. With men, it strikes at the very heart of measuring up to the father. The client continues to perceive himself as a son and unable, except by "killing" the father or dissolving the father imago, to grow up into a full man and potential father himself. His task is to come into his own authority. For a woman it is more likely to take the form of an introjected and negative, cruel "judge." We will discuss this further on. The issue may involve claiming power.

The Sun in the chart points to the spiritual hero or heroine in us who is setting forth on life's journey. It will in

82

every case be modified by sign, by aspects, and by the house it occupies. And since the Sun rules Leo, one must look to which cusp that sign rules, as you will learn.

This has been a longer letter than I anticipated, and yet I am not through—is one ever? Nevertheless, the Sun is beckoning me to stop writing about it and to go out for a walk in the snow.

I leave you with a pleasant assignment: make a list, if you will, of things that you might associate with the creative powers of the Sun.

I send you my love (that's one of them),

growth - /green
Warmth :
birth - : why

11
The Sun in India

Dear friend,

A few years ago, my husband and I, still newlyweds, went to India with an unusual group of people wishing to travel more as pilgrims than as tourists. It was my task to discuss what we were seeing and experiencing in terms of history, myth, and Jung's concept of the Collective Unconscious. When we reached Varanasi (Benares), we were joined by a young American woman who had spent several years traveling about India, visiting gurus and ashrams, and learning (or relearning) the depth and mystery of the country. Her name was Paula.

The night of our arrival, we set forth in the dusky oven of the dark in rickshaws. Our driver, who pedaled the bicycle attached to us, was a wiry old man of incredible strength. He set off confidently into the darkness. There were no lights anywhere. When we asked him about this, he answered, "My eyes are my lights."

It is impossible to describe the ancient primeval stench of Varanasi. It is a combination of charcoal, urine, curry, spices, dung, and burning cadavers, mixed with flowers and incense. When we reached the heart of the city, the crowds stretched everywhere, an immense sea of bobbing heads. The falsetto barking of the horns of three-wheeled taxis punctuated a traffic jam that halted everyone. Overhead was misty saffron-colored light which, I discovered, came from the dust hanging perpetually over the city.

There are no glass windows, only corrugated metal doors and wooden shutters. People sit, talk, smoke, sleep, pee, and wash in slow motion on the doorsills and sidewalks, while cows and goats and water buffalo shuffle along in an amiable way. All eyes are limpid black and full of friendliness, and hundreds of holy men in stained garments pick their way in gaunt abstraction on leathery feet, headed towards the sacred river Ganges.

It was decided that we should dismount and go a back way. So, with Paula leading, we set out through the back alleys, our goal the burning ghats on the river. Thanks mainly to Woodstock, my stick, I made it. The temperature must have been in the high nineties, the alleys were rough stone and dirt, filled with slippery cow dung, rotting vegetables, rats, sleepy children, and that heavy, smoky, faintly familiar odor of burning flesh.

As we drew closer, ashes fluttered here and there. We passed houses with orange-lit windows, with chanting and music drifting out of them. We walked with flashlights lighting each other's steps, I think each of us wondering at our rendezvous with life and theirs with death. Finally we reached a terrace. It was lit by the glare of what, at night, seemed an inferno of crackling, snapping heat. Eleven bodies were burning below, each on a bed of fire. The temperature now must have been over a hundred. Dogs were trotting here and there, snapping up bits of roasted flesh. When they looked up at us, their eyes were glaring red balls, like hounds of hell. Next to the terrace was a hospice, a large building with balconies on which huddled the sick and dying, each awaiting his turn. The black stretch of the river lay ahead, and on its far side lights twinkled peacefully, as if everything was quite normal, and, of course, it was. The collective effect of that holy city's consciousness is overwhelming, so completely united are all the paradoxes that make for a greater life. Nothing, absolutely nothing is held back, and the result is the impression of the ultimate dignity of the human spirit, of its triumph in the midst of acceptance of life in death and death in life. Instinctively, we reached for each other's hands and made a circle, and the few Indians present joined us, as we stood stunned by it all.

The next morning we rose at three, after little or no sleep, to return by bus to the edge of the Ganges to witness the sun rising. Already the mobs were there: holy men lined up with their bowls, music blaring prayers from loudspeakers, and in the dim light the people making ready to greet the rising sun. We got into boats and pushed out into the river and gently floated downstream past thousands of people of all ages. They waded into the heavy green waters, the saris of the women like wet flowers blooming. A young boy with a flute followed us on shore, stepping over the faithful, running past the geometric stacks of drying cow dung patties. Some men were slapping their wet clothes on stones to clean them. In the water floated candles in flowers, sticks, turds, a bloated pig, part of a human foot, and hundreds of flower petals. At the river's edge women were collecting holy water in little brass jugs and drinking it. And then it happened.

You saw it first on the faces of the thousands lined up—a blush of oncoming light. Men and women and children turned to the east and folded their hands in prayer. An old grasshopper of a holy one went into ecstatic yoga asanas, his own grizzled face lit by the face of God. His fingers danced the mudras while he faced the vision that racked his body with joy. And then I knew what it is that makes these people so rich in the midst of their poverty: they know something that most of us have forgotten. They know what it is to lead a symbolic life, to accept the gift of a sunrise as if it were the most precious golden treasure, as if each day were a gift from God. I believe this changed my life.

This experience makes it easier to understand the meaning of the Sanskrit poem:

THE SALUTATION OF THE DAWN

Listen to the Salutation of the Dawn
Look to this day!
For it is Life—the very Life of life!
In its brief course lie all the

Varieties and realities of your
Existence:

> The Glory of Action
> The Bliss of Growth
> The Splendour of Beauty

For yesterday is but a dream
and tomorrow only a vision
but

> today well lived

makes every yesterday a dream of happiness
and every tomorrow a vision of hope

Look well, therefore, to this Day.

Such is the Salutation of the Dawn.

We passed the very ghats we had stood above the night
before. The smoke was still curling from the embers, and
fresh bodies were being brought down. A cow stood munch-
ing away among them, and there were the awesome death
dogs, but one was a bitch with two wee puppies frolicking
at her heels and stumbling over themselves and the dis-
memberings.

Another experience we had on that trip was in Nepal. We
went to the Temple of the Sleeping Vishnu, which lies in
the countryside outside of Kathmandu. This time it was
dusk and just before sunset.

The countryside of Nepal is very beautiful. It is lush,
green, with tiers of rice paddies on the slopes of high and
higher mountains receding into the distance.

The temple itself was small, and the other members of the
group went into a building to listen to some music. For
some reason, Walter and I decided to stay outside. The
Sleeping Vishnu is an enormous stone figure of the god lying
recumbent on the world serpent in a rectangular pool of
water. His serene face is turned up to the sky, and his hands
lie open at his side. The pool is sunken, and a walk with a
railing surrounds it on three sides. In a corner behind the
god's head stands a tree filled with tiny twittering birds.

87

We stood looking at Vishnu lying in a pool made of gold by the setting sun. There was a handful of Nepalese standing by and watching the sunset. As the rim of the sun touched the earth's horizon, they all sprang into unexpected action. A man blew a deep horn, someone beat gongs, and a teen-aged boy, a young brown stripling, walked delicately down a plank onto the god's body. He was bearing a taper of fire, and as the sun slowly disappeared, the boy leaned over and lit a lamp in the god's right hand. Vishnu would watch through the night bearing the light. Slowly, we watched the stars pricking into the deepening vault of blue above. All was hushed except for the plaintive begging of a baby—she cheeped like the birds, holding up her grubby little hand as a kind of duty. The chanting wavered on in the temple.

Here again I was reminded of Jung's remarks on the necessity of the symbolic life.

Compare, if you will, the descriptions above with two excerpts from ancient Egyptian sources written possibly as far back as five thousand years in *The Book of the Dead*. Both are translated by Robert Hillyer and appear in *An Anthology of World Poetry*.

THE DEAD MAN ARISETH AND SINGETH
A HYMN TO THE SUN

Homage to thee, O Ra, at thy tremendous rising
Thou risest! Thou shinest! the heavens are rolled aside!
Thou art the King of Gods, thou art the all-comprising
From thee we come, in thee are we deified.

Thy priests go forth at dawn; they wash their hearts
with laughter......

Between the Turquoise Sycamores that riseth, young forever

Thine image flashing on the bright celestial river....

Homage to thee, O Ra, who wakest life from slumber
Thou risest! Thou shinest! Thy radiant face appears!
Millions of years have passed—we cannot count their
    number—
Millions of years shall come. Thou art above the years!

ADORATION OF THE DISK BY KING AKHNATEN
AND PRINCESS NEFER NEFERIU ATEN

Thy dawn, O Ra, opens the new horizon
And every realm that thou hast made to live
Is conquered by thy love, as joyous Day
Follows thy footsteps in delightful peace...

Dawn in the East again! the land's awake,
And men leap from their slumber with a song;
They bathe their bodies, clothe them with fresh garments

And lift their hands in happy adoration.

Both north and south along the dazzling river
Ships raise their sails and take their course before thee;

And in the ocean, all the deep-sea fish
Swim to the surface to drink in thy light....

The chick within the egg, whose breath is thine,
Who runneth from its shell, chirping its joy,
And dancing on its small, unsteady legs
To greet the splendor of the rising sun....

And lo, I find thee also in my heart
I, Khu en Aten, find thee and adore,
O thou, whose dawn is life, whose setting, death,
In the great dawn, then lift up me, thy son.

Here we can see almost the erasure of time, as well as the unity of the human family through time and space, in this honoring of the primal source of life.

I have spent this time, as you can see, away from textbook definitions of the Sun, and I read with such pleasure from your last letter that you are beginning to experience it within yourself in a new way. Seeking our own God helps us and our patients, too. Too often one goes through a whole lifetime accepting someone else's definition. To whom do we cry out, "My God"?

Yours in the Light,

12
The Sun in the birthchart

Dear friend,

When we begin to study the signs and the houses, it will be easier to understand what is meant by a "strong" Sun, or a "weak" Sun, or what the negative side-effects of these can be. Today I will enclose a chart, something I call the "Handy Dandy Summary." It will give you something to consult when I talk about exaltations and falls, and the like.

The planetary processes are modified by the twelve signs by virtue of their elements. There are four elements: fire, earth, air and water. Each is further differentiated by being expressed in one of three ways: cardinal, fixed, or mutable. At this point it is enough to know that the fire signs work most happily through action; the earth signs through practical manifestation; the air signs through mentality; and the water signs through the emotional nature.

If you look at this, you will see that the Sun rules the sign of Leo. Whatever sign a planet "rules" is a sign compatible with the nature of the planet. In other words, the process functions easily in it by virtue of its element (fire, earth, air, or water) or quality (cardinal, mutable, or fixed). The opposite sign, however, will be contradictory, and therefore will be said to be that planet's "detriment."

The Sun rules Leo. Aquarius is opposite Leo. Therefore the Sun is in its detriment in Aquarius. This sounds bad, but it isn't. It only means that the intrinsic nature of the Sun is now modified.

Planet	Rules	Detriment	Exalted	Falls
☉	♌	♒	♈	♎
☽	♋	♑	♉	♏
☿	♊/♍	♐/♓	♍	♓
♀	♉/♎	♏/♈	♓	♍
♂	♈/♏	♎/♉	♑	♋
♃	♐/♓	♊/♍	♋	♑
♄	♑/♒	♋/♌	♎	♈
♅	♒	♌	♏	♉
♆	♓	♍	♌	♒
♇	♏	♉	?	?
	+	−	+	−

Table of Cosmodynes

Leo rules kings and monarchy; Aquarius rules the common man and democracy. The Sun as "king" must learn to serve the common people, or reversed, we must learn that everyone has a "king" inside. Since we are entering the Age of Aquarius, this is one of our great tasks: to find that Royal Self within our own psyches and to recognize and love it in others. The Indians do this symbolically when they meet: they press their own hands together, bow, and say

91

"Namaste" (I bow to the divinity in you). In this way, Aquarius is the balance of Leo, as are all opposing signs.

The next thing you may observe from the Handy Dandy is that the Sun is "exalted" in Aries and "falls" in Libra. The exaltation of a planet is a description of the sign which is the best of all for the process of the planet to operate through. Aries is the first sign and also a fire sign, so the Sun with its fiery nature goes "ramming" enthusiastically into spring and running a fresh race through the zodiac. Perhaps you remember the lovely lines of Chaucer from *The Canterbury Tales:*

PROLOGUE

Whan that Aprille with his shoures sote
The droghte of Marche hath perced to the rote,
And bathed every veyne in swich licour
Of which vertu engendred is the flour;
Whan Zephirus eek with his swete breeth
Inspired hath in every holt and heeth
The tendre croppes and the yonge sonne
Hath in the Ram is halfe cours y-ronne
And smale fowles maken melodye
That slepen al the night with open ye
(So priketh hem nature in hir corages):
Than longen folk to goon on pilgrimages.

It is marvelous to read this for pleasure, rather than education, and to feel the rising sap which is the gift of the Sun exalted in Aries.

The opposite sign is the "fall" and comes on the first day of the Autumn Equinox when the Sun enters the Sign of Libra, the Sign of the Balance. If you look at the circle below, you will see the horizontal line of the horizon. Aries the Ram occupies the First House of the Natural Zodiac. It has the distinction of being the first to rise. (The signs move clockwise.) The Sign of Libra, the Scales, thus, is the first to set.

In astrology the First House is "I" and the Seventh "Thou." It is contrary to the nature of I to think of Thou.

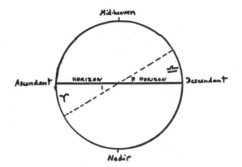

The houses remain stationary; signs move clockwise.
Planets move through the signs counter-clockwise.

But the nature of all relationships (and all opposites) lies in the "balancing" of I and Thou. Here are intimations to why the Sign of Libra rules justice, harmony, beauty, art, and marriage, and, negatively, rules open enemies or opponents. Venus rules Libra, and her ancient counterpart Ishtar was the goddess of both love and war.

How, you may ask, can the nature of the Sun be negative? It becomes negative through excess or weakness, when it is out of balance. In nature, the result is aridity, heat, drought, and barren desert—a fierce, blinding, and destructive heat. Or, it can be pale, wan, cold, vapid, and listless. The parallels in the psyche are the destructive aspects of tyranny, obsessive will, and the inflation and sub-sequent corruption of power and unbridled anger; or the cold cruelty and heartlessness of someone locked in a sunless inner world. One does not know whom to feel sorrier for— such a person or those around him or her.

I once had occasion to do the chart of a woman who was a Capricorn with Aquarius rising and Saturn in the First House. As I was drawing up the chart, I casually asked her if she did not feel the cold. It turned out that she suffered from Reynaud's Syndrome, an unusual disease that shuts off the circulation when a person touches something cold. The chart went on to show that this woman was almost frozen inside with a forbidding intellect (she had two Ph.D.s), which destroyed all hope of faith in any religious experience or allowing for the existence of something greater than her own mind. Her father had been a lofty professor and her mother a mouse. Her husband had left her as a cold and unfeeling ice queen. As the session continued, the synchronicity of my very first question began to touch her, and I noticed a long trace of a tear on her cheek and then another. She was deeply ashamed to show any emotion, but I rejoiced and encouraged her, pointing out that she was not dead at all—she just *thought* she was. Just because we think things are a certain way doesn't mean that's the way they really are. I gave her a mantra: "It ain't necessarily so!" I urged her to set this cruel judge in her psyche to judging his own judgment—I hope the resultant tautology has tied him up in fits of laughter!

The nature of the Sun in Aries is to lead and in Leo to rule. When life conspires to permit this in a constructive way, good things happen. But whenever this energy is frustrated, a complex is set up: the need to be recognized becomes imperative and the person becomes dominated by a subversive insistence which causes troubles in relationships and triggers anger, resentment, and sometimes downright hostility. This, in turn, interferes with the success and achievement the Sun is craving for.

With the chart, or in a good analysis, the way can be opened for the Sun to shine through. But I hope you can see that the Sun needs the help of the other planetary archetypes in the psyche, just as the Supreme and Unknown God would seem to need a host of humbler ones (us!) to make the world a more fruitful and interesting place.

Let your Sun so shine...

or, as it is written in *The Book of Common Prayer:*

> The Lord bless you and keep you
> The Lord make his face to shine upon you
>   and be gracious unto you.
> The Lord lift up his countenance upon you
>   and give you peace.

My love,

13
The Feminine

Dear friend,

Currently I have a client, a man, who not too long ago was working for a film company in London. The other day, he told me a remarkable story. It seems that the day after a huge antinuclear demonstration had taken place, an elderly Turk from Manchester showed up with an urgent message, which he felt should be delivered to the world.

As a boy in Turkey, he said, he had met a very old and wise man. This man had drawn him aside and prophesied there would be two great World Wars, and that he, as soon as he could, should leave Turkey and make his way to England, where he would be safe. In return, he should deliver a message to the world, and the message was this: *Only if the feminine is restored to the world can the earth be saved from destruction.*

The Turk had obeyed and gone to England and settled in Manchester. He had watched two World Wars come and go, and now he was seeing the dark threat of nuclear war. Suddenly he remembered the message he was to deliver, but he had no idea to whom to deliver it, so he had come to the film company in London. It happens that my client is a Sufi, and so the message did not fall on deaf ears. I repeat the story because, though we all know the truth of the message, it is remarkable that the wise old man was so prescient in a land and a time very caught up in patriarchal thinking.

The return of the goddess is at hand, and I suspect she too has evolved, or rather that we now are able to perceive new aspects of her, since we ourselves have evolved. Jung, as you know, was enormously excited by the Roman Catholic dogma of the physical Assumption of the Virgin Mary, and saw this as symbolic of positive things to come. Nor should we forget one of the few memories we have of Pope John Paul I: his public evocation at the Vatican of "God our Father and God our Mother."

Symptomatic of the need for change are the swamis, gurus, abbots, priests, and rinpoches who have been accused of having been unfaithful to their holy vows of celibacy. It is my personal opinion that this results not so much from human weakness, but from men reaching a certain level of consciousness and learning they can go no further without "knowing" the feminine. It just may be that at a transpersonal level something stronger than all of us is trying to get a message across: *spirituality can no longer exclude the feminine*. It must now arise within the context of a true *coniunctio* of masculine and feminine. The rule of the old goddess is no longer valid, since it was based on a matriarchy which swallowed up the masculine. The Mother Church who "castrates" her son-priests is still with us, and the very real and justified fear men have of "priestesses" handling sacred objects may be an unconscious memory of days when the priests of the Mother Goddess had to emasculate themselves and wear women's clothing. Such memories of these images are too strong and too potent. Though, slowly, women are being ordained in Protestant and Jewish faiths, they are not called priestesses. New images must emerge.

This could presage a new feminine archetype: that of Holy Wisdom: Hagia Sophia, the Holy Ghost aspect of the Trinity, whose only hint of femininity, as Jung has pointed out, is her symbol of the dove. If this aspect can emerge, as predicted by the medieval monk Joachim of Flory, then the precious balance of masculine and feminine may be restored. Women's Lib and an angry enantiodromia of women into Amazonian men will not do it, and too many tenderhearted *pueri aeterni* will not do it, either. We need kindhearted men who are men and not boys, and wise women who are loving and strong. No small task ahead! The men to respect and not use women, and the women to raise sons who become men because their mothers know when to let go. This is especially hard for us in America, since we are a Cancerian nation (July 4th) and that sign rules motherhood. Our national mandala is an apple pie.

A delightful example of our problem appeared a few years ago in a cereal box (Ceres!) which I found in a supermarket. In it was a decal of a red-blooded archetype: the Seven-million Dollar Man wearing a red (Mars) suit and warding off boulders (Saturn) that were falling on him. I was so intrigued that I bought another box. In this one was a decal of a feminine archetype: the Bionic Woman. She was dressed in a blue pantsuit (androgynous Uranus) and leaping over an electric fence. On the back of each decal were printed the words: DO NOT APPLY IF MOM DOES NOT APPROVE. A psychological and astrological summary of our culture! The United States has the Sun in Cancer and the Moon in Aquarius.

You may be wondering what I am leading up to astrologically. I am coming to some of the complexities around the archetypal processes of the Moon in the chart. Perhaps the best way to begin is with an ancient alchemical text quoted in Manly Hall's *The Secret Teachings of All Ages:*

THE EMERALD TABLET OF HERMES TRISMEGISTUS

The Secret Works of Chiram One in Essence but Three in Aspect:

It is true, no lie, certain and to be depended upon, the superior agrees with the inferior, and the inferior with the superior, to effect that one truly wonderful work. As all things owe their existence to the will of the Only One, so all things owe their origin to the One Only Thing, the most hidden by the arrangement of the only God. The father of that one only thing is the Sun, its mother is the Moon, the wind carries it in its belly; but its nurse is a spirituous earth. That one only thing (after God) is the father of all things in the Universe. Its power is perfect after it has been united to a spirituous earth.

Separate that spirituous earth from the crude by means of a gentle heat, with much attention.

97

> In great measure it ascends from the earth, up to heaven,
> and descends again new-born on the earth and the superior
> and the inferior are increased in power.
>
> By this thou wilt partake of the honours of the whole world
> and darkness will fly from thee. This is the strength of all
> powers. With this thou wilt be able to overcome all things
> and to transmute all what is fine...and what is coarse....
>
> In this manner the world was created. The arrangements to
> follow this road are hidden. For this reason I am called
> Chiram Telat Mechasot, one in essence, but three in aspect.
> In this trinity is hidden the wisdom of the whole world. It is
> ended now what I have said concerning the effects of the
> Sun.

If Jung is right, the opus described by the alchemical texts
is symbolic of the individuation process, and the result is the
rebirth of the Self. The key to such a mysterious text, of
course, is not to read it literally but in terms of processes.
The emphasis is on the One in Three, and the necessity for
a father Sun and a mother Moon and the "spirituous earth"
as nurse; the *opus* is accomplished with the help of all the
planetary processes, and it ascends and redescends. Psychologically interpreted, both the masculine and feminine are
required, and their union must be grounded (applied) on
earth or in the world.

It seems as if a father Self and a mother ego, together
with the help of daily life experience, are required to bring
forth the *spiritus renatus,* the reborn or twice-born Self.

What I am suggesting is a view different from the traditional one of the Moon in the chart, but I am basing it on
the "as above, so below" process put forward by Paracelsus
and by Jung himself. If the solar system is a paradigm for
the psyche, then we have to take a closer look at the position and function of the Moon vis-a-vis the Earth.

The Sun is special by virtue of its being the only fiery
"star" at the center of the system. The Moon is special in
that it is not a planet but a satellite of the Earth. It
mediates between Sun and Earth, always showing the same
face to us, waxing and waning, constantly changing the
amount of sunlight reflected. At the same time, the back of
the Moon always faces the other planets.

The effect of the Moon is familiar to us in its pull on the tides and as it coincides with the menstrual periods of women. Science is slowly validating some old wives' tales (I sometimes wonder if the day will not come when the Nobel Prize will be awarded to an old wife). Scientists now have instruments delicate enough to measure the tide in a cup of tea. It is ridiculous to assume that the water in human bodies is less sensitive to such a pull, or that the water rising and falling in the stems of plants is not affected. Science has even proven that there are earth-tides and that the crust of the earth rises and falls several inches a day, as though the earth were breathing. According to Lyall Watson, a biologist, in his book *Supernature,* scientists have found that whole forests breathe in unison.

A Japanese scientist, Takata, has discovered that the contents of human blood are very subtly affected by eclipses and even at the moment of sunrise and sunset. Yogis maintain that these are two times during the day when we are likely to breathe equally through both nostrils, and since the nerve endings of the nose go directly to the brain, this may balance the Ha and Tha (Sun/Moon), and it may explain the ritual greeting of the Sun at dawn and sunset described in an earlier letter.

We need to "redescend" and to realize more consciously and actively what we are doing. To return, as T.S. Eliot puts it, "and know the place for the first time."

The way I see the process of the Moon in the chart is that it functions as the *matrix* of consciousness: it has the capacity to give birth to those limitless little or big attacks of insight through which we turn experience into empiric knowledge. All else goes in one ear and out the other, is memorized or swallowed whole in an unexamined way.

One side of the Moon is turned to the outer world of daily life and one to the inner world of the psyche and the world of the Unconscious. Jung defines the ego as the center of consciousness, and I would define the Moon as the mother of consciousness, the process of the ongoing weaving of life experience and inner meaning into a web of wisdom.

The Moon can be seen as dispensing the light of the Sun according to the needs of the Earth. As the Great Mother she gives birth to outer life in terms of form and to inner life in terms of consciousness. She is not consciousness herself but the matrix of it.

In *Ego and Archetype,* Dr. Edinger's moving book, is a diagram of the "Psychic Life Cycle," illustrating the inflation and deflation of the ego. It could serve as a diagram of the waxing and waning of the Moon. Jung himself said:

> In every individual it is the same; we have a large indefinite unconscious and only a part of it is definitive; whether it is central we don't know. Perhaps it has the same relation to the center as the earth has to the Sun. The center of our solar system is the Sun, and our center, our world is revolving around the Sun; we are the children of the earth, and so our consciousness is excentric relative to the Sun.... our consciousness may also be like a planet revolving round a central invisible Sun, namely round presumable center of the unconscious, which is called the Self, because that is the center of the conscious and the unconscious.

It is the ego which is exposed to daily life; it is the mortal spouse coping with moods and responsibilities, joys and pains, and the "banality" of every day. In fact, one way of knowing that a person is identified with the ego is if his or her definition of life is "just one damn thing after another." We hear the expression "ego death," but I wonder if you would not agree with me that what has to die is not the ego but the identification with the ego.

Apropos of this, I came across a passage in the *I Ching* which puts the potentially ideal relationship between the Self and the ego in perspective. I take the liberty of interpolating the words *ego* and *self* next to the terms *Creative* (yang) and *Receptive* (yin).

> But strictly speaking there is no real dualism here, because there is a clearly defined hierarchic relationship between the two principles. In itself, of course, the Receptive [ego] is just as important as the Creative [Self], but the attribute of *devotion* defines the place occupied by this primal power in relation to the Creative [Self]. For the Receptive [ego] must be led by the Creative [Self]; then it is productive of good. Only when it abandons this position and tries to stand as an equal side by side with the Creative [Self] does it become evil. The

> result then is opposition to and struggle against the Creative
> [Self], which is productive of evil to both.

This is most clearly and beautifully expressed. When the ego steps up in pride and we identify only with it, it becomes another Lucifer and we head for an inevitable fall.

Thus the harmonious process of the ego is not unlike that of the Virgin, the handmaid of the Lord, who is chosen by the God within us, if you will, to bring forth the Christ Child, the individuating Self. The very same process of natural reproduction is internalized and carried out within the psyche. In this way the symbolic images contained within the Christian mythos (and others) reveal a truth which is both psychologically and spiritually valid.

If we look to the body for verification of these processes, we find that the Moon rules or is associated with the breasts, the stomach, and the womb—all three variants of one process, containment. The womb receives seed, gestates, and brings forth form—the triple function of the feminine in response to the masculine creative. The stomach ingests food and transforms it as an alchemical alembic into nourishment for the body. The breasts have the capacity to fill with milk (of human kindness) for the nourishment of others. To nurse is not only to breast-feed but to care for the sick and to heal. All three of these functions are open to the human ego, regardless of sex. We all have the capacity to ingest daily life, to bring forth new consciousness, and to share it for the nourishment (nursing) of others.

not a bad definition of feminism

These are all positive aspects of the Moon. There are also negative ones, cathartic and destructive. The tomb is a container, but one which cannot hold the resurrected Self. The images of the dark chthonic aspects of the feminine are those of Erishkegal, Kali, Hecate, and a host of bloody furies, harpies, witches, and sorceresses. The goddess in the psyche also has to know how to deal with filth, corruption, destruction, pollution, and decay. The body packages it neatly in feces, and at the end of life in what the Dutch refer to as *stoffelijk overschot* (stuff left over, mortal remains). All of which Mother Nature simply recycles into more grass and flowers. What is fascinating to me is that

101

the yogis in India and Don Juan in Castaneda's books find extraordinary "life" in putrescence. Just as the form is disintegrating, it releases all kinds of fresh, sparkling energy.

The alchemists were aware of this too, since the *prima materia* was inevitably a kind of excrement to be worked on. And certainly this is true at the psychological level. Again it is the ego which has to do the work, recycling mistakes and sins into greater wisdom. The Black Madonna has white palms. Kali always has one of her six hands up, waving as if to say, "Don't worry, I know what I'm doing!" The other hands are holding severed heads and dripping knives.

As women somehow know and men fear, females have an incredible access to strength and natural wisdom if left to their own devices. People in ancient times saw the feminine as the triple goddess: maid, mother, and hag. I see them as one enfolded within the other: bud, flower, and fruit.

Astrology would seem to bear out both nature and alchemy. All men and all women contain both masculine and feminine, only in different ways. Thus, the Moon in a man's chart will point to something different from the Moon in a woman's chart, just as this was true for the Sun. In both cases, the first experience will be projected onto the "mother," but from then on it will be experienced as "other" for a man and as her identity for a woman.

A man's relationship to his mother can be read in the chart, and so can his potential for ego development and strength. If he is living the chart unconsciously, his relation-ship to his wife will have unconscious components, since the latter will so often depend upon the former. This is a psychological fact.

The Moon in a woman's chart will show a different nu-ance. It will show, among other things, her own relation-ship to herself as woman/wife/mother. Much of women's ego strength has, in my opinion, been confused with animus strength (or the inner masculine side). I see many clients who are independent, strong Amazonian women in their mid-to-late thirties. Their very "masculine" strength has become their weakness. They feel cut off from their woman strength and are facing or dreading a childless future without a loving relationship with a man rather than a testy one. They are not secure in their feminine egos.

The fault may be a cultural one. These are the angry young girls who were not going to end up household drudges. Who can blame them? The times conspired against them; they had no models or archetypes to fit the age. Not only have we lacked heroes, but we have lacked heroines. The most admired women of the last fifty years have been Helen Keller, Eleanor Roosevelt, Margaret Mead, and Mother Teresa, not for their outer beauty but for their inner character. Some of the beauties have been Marilyn Monroe, Jackie Onassis, and now Princess Diana. Obviously, what is wanting is the goddess aspect potential in every woman. As an ideal, she waits in every psyche smiling and waiting to be discovered.

Looking forward to hearing from you.

Love,

14
The Moon

Dear friend,

Is the Moon as important as the Sun?

I would have to shout "yes"! If the Sun is the life giver and symbolically connected with the spiritual dimension, the Moon is connected with the manifesting of the Spirit. In every way, it deals with the practical expression of mundane matters: planting, growing, cooking, washing, working—the "one thing after another" of daily life. The Moon passes through every sign and touches off every aspect in every chart once a month. Today, you could say, psychologically, it represents our psychic "homework," learning and applying. But in prehistoric days, it was the cosmic clock by which all things were measured.

A few years ago, I found myself, with four of my students from the school where I taught, on the Isle of Lewis in the Outer Hebrides. At Callanish are some of the most remarkable standing stones in the world. They lie to the west of the island, and their antiquity may be greater than Stonehenge. They consist of a circle of thirteen tall stones of Lewis gneiss, with the tallest in the middle, and avenues of stones are spread in four directions making a cross. At the head of one of these avenues is a natural outcropping which has platforms for three people to stand, one on top and two flanking. You can just picture the leader standing there.

We arrived at sunset, after a grueling drive through the endless stony and barren wastes of Harris. The four teenagers were thrilled. They had seen the stones from a distance and swore they were grotesque people outlined against the sky.

We clambered and shouted and enjoyed, all in the golden air, and then went to the small hotel at Carloway. I got them fed and finally to bed. At about 11:30 I decided to return alone to the stones. I wanted to feel and experience them in silence.

To my amazement when I stepped out of the hotel, the weather had changed drastically. The moon was glaring down through ragged clouds, and a gale was rising. I really hesitated, but then resolutely pulled up the hood of my rain-cape and marched out to the car. By the time I had reached the stones, it was pouring. The wind hurled the car door shut as I got out, and it flung so much rain in my face that I couldn't see through my glasses. But it was not pitch dark; there was that eerie light that prevails that far north in the summer, plus what I now realized was the moon behind the rushing clouds. Nevertheless, it was spooky. In fact it was so spooky, all I could do was chuckle. Now what to do? I forced myself through the opening in the wall, and with Woodstock in hand, pressed onwards into the night and the wind, up the solitary avenue of stones until I reached the circle. You will have to see them for yourself. They really do feel like presences and, with a little imagination, they conjure up a gathering of wizards in conference.

Suddenly, I became self-conscious and embarrassed in their presence. What was expected of me? Feeling foolish, I decided I should greet the "leader," so I climbed clumsily to the huge center stone, threw my arms about it, and gave it a great hug. Then came the shock. Though the temperature was at best in the forties, the stone was as warm as I was—wet and warm. In its shelter all was hushed. I just laid my cheek gratefully against it and patted it, praying that I might return again to such a magical place. (I did.)

As I went back to the car, the moon peered through again, as if she were an old woman opening a drawer to find something lost in the bottom of it—me. As I got back into the car, I noticed a woman's bicycle propped up against

105

the wall. I had not seen it before. To this day, I wonder whether I was alone or not among those stones.

Needless to say, these standing stones are moon-oriented as well as sun-oriented and are judged to be pre-Celtic. The most recent studies have noted that they point to the rising of the Pleiades. They may be 4,000 years old. They seem to gather the heat of the sun like dynamos; some have been tested with rheostats and found to be magnetic and electric at different levels. It is all one big mystery, but I can assure you that if there are such things as "power points" on earth, Callanish is one of them.

Serious research is now being conducted in Britain by scholars, the late Dr. Alexander Thom of Cambridge, for one, and John Michell of R.I.L.K.O. These are just a few of a growing number of people bringing information to light which is challenging historians to new views. Most stone circles seem to be moon-oriented.

The glyph for the Moon in astrology is:

According to Bachofen, the Moon is masculine for some people when waxing and feminine when waning. It certainly has androgynous qualities. But one can easily be drawn into literalism here, thinking gender instead of process. The feminine process relates and unites. It includes opposites. A woman is feminine, but she can bring forth sons as well as daughters.

The Moon has also been said to be yin in its relationship to the Sun, but yang in its relationship to the earth. If we translate this psychologically, perhaps we can say that the relationship of the ego to the Self should be seen as receptive, but in relationship to self-expression it becomes creative.

Think of the actual process of birth itself. Conception takes place in a mysterious, warm concavity of vagina and womb. It is "a garden enclosed," but at birth all that was concave becomes convex. The genital area balloons out, and the head of the baby "crowns" as it comes out the birth

106

canal. Having seen this for myself in slides presented by a midwife, I readily can see that the tonsuring or shaving of the heads of monks was a reenactment of a "birth."

Erich Neumann wrote, as you know, a very fine essay, "On the Moon and Matriarchal Cosciousness." It clarifies those differences between the masculine and feminine ego. He states:

> the male faith in the ego and in consciousness is alien to women; indeed, it seems to them slightly absurd and childish. From this stems the profound skepticism and the kind of indifference with which they tend to react toward patriarchal consciousness and the masculine mental world, especially when, as frequently happens, they confuse the two worlds of spirit and consciousness. Masculinity is attached to the ego and to consciousness; it has deliberately broken the relation to nature and to destiny in which matriarchal con- sciousness is so deeply rooted. The patriarchal emphasis on the ego, on will and freedom, contradicts experience of the "potencies and powers" of the unconscious and of fate, of the way that the experience depends on the non-ego and the "thou."

and

> So the moon has not only a male manifestation as the center of the spiritual world of matriarchal consciousnesss; it has also a feminine manifestation as the highest form of the feminine spirit-self, as Sophia, as wisdom. It is a wisdom relating to the indissoluble and paradoxical unity of life and death, of nature and spirit, to the laws of time and fate, of growth, of death and death's overcoming. This figure of feminine wisdom accords with no abstract, unrelated code of law by which dead stars or atoms circulate in empty space[!!]; it is a wisdom that is bound and stays bound to the earth, to organic growth, and to ancestral experience. It is the wisdom of the unconscious, of the instincts, of life, and of relationship.

Hence, matriarchal consciousness is the wisdom of the earth.

Then

> Only in later periods of development, when patriarchy has fulfilled itself or gone to absurd lengths, losing its connection

with Mother Earth, does individuation bring about a reversal. Then, patriarchal sun-consciousness reunites with the earlier, more fundamental phase, and matriarchal consciousness, with its central symbol, the Moon, arises from the deep, imbued with the regenerating power of its primal waters, to celebrate the ancient *hieros gamos* of the Moon and Sun on a new and higher plane, the plane of the human psyche.

In rereading these passages, I cannot help but be struck by the application of these words today in the new developments in holistic healing and medicine, and, in fact, to the direction towards holism in many different disciplines and by the synchronistic development of the hologram itself. I think the icon of the New Age is the photograph of our planet Earth taken from the Moon. We have a reversal of view enabling us for the first time to see the Earth objectively as a whole. We have become *conscious* of where we are and what we have.

It is obvious also that these letters of mine are a weaving of text within texture. It is feminine to tell stories or to clothe the facts within a uterus of lived experience. It might drive a man nuts to read them, as it does my animus, which wants to have the facts condensed and organized into a neat package of formulas. But that will not make one an astrologer, only a logical speculator. One cannot touch a chart without touching the hem of the universe.

In *Psychic Discoveries behind the Iron Curtain*, I read an interesting chapter about the effect of the Great Pyramid on metals, and about a Czechoslovakian engineer who obtained a patent to produce little pyramid-shaped boxes for sharpening razor blades. The patent office was very sceptical, but they became convinced when they experimented with their own razor blades. It worked, and the inventor got the patent. Hidden in the chapter was a reference to a Russian custom in the old days in the army. When a man wanted to play a trick on a buddy, he would take his knife and put it on the windowsill in the light of the full moon. In the morning the blade would be dulled and useless until resharpened. That stuck in my mind because in astrology the Moon and Mars (knives) are inimical, or rather incompatible, when conjunct in a chart or inharmoniously aspected. This is the kind of trivia the astrologer notes and puts in the sack of goodies or in the computer, depending on the type of mind you have. It shows you that once you have astrology programmed into your psyche, there will always be a place to hook a piece of information. For me, it is the best mental filing system in the world. A person with Moon conjunct Mars will be easily irritated by "mother," and if the complex is not dissolved, may go on later in life to suffer acid (Mars) indigestion (Moon) or stomach (Moon) ulcers.

The Moon in the chart is also going to be modified by sign and house position, and it will be profoundly affected by its aspects or the company it keeps, since like milk, which it rules, it tends to take the shape of its container and the flavor of its neighbors.

Another interesting thing about the Moon is its relationship to time (Saturn). The Sanskrit root of moon is *ma* or *men* which is at the base of our words for measuring, and even for *man* as "mind." The Sun takes a year to make its apparent orbit, but the Moon only a month, and so in early times it was natural to measure time by months. The Sumerians, for instance, as you must know, had two number systems: a sacred one based on multiples of six, and a secular one based on fingers and toes, the decimal system. It was the Egyptians who developed the solar calendar, but though we are about to abandon our lunar measurements of inches, feet and yards, we cannot escape the twenty-four-hour day and the weeks, which seem best to agree with our body clocks. I think that the French under Napoleon experimented on lengthening the week, but it didn't work.

I remember being invited to a party when I was little, which was to take place on a Saturday. The invitation arrived on a Tuesday, which meant waiting, which did not appeal to me at all. Highly affronted, I asked my mother, "Who said it was Tuesday?" When was the first Tuesday? And couldn't they have been wrong, maybe it was really Saturday and nobody but me realized it. My mother could not answer me, but the question bothered me for years.

109

Finally one day, waiting at an airport, I found a copy of Esther Harding's *Women's Mysteries,* and there I found the answer. It began in Sumeria with the *sabat* (rest), which was the dark of the moon, when the goddess was having her period. Maybe she suffered cramps. Anyway, the Sumerians rested with her. Eventually the month was quartered into four six-day weeks with a Sabbath for rest. The ancient Hebrews took the custom with them when they left Ur with Abraham, along with a complicated sacred calendar of movable feasts based on the moon. The Christian liturgical calendar is a mixture of solar and lunar stations. The most renowned lunar-based feast, of course, is Easter, which falls on the Sunday following the first full moon after the Spring Equinox.

The number (besides thirteen) associated with the Moon is nine in many cultures. Nine (3x3) is the number of months of gestation. It is also the number of Muses and Valkyries, and in the Sacred Medicine Pipe Count of the Amerindians, the number of emotions and lunar influences. It was the number relating to the great goddess, the Moon, and for Pythagoras the number of wisdom, the number of the orgiastic moon-priestesses devouring the Dionysus-bull, and a host of other things which you can look up. It also is the last number before starting over with ten. Hence "casting out nines," which I always forget to do.

Finally, the Moon in the chart is where you look to see how a person is likely to react. A spontaneous question arises in the person: For Moon in Aries it will be, What should I do? For Virgo, What does it mean? For Libra, Is this fair? For Scorpio, What's *really* going on? These are oversimplifications, to be sure, but they are descriptive of a posture a person takes in life, the way experience finds an entry into the psyche.

The Moon rules Cancer, is in its detriment in Capricorn.
The Moon is exalted in Taurus, falls in Scorpio.
Psychologically interpreted, the Moon is happy transforming, gestating, and bringing forth, and it is happiest giving form to life in the "merrie monthe of May." The Empress card in the Tarot depicts that burgeoning, rich green energy

of spring. It is quite different from the card of the Priestess, and yet we all have both somewhere in our psyches. The Moon in Capricorn is Persephone in the underworld, Inanna descended. The Moon in Scorpio suffers suspicion of all motives including its own. It has the best "crap detector" in the business. It has to experience the dark side before it can accept the light. It's rooted in the tragic view of life and cannot accept happiness easily without guilt. I say this to point out that the so-called negative aspects are by no means all bad; they often offer a more complete view in the end.

Love from a friendly lunatic!

15
More on the Moon, and we meet Saturn

Dear friend,

Well, we just went for a walk in the snow, and it was lovely if cold, and we came in and had a cup of hot tea. Among the gifts of Saturn are winter, old age, white snow, icicles, white hair, and beards. But Venus creeps in with all those exquisite lacy designs in each snowflake. No wonder Saturn is exalted in her sign of Libra. I am testing you to see if you can field a remark like that!

Also, there is an important relationship between the Moon and Saturn. The late Dane Rudhyar, the grand old dean of astrologers, wrote of this in his brilliant book *The Astrology of Personality*.

> Psychologically speaking, Saturn symbolizes, therefore, that process which leads to the realization: "I am". This may not be, however, such a simple realization as it may seem and has seemed to many. Thus the modern psychologist speaks of the "ego-complex", as previously defined: "A complex of representations which constitutes the center of my field of consciousness."
>
> Within the "field of consciousness" life flows; in other words, changes take place, energy is released in actions and re-actions. This "psychic energy" which is contained and operates in the field of my consciousness (within the boundaries of my ego, set symbolically by Saturn) is represented astrologically by the Moon. The Moon is that portion of the Sun which is enclosed by Saturn—if such an astronomically

112

peculiar sentence may be allowed. It is that portion of the
life energy of the total being which I am aware of as myself,
as the conscious ego which I am. Saturn refers to the abstract
structure of this ego. The Moon pours into this structure
"psychic energy"—and the result is a conscious entity, a particular living entity. The relation Saturn-Moon is therefore
the relation: form-to-energy. Form conditions energy, though
there is really a deep reciprocal action, which would be too
long to discuss in such a brief survey.

It is interesting that Saturn rules Capricorn and the Moon
rules Cancer. These two signs are opposite each other and
therefore involved in reciprocal action. Nor is that all.
When the natal chart is "progressed," which means progress-
ing the chart a day for every year of the life of the individual, the progressed Moon travels at almost the same pace as
the *transiting* Saturn. This means Saturn is traveling along
seeing to it, metaphorically speaking, that the "task" is done
(or at least remembered), and that we learn our psychological homework (home—Moon, work—Saturn). This is
sometimes referred to as karma but is more what the word
implies: the law of cause and effect. What binds us is not a
"planet" out there, but the inner process that we persist in
using to perceive our reality.

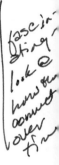

We are so often convinced that the world "out there" or
"people out there" are to blame for our misfortunes. If only,
if only, we cry, circumstances were different! Saturn is
always involved in projections of the Shadow, but behind
the cruel-seeming scenario always lies a lesson. Once the
lesson is learned, we are invariably given the opportunity to
prove it in outer life. Then only are we released from that
lesson, and life serves up the next.

In one of his letters, Jung audaciously questions: "What if
Satan were to remove his mask, and we were to find the
face of Christ behind it?" What humility this implies! Yet,
this is astrologically true: the "old devil" Saturn is really
only reflecting the Spirit of the Sun. Once unmasked, the
Wise Old Man or the Wise Old Woman emerges. It is the
bitter medicine that heals. There is much genuine humility
in Saturn.

Another place where the Moon and Saturn meet is in the

image of the egg. The process involved in the shell (calcium is ruled by Saturn) is one of protection through limitation. This is its positive purpose. However, if the shell is not sacrificed at the right moment, the unhatched new life would succumb as if in a tomb. This is a powerful symbolic image for some people who are paralyzed by a shell of fear (Saturn) and unwilling to hatch, as it were, even if it means stumbling around on wobbly legs a while. Eggs per se are ruled by the Moon, and I have found that people will even dream of eggs or egg-shaped ovals when they are going through this agony.

Reluctance to hatch is very often experienced by Taurians and Virgos. Taurus hangs on to the status quo, and will endure almost anything rather than change. Virgo waits to hatch "perfectly," which any old chick will tell you is impossible.

Another helpful image is that of scaffolding, which enables a structure to be built, but is no longer needed later on. Once the building is up, down goes the scaffolding, but psychologically, this kind of scaffolding is hard for some to sacrifice. An example of this lies in academia: professors publish papers carefully, oh so carefully, quoting other professors. In the end, all you have is a rehash and nothing genuinely new. I was recently sent such a paper by a young man. It was a perfectly organized pudding of quotations. In his timidity and fear, nothing else emerged from the paper.

I remember my teacher shaking his head at me because of all my books. We argued about it. They were only a ladder, he told me, to get up to where I was going, but once there, I would see they served only a limited purpose. I had to live what I learned.

Since I have Jupiter conjunct Mercury, books are still my passion, but now I see the trap. If I have to read a book about it, I am actually using my ego to convince itself of its distance from what it seeks. This is a dreadful paradox when it comes to reading books about religion, spirituality, or even individuation. We learn best by teaching, my teacher would say; only in that way is the flow at both ends kept open.

Later I tested this with my students. I placed strong and weaker students, side by side, and I often found they could teach each other better than I could. I used to teach a "Cultural History of Civilization" and had the children write "monographs" on their favorite topic as it applied in the various civilizations we studied. Thus a student who was interested in writing, say, would become a mini-expert on Chinese, Sanskrit, Hebrew, Sumerian cuneiform, Egyptian hieroglyphics, Coptic, Greek, and Roman alphabets, another on medicine, etc., by the end of the school year. Then we would have a week's seminar in which they would present their monographs. Each student was able thus to do research at his own reading level, the smarter ones using adult sources with which I lined the classroom. (Aha! there was a use for those books!) Anyway, something happened that I had never anticipated. The kids would get excited about something, a picture, or an odd fact, and then they would share, thus indirectly learning from each other, unaware that this was "education." And guess who learned the most of all? Me! Where else would I have learned the definition of Jung's Collective Unconscious: "It's when a whole bunch of people don't know nothing and don't know why they don't."

I also learned from Jung that if you seek to honor the Self in the child first, then the ego will take instruction, correction, and affection. All too often, as I myself experienced as a child, teaching is conducted between the ego of the teacher and the ego of the child, and much is suffered, little learned. I was blessed by three wonderful teachers as a child, and they all had the same things in common: a loving faith in and respect for their students, an enthusiasm for their subject, and a healthy tolerance for mistakes, providing you learned from them. But now that I am older, I do see what my teacher was trying to convey: we really only learn to recognize what we already know. But there are certain books, I maintain, which like music put you in a right frame of mind to learn or even to delight. Dear God, I pray these letters of mine will contain something for you!

Now I would like to introduce the application of astrological thinking. It helps to use the thought of "by extension." You take the planet, in this case the Moon, and you think of the body part it rules. Let us take the womb. What is the process of the womb? Containing, protecting, building, etc. By extension, where else can you curl up, even in the fetal position, secure and warm? Your bed...by extension your bedroom...by extension...your house... home...wife. If these all suggest Mother, keep going...by extension...the Church...the Motherland...Mother Earth. Eggs, boxes, chests, caskets...and so forth.

Or take the breasts, ruled by the Moon. The process is nourishing and nursing...feeding...by extension...bottles...the kitchen...the restaurant...the supermarket...the "breadbasket" of the country...agriculture...social services...hospitals...CARE packages...Red Cross...Save the Children...UNICEF.

Or by extension...a cup...a holy cup: chalice...a mythic cup: Holy Grail...by extension...Mother Goddess.

Look around any room and list the things in it which might be ruled by the Sun or might be ruled by the Moon. If in doubt, give your reason in terms of processes.

List the goddesses you know who are associated more with Moon processes than Venus (puella-hetaira) processes.

Drink a glass of milk slowly—really experience it.

Take a bath, not a shower—really observe the miraculous fluidity of water.

Meditate on the process of being an apple tree. From the very beginning, mind you!

Compare an apple tree to a teacher.

Feel yourself a woman—why are you strong? (A man can do this, too)

Love a man because he is a man. Love a woman because she is a woman.

Have fun!

16

Sun and Moon as the Royal Pair

Dear friend,

It is snowing hard, big thick flakes dropping heavily, enclosing the house in a white muffler of silence. Your note of appreciation spurs me on. The "by extensions" of astrology would be familiar to any psychologist, since this is the key also to dream interpretation.

We have met the "Royal Pair," the Sun and the Moon. Theirs is the *hieros gamos,* or sacred marriage, *mysterium coniunctionis* Jung wrote about: the great union of opposites required of the psyche. Not the triumph of one over the other, but the balanced acceptance of both polarities. He felt religions too often stressed the good through denial of the bad. The bad doesn't go away, it just goes down into the Unconscious to be projected onto others, thereby causing all kinds of troubles.

The symbols for the Royal Pair are many: the king and the queen, the gold and the silver, the Ha and the Tha, the ida and pingala, Siva and Shakti, Kether and Malkuth, and in the nursery, even, they reign with little candy hearts on their chests which say, "I Love You - Raggedy Andy and Raggedy Ann."

This Royal Pair of Sun and Moon is to be distinguished from Mars and Venus, "the lovers," the prince and princess, only by virtue of their elevation as processes in the psyche. They hint at the love and yearning of the Self and the ego for one another. It is the Self, the Christ Within, the Atman, the Spirit whom the ego is longing for, because that alone is the touchstone to wonder, to the direct experience of God as Spirit within us. But I suspect the Self yearns as poignantly for recognition and acceptance from its human incarnation in the ego, and plays this out in the divine drama of its potential rejection and crucifixion in the passion of our lives. We struggle so hard to acquire an ego, but if we then identify with it, we forget the Self, deny it either through ignorance or pride, until our suffering becomes unbearable. Finally, we become humble enough to hear the voice within us which was always there. Or cry out from deep despair for help. For me, what Jung was saying is that the task of analysis is to guide the patient to where he or she can begin to hear that voice. He stressed the spiritual dimension of the task, for therapist and patient alike. It is not *just* psychology or a "medical solution," as you know better than I.

Unfortunately, part of the process means traveling almost daily with the demon of doubt: dear Mephistopheles whispers, "I am the spirit that ever denies." Saturn can be the Lord of the Morning After. Hence the wisdom of:

Before enlightenment, chop wood and draw water
After enlightenment, chop wood and draw water.

First the mountain is there
Then the mountain disappears
Then the mountain is there again.

These verses warn us of the necessity for grounding and regrounding every peak experience in the very "banality" of everyday life. And then you wonder, of course, if it had been real in the first place.

I remember—how could I ever forget!—an experience I had several years after meeting M. It happened on October 9th, 1949, in Newport, Rhode Island. I had gone to visit my parents (who had finally settled down) bringing my two little ones, both under three. I was already four months pregnant with a third child, and for financial reasons had not been to a doctor, thinking I knew the ropes. What I didn't know was that the over-the-counter new drug for hay fever, from which I was suffering as never before, was also a blood decoagulant.

Near the end of September, I suffered a sudden miscarriage and a few days later, a severe hemorrhage. Finally, I was released from the hospital and told I needed only to rest and recover. I trusted this and returned to my parents' house, but on the night of October 9th, I again began to hemorrhage. I filled two bedpans with blood, before the doctor took the matter seriously enough to send an ambulance. No sooner was I at the hospital than some other emergency took everyone's attention, and I continued to bleed. By the time my husband appeared, the bleeding was unbelievably severe.

After several hours, it was evident that I was dying. My mother was called to the hospital, and she subsequently verified that my impression of the special nurse, who was called in to help, was not exaggerated. This nurse walked in like a diminutive skeleton with a death's head, pale, sunken, with enormous black eyes. The minute I saw her, I recognized her as Death, and accepted that I was doomed.

Things worsened rapidly as the ligaments to my uterus were stretched and ripped. I was racked with searing pain and terror. I kept my face turned to the wall, screaming inwardly, and yet at another level aware of my teacher's presence. My task now was to turn around and look Death in the face. Should I fail to do this, I knew somehow I would have failed this life. I must look at Death and love her.

I remember turning and searching for her face. I found it. I found the pallor of it and those terrible eyes, and when I looked into them, to my astonishment, I found strength, compassion, and understanding. (This nurse, whose name I will never know, stayed with me all night. When I tried to find her later on, I was told that she herself had died the following week.) How many times have I blessed her.

My husband called another doctor. I was taken to the operating room. The next thing I remember was a deep buzzing in my head, and then the somehow familiar journey through the tunnel, only I did not come into a light but into

119

outer space, looking back at an earth about the size of a dime. The brilliance of the stars was all about. I remember facing an undulating blackness, a velvet cloud. It asked me a question and told me that the fate of the world hung upon my strength to answer it. I summoned all my energy in one enormous surge. The question was, "Can you love *enough?*" I screamed and groaned and sobbed all at the same time— "YES!!" And I called on my teacher to witness my pledge. I know at that moment he was there. In the hour of my death I could trust. Somehow I had passed the test, but so had he.

Then I awoke on the operating table. They had the round lamp about three inches above my body and hot water bottles on every side. If someone touched me, it felt as if they were feeling their way through two feet of dry leaves. My husband and my mother were brought in to talk me back, and I was given strong hot sweet tea as I lay there. (To this day, I drink tea with honey in it, the taste of life returned.)

I was brought back to my room and to Death, the nurse, now become my dear helper. She tended the transfusions, gently squeezing the fatal air bubbles out of them. She rubbed the arm that was so painfully strapped to a board, and she must have heard my prayers. Just before dawn, I was seized with a paroxysm of strength. I can scarcely describe the inflation of that moment. I felt strong enough to lift the city of Paris (that was the image) with one hand. At the same time, I was so weak I could not raise my head or even my hands. (My blood pressure had gone down to 3 on the operating table. They really thought I was gone.) Now I observed that my strength, which I had always thought of as physical, was, in fact, nothing of the kind. It was psychic. It was "I," not Alice, and the two seemed quite distinct.

For those few hours, in and out of this reality, I realized the paradox of what one emphasises in the two worlds. What I thought important here was nothing of the kind. Life was like the negative of a photograph, where light and dark are reversed. The worries and concerns peculiar to the ego (though I did not know the term in Jung's sense) were *maya,* of no consequence in the face of this *mysterium tremendum;* what mattered was how I had dealt with them. All that remained was what I had given away, which wasn't much. I realized I had received a great gift in the maw of death itself. Love had conquered death, and for this reason I no longer really fear it. "Die before you die."

It was comforting and exciting to read a few years later that Jung, when he suffered his heart attack, had had the same kind of experience in "outer space," and I have read that Emerson did also and probably many others.

This was my lesson on doubt. Before that time, I sometimes doubted the magical dimensions, as they seemed to me, of my teacher. But that night was also a birth into a place inside myself where I can no longer doubt the validity of that greater dimension. I was finally convinced. I know.

I mention the date, because on that day the Sun was conjunct my Saturn in the Eighth House to the degree, the House of Death and Rebirth, and Saturn was conjunct the Moon. Twenty-nine years later, a similar configuration loomed. I confess I gulped, wondering what would happen this time. It was the first day of a course I was scheduled to teach at the Jung Foundation in New York. I went into the city, saw clients and patients, had supper, and arrived at the Foundation only to discover that instead of being assigned the nice big room upstairs, the class had been relegated to the absolute foundation (Saturn!) of the building. The very bottom in a windowless storage room, no less. But there was a blackboard on which I could safely write: AS ABOVE, SO BELOW. Talk of being grounded!

Which goes to show that we can never anticipate how a transiting aspect will work out. The process was carried through the symbolic situation, and the cosmic joke was on me, an astrologer!

In retrospect, that searing experience of near-death was also one of encountering the Shadow and hearing its challenging question about love. It confirms for me that our darkness is crying out for redemption.

Which brings me to a true story about a child's encounter with trying to be only good. When my thirteen-year-old son

121

was on scholarship at a fine prep school, he was so deeply affected by his religious studies that he came home for his holiday seeming to have taken up the vocation of sainthood. He was obedient to his father, helpful to his mother, kind and tolerant of his three pesky sisters. He asked that his bed be removed, so he could sleep simply on the floor; he ate sparingly. Our amazement beggars description.

Then one night as I passed his room, I heard sobbing. Timidly, I knocked and was invited in. There he sat, tears streaming down his face, pounding the mat he slept on. "It's not fair," he cried, "it's not fair!"

"What's not fair?" I asked in bewilderment.

He shook his head in desperation and looked up at me. "I've tried to be good, I've done everything I know how to be good! But all that's happened is that I have fallen into the greatest sin of all!"

"What do you mean, dear?" I asked.

"Can't you see?" he agonized, "I think I'm better than other people!"

I really quite agreed with him; it didn't seem fair. He had me stumped. All I could do was hug him and tell him to go to sleep. We'd talk about it tomorrow.

The next day, I found my kitchen supply of paper towels was used up. As I removed the cardboard tube from the dispenser, the sun flashed through it. Somehow, this seemed significant. And then it hit me. Here might be the answer. I stuffed one end with tissue and ran to find my son. "Hey, look through this!" I cried. Indulgently, he looked into the tube and saw nothing. Then I took the stuffing out and told him to look out the window. He thought I was nuts, but he looked.

I told him that his dilemma with pride was from perceiving that his "goodness" came out of him, rather than through him. If he could see himself as a paper-towel roller, he could avoid the problem of conceit. All we can ever do is remove the obstacles and let the light shine through. Thoughtfully, he put the tissues in and out. It seemed to make sense even to him. At any rate, the rest of the summer was more relaxed, and as far as I know sainthood had been postponed.

I have often had to remember the cardboard tube myself, because in our professions, as you know, frequently expressions of praise come pouring out from grateful clients and patients. The Self is at one end of the tube, so to speak, and the ego at the other, and between them the axis or the channel. If you stuff one end of the roller and try to see the Sun, there *is* no Sun.

I remember discussing the problem of inflation with Edward C. Whitmont once and his wise advice: "Don't deny the inflation, enjoy it for about ten seconds, then see it for what it is and offer it up!" For me, that's sending it back up the paper-towel roller.

I remember that as a child I used to worry about those stories of rejecting the devil. My sympathies were more often with him than with the righteous ones. I felt sorry for him. Then Hermes gave me a most beautiful poem by Edward Carpenter, which I have never forgotten. It offers the best solution to the problem of evil I know.

And so at last I saw Satan appear before me—
magnificent, fully formed.
Feet first, with shining limbs, he glanced down from
among the bushes,
And stood there erect, dark-skinned, with nostrils
dilated with passion;
(In the burning, intolerable sunlight, he stood, and I
in the shade of the bushes);
Fierce and scathing the effluence of his eyes, and
scornful of dreams and dreamers (he touched a rock hard
by and it split with a sound like thunder);
Fierce the magnetic influence of his dusky flesh; his
great foot, well-formed, was planted firm in the sand—
with spreading toes;
"Come out," he said, with a taunt, "art thou afraid to
meet me?"
And I answered not, but sprang upon him and smote him.
And he smote me a thousand times, and brashed and
scorched and slew me as with hands of flame;
And I was glad, for my body lay there dead; and I sprang
upon him again with another body;
And he turned upon me, and smote me a thousand times
and slew that body;
And I was glad and sprang upon him again with another
body—

And with another and another and again another;

And the bodies which I took on yielded before him, and
were like cinctures of flame upon me, but I flung them
aside:

And the pains which I endured in one body were powers
which I wielded in the next; and I grew in strength till
at last I stood before him complete, with a body like
his own and equal in might—exultant in pride and joy.

Then he ceased and said, "I love thee."

And lo! his form changed and he leaned backwards and
drew me upon him,

And bore me up into the air, and floated me over the
topmost trees and the ocean, and round the curve of the
earth under the moon—

Till we stood again in Paradise.

From *The Secret of Time and Satan*

This poem shaped my way of thinking profoundly. We
know from Jung and others that we cannot lock up our evil
in the Unconscious. It won't work. It only gets projected
onto others. I believe we should try to redeem our personal
"devils" (Shadows) rather than banish them. Jung said that
only by working on our own Shadows can we deplete, little
by little, the collective Shadow which hangs over the world
threatening to destroy it. The darkness I encountered in my
out-of-body experience, if that is what it was, did not seem
malevolent, it seemed more an impersonal emptiness, a
hungry void. There is a mystery to it.

But speaking of a hungry void, it's time for lunch.

My love,

17
Mercurial Mercury

Dear friend,

Today, I suggest that you take ten pages, one for each of the planets, and begin to list the archetypal figures (processes) which are associated with each. For instance, the Sun will give extensions of the experience of authority: father, husband (don't flinch, ladies, this means an inner one, which may or may not be projected onto an actual man), boss, mayor, governor, president, king, bishop or pope, *imago dei*, Self, Atman, Christ Within, Buddha, Krishna; or try a mountain top, star, heart, etc. List as many as occur to you as the weeks go by until it becomes clear that every organism or entity has a central energy which could be called its Sun. Classic novels usually contain these archetypes, and certainly every myth or fairy tale. In *Winnie the Pooh*, for instance, who would be the "Sun," Pooh or Christopher Robin? Do the same for the Moon and the others as we go along.

Today we'll be looking at a rich and complex planetary archetype, one I've mentioned before, and one I often discuss first, because he represents the master of ceremonies, the guide, the connector, the joker in the pack, the *passepartout*. Let me introduce this master of disguises, Mercurius himself.

He, too, is special and different, by virtue of his nature being hermaphroditic. He is neither exclusively masculine nor feminine, but both. If you were to see the planets lined up in a great Virginia Reel, you would find a group of couples whose processes are balances to one another. Mercury would be the caller, directing the exchange of partners. Or if you contemplate one of your sneakers, the eyelet holes would be the planets, and Mercury would be the shoelace criss-crossing and binding the shoe together. The process of a shoelace is a humble example, like that of the aforementioned zipper, of the same process which appears in the ida and pingala of kundalini, or in the caduceus of Hermes, or the DNA/RNA of the body. It is one of those ubiquitous principles in the universe binding the different levels of existence together. It is like the stairs and elevators which lead you from one floor to the other in a building. (Stairs and elevators are ruled by Mercury.)

This talent of Mercury's is symbolized in his glyph:

$$\ddot{Q}$$

As you can see, it contains the Sun of Spirit, the Moon of growth, and the cross of matter. So Mercury, by his very nature as Messenger of the Gods, can go from the manifest to the Source faster than Mighty Mouse (another of his disguises), which if not at the speed of light is at the speed of thought. And I wonder which is faster?

It used to puzzle me as a child that when I was hurt or sad, wet stuff came out of my eyes. How did my body know when to cry? Sometimes I would get so intrigued, I'd forget about the pain and just wonder. I didn't know about Mercury then.

If we look at what Mercury rules in the body and at the signs that Mercury rules, we will see how much sense he makes and how much trouble he gets us into—as Trickster—and how much fun and delight, as well.

Mercury is said to rule two signs: Gemini (the Twins) and Virgo (the Virgin). The former is an air (mental) sign, and the latter an earth (practical) sign, so Mercury will show two different aspects of his nature in terms of bodily processes.

Let us begin with the Gemini aspect. Here Mercury rules all matters dealing with communication. It takes no stretch of the imagination to see this would involve the nervous system. Now the glyph for Gemini is the Roman numeral II, and Mercury functions through dualities everywhere: in the body, in the psyche, as well as in the outer world. There are two nervous systems, two hemispheres of the brain, and a wiring, as it were, of sensitivity connecting our thoughts with our bodies psychosomatically. Mercury's effect is both afferent and efferent: you decide to touch the table, and this decision is communicated by the nerves to the muscles, and you touch the table; when you do so, the nerves of your fingers transmit the feeling of the table back to the brain. You can also put the whole body on "automatic," and it will run itself without conscious intervention, as for instance when you sleep.

Mercury also rules the lungs; the lungs provide the oxygen necessary to life. The connection between breath *(spiritus)* and consciousness is obvious. Too much oxygen as in hyperventilation will result in passing out, and too little in brain damage. Normally we breathe automatically according to the body's physical needs. We pant with exertion and slow down when resting. However, the yoga science of breath *(pranayama)* is a complex and highly scientific method of breathing, by choice, to reach higher levels of consciousness. All this comes free, and seems to be unknown to those poor addicts who are spending fortunes on sniffable and dangerous drugs! So the link between breath and con-sciousness comes under Mercury's rule.

Perception and vision also belong to Mercury. The eyes are ruled by the Sun and the Moon, but conveying what they see is Mercury's job, and here is a most fascinating clue to the process, I suspect, of "inner" vision. What we see originally is received by the eyes upside down, so the image must be reversed and is then sent crisscrossed to opposite hemispheres of the brain. It is only in the last few decades that we have become aware of the different perceptions in right and left brain thinking: one side sees the whole, and the other the parts in linear thinking. Mercury hints that both are necessary.

When I was a teacher of children, I observed that left-brain (masculine) thinking was the kind rewarded, and right-brain thinking hardly at all. I also wondered about the generation of children who sit before TVs for hours. Images are perceived by the right brain (feminine), and it was this first group of children who grew up with greater difficulties in reading and spelling, but also became peace-loving "flower children" who were reconnecting to nature and to one another. These image-oriented ones baffled their elders. Could there not be a connection?

Some languages are written in pictographs not alphabets. You cannot read Chinese with the left brain. Pictographs and hieroglyphs are infinitely more subtle, as are symbols and glyphs. One of my hopes is that as more and more people develop right-brain thinking, astrology will seem easier to comprehend, because the glyphs are symbols and lead to symbolic (connecting) thinking on many levels. The higher octave of Mercury is Uranus, the planet of the intuition and the making of connections through symbols. Needless to say, astrology is ruled by Uranus, ruler of Aquarius and of the New Age as well.

Mercury also rules the arms, hands, fingers, and the faculty of speech. When we are unable to speak, we wave our hands in many recognizable gestures (my youngest daughter and I thought of over 150), such as saluting, or a finger to the mouth, or a fist or a *V* for Victory sign, to say nothing of the complex digital languages for the deaf and those of the semaphore at sea, or even the dot and dash of Morse code.

Dot and dash are not far from Mutt and Jeff, the short and the long of it, and we are back to the archetypal twins (Gemini) or rival brothers or best buddies, who exist all the way from Gilgamesh and Enkidu to R2D2 and C3PO in *Star Wars*. Tweedledee and Tweedledum, Cain and Abel, Romulus and Remus, and Balor and Balin, and a host of others in every mythology conceivable are all expressions of Mercury's masks of laughter and grief. "Life is a comedy to those who think, a tragedy to those who feel."

A curious aside is that one of the symptoms of tuberculosis is a thickening of the fingertips, a clubbing, which demonstrates a resonance between the lungs and the fingers. Further, Mercury's connection to the hands and fingers is shown in the way we reveal our natures in the individuality of our palms and the uniqueness of our fingerprints.

This process of communication extends beyond the body, of course, in letters, alphabets, words, numbers, semantics, newspapers, books, writing instruments, printing, calligraphy, dictionaries, and the like, to say nothing of reading and writing and 'rithmetic! The words for *mark, marking, market, mercurial* all have *Mercury* at their root, and so the business of buying and selling and com*merce* belong also to him. Tradition has it that "trivia," which means "three roads," originated with a statue or herm (Hermes) being erected where three roads met. People in ancient Rome would dismount and stop to chat and gossip about trivial matters, hence the term.

Mercury rules all opposite motions: up/down, here/there, in/out, now/then, etc. (and even et cetera). And the process behind "now you see me, now you don't." So the Trickster aspect is his, and he runs rampant through our funny papers and cartoon strips as Bugs Bunny, Woody Woodpecker, and through our jokes and jokesters. Brer Rabbit, Til Eulenspiegel, Max & Moritz, the Katzenjammer Kids on one level, and on another the figure of the comics, Laurel & Hardy, Abbott & Costello, the Fool, the harlequin, the jester. Some, but not all, clowns are Mercury, because the sad ones are Neptunian and have a sacrificial element to them.

Mercury rules children. It is hard to tell sometimes just by looking at them which sex they are. The *puer aeternus*, Peter Pan, the boy who will not grow up belongs here. This archetype often appears in Geminis, and to be truthful, the gift of this *puer* is the gift of childlike wonder. It confers a youthfulness.

Geminis come big and little. The little ones are easy to spot—there is something delightfully leprechauny about them. They suggest the wee folk. But harder to spot are the "big" Geminis; they lack this spritely quality. Curiously, they think not so much in terms of opposites as in terms of large and small, another aspect of Gemini. Stories involving giants and dwarfs or people growing enormous or tiny, like djinns in a bottle, or Alice in Wonderland, belong in this category.

The funny experience astrologers often have with a Gemini, or Gemini rising, or someone with Moon or Jupiter in that sign, is that such clients will never stop talking. They talk and talk and talk, and leave raving about what a wonderful astrologer you are. Now that we have tape recorders, I have not been surprised to get a call from such a client sheepishly requesting another session, because all they can hear is themselves!

That Mercury in Gemini should rule words, languages, books, papers, pens, pencils, cartoons, etymology, grammar, writing, punctuation should come as no surprise. Consider the humor of quotation marks: they come in pairs and are little glyphs of Gemini ("!"). When used, they can invert the meaning of a word. What would be meant by: Mrs. Jones is a "good" woman?

The profoundest expressions of Mercury within the psyche are those of the psychopomp and the Divine Child. The psychopomp (marvelous word) is the guide within us, the one who like Virgil leading Dante down into the Inferno, also leads us back up, as Dante was led up. Hermes, the Greek Mercury, led souls down to Hades. This guide within us is none other than the voice of the Self. It descends into our worst times of suffering and does not forsake us, if we will only listen and try to put "two and two together" and become more conscious of our situation, of our mistakes, or how we can accept and understand better the misery we are experiencing. In that sense, our inner guide can remain detached and observant, and with Mercury as ruler of Virgo, more analytical. But a psychopomp can also write captions under the images of our life and show some humor in our dilemma, grim as it may be.

Mercury teaches us that *the laws of nature remain the same, but are mirrored within the psyche.* Just as children in the outer world require a father and a mother and the physical coniunctio, so also does the birthing of the Divine Child, the reborn incarnate Self within us, require the same:

the presence of a Mother Virgin (Sophia) and a Father God. And a coniunctio.

The nature of this inner coniunctio was what Jung perceived to be the symbolic goal of alchemy. The figure of Mercurius in the texts is purposefully ambiguous. I once dreamt that the secret of alchemy was never ever committed to writing, but was encoded, so that only one who had vision could see it, thus safeguarding the texts from the profane. The secret could be imparted by mouth to ear by an initiate or perceived by higher intuition. The key to the code was "Mercurius"!

A whole treatise could be written on the childhood of various gods and saviors, of the archetypal events that befall them. So often they are cast away or grow up in exile. Sometimes they are put in baskets to float on the sea or a river (the Unconscious) or brought up by animals or poor peasants (instincts) or threatened with annihilation as Jesus and Moses were. The motif shows our experience of losing this inner child until it is reborn to lead us into our ultimately greater life. That child, that little golden one, trusts and knows its "real" parents, the ones we so often seek in vain in our everyday lives. We have seen countless tears shed, and I confess I have shed some myself, in that search. Mortal parents can never satisfy so deep a need.

I hope you can see in this letter, which flits from topic to topic, some of the essence of the process of Mercury in his Gemini role. Of course, our correspondence itself comes out of his process. So I send him your way, as ever, with much love,

18
Grounded Mercury

Dear friend,

Now we have to come down to earth again, because the nature of Mercury, as ruler of Virgo, is grounded, sensible. Virgo rules the intestines in the body, and their function is to analyze and break down what we ingest into that which is useful and that which is not. The useful is kept and distributed throughout the body, and that which is not is neatly compressed or distilled and expelled. The worm is the simplest expression of this process, because what it takes in is improved by the time it is cast out. My teacher told me that food passing through the various kingdoms is heightened infinitesmally in vibration as it does so, from minerals through plants through animals through human beings. Anyway, Mercury's process here is sorting, discriminating, and improving.

One is reminded of Psyche's first task of sorting the grain. Grain is ruled by Virgo, and so is the miniaturizing process of wholes into parts. Polka dots and tiny flower prints are fancied by Virgos, and they surely are the only ones in a sign that can get a real thrill at the sight of graph paper! Sand is ruled by Mercury in Virgo. What keeps a grain of sand from getting any smaller is that eventually each attracts an envelope of water which keeps it from annihilation. Pisces, a water sign, is opposite Virgo. And Pisces rules synthesis, the balance to Virgo's analysis.

The mercurial Trickster grows up and becomes orderly and logical, helpful and problem-solving in Virgo. The shadow aspect is an almost obsessive need to criticize and evaluate. The Age of Pisces, which we are emerging from, marked the first true impassioned concern with morality, punishment, and the opposites of sin and virtue. Virgo can be a Goody-two-shoes and a scold.

Neatness, filing, and ordering belong to Mercury in Virgo. The archetypal Old Maid belongs here, the Virgo Prunefiddles of this world. Here he becomes the quartermaster general of the cosmos, the watchmaker with patience for every detail. He can also be the faithful servant, the disciple, the obedient and humble chela, who shuns the limelight.

Recently my husband was in the hospital in Switzerland (the Swiss are a Virgo people), and I was beside myself with anxiety and distress. I went to provide his statistics to a woman in the admissions office, whose job it was to feed them into a computer. She was middle-aged, sharp-nosed, with permed hair and a kindly old-maid look. She would repeat aloud everything I said, slowly, and type it into the computer. Then she would peer into it, nod her head a few times, and say with great satisfaction: "Alles in Ordnung" (all is in order). I could have wept at the comfort of those words spoken in that manner. They were healing to hear, and, indeed, prophetic, because everything in the end was returned to order and to health. (Health is ruled by Virgo.)

The practical Mercury rules precision, skill, diagnosis, and the solving of problems, punctilious and thoughtful service—Mrs. Fix-it and Mr. Clean, all fastidious perfectionists. But where mercurial Mercury is full of wit and humor and plays on words, practical Mercury is often humorless, seriously logical, and literal minded. The only cure is seeing the common sense of nonsense.

Mercury in Virgo also extracts and dehydrates. It is the process of *The Reader's Digest* (sic). It loves to read and to take notes and fill little black notebooks with helpful quotations. (Where do you think mine come from? Me, with my Moon in Virgo!) Mercury in Gemini is curious and hates to miss anything; Mercury in Virgo doesn't miss anything, period.

I simply cannot resist interpolating one of my favorite experiences of a Virgo. I had occasion to visit a small town in

England one winter. I was alone. I found all the hotels were filled because of a business conference in town, and I was lucky to find a cubicle in a boarding house. When I came down to dinner, the dining room was completely filled. There was only one table free, which I took. I noticed a quivering smile pass over everybody's face. Presently, a man came in, looked at the table and me, and glared. He spoke to the person in charge and was redirected to my table, which obviously was his. I observed that he was probably thirty going on seventy. His hair had been parted with a razor and presumably his lips as well. He sat down and opened up his paper, blotting me from sight. I murmured something about the difficulties the world was in. He lowered the paper and looked at me balefully, indicating that he was in no mood to converse. Finally supper was served. Each of us had a small piece of meat, some carrots, some fried potatoes, and a plate of bread and butter. I began to watch what happened next, and judging from the hush in the dining-room, so did everyone else. My companion proceeded to butter his bread and to cut it horizontally and vertically into neat squares. Next he cut his meat into squares and his potatoes and carrots into cubes, all with utmost attention. This concluded, he began to eat ritualistically and in order: one piece of bread-and-butter, followed by one piece of meat, one carrot, and one cube of potato. He didn't miss once until dessert came and turned out to be applesauce, much to my disappointment! The entire meal was consumed in silence. At the end, I could not resist asking, "Excuse me, but were you born in September?"

"No, madam, I was not. I was born the end of August." This was said with grim satisfaction, but confirmed my suspicions: I was eating with the Virgo of all Virgos.

I managed to find out from the landlady that my table companion was a chief pharmacist. She said he was a pinchpenny all right, but quite a good pharmacist. I just bet he was! And he probably is dispensing food for himself to this day, though I fervently pray he fell for some girl who could teach him a lesson or two. I can't think of any other cure.

Mercury is said by some to be exalted in Virgo and by others in Aquarius. I lean personally to the Virgo concept, because the "fall" in Pisces makes more sense to me than if it were in Leo. The music of Bach and the music of Debussy are two ways of expressing these opposites. One is built on precision and order, conveying the grandeur of the human spirit in its quest for the divine; the other sweeps and sways and flows through chaos yielding up a beauty of freedom which has its own kind of order. One could say that Mercury is threatened by chaos but needs some disorder to set it in order; and that the Piscean fears precision and analysis lest it kill the flow of the spirit. We can see this dichotomy played out over the last 2,000 years in the Piscean Age in the arguments of faith and reason, of religion and science, of Romanticism and Rationalism. The Newtonian view of a mechanical structuring of atoms is certainly Mercury's Virgo approach, but the Romantic expressions of art and literature and music are pure Pisces. The pendulum has not stopped swinging, but now it is swinging between new opposites, as we learn to reconcile the former ones. Other names for this god in other cultures are Hermes (Greek), Ganesh (Indian), Thoth (Egyptian), and Woden (Norse). The latter two were associated with bringing the written word to mankind. We remember them on *Wodensday* and *mercredi*.

So far, I have not spoken too much of the Shadow or negative archetypal processes associated with the three we have studied—the Sun, the Moon, and Mercury—or how we would expect to find them expressed in a chart. As we go along, we need to add this possibility. The negative is shown mostly through stressful aspects, but these can be aggravated, either heightened or weakened by sign or house position. In every case, the problem arises from imbalance.

I now charge Mercury to bring you this letter with all speed and with fond affection!

Love,

19
Venus

Dear friend,

You have now met three members of the planetary family, and you can begin to see that, like any other family, they have their own natures and will interact with one another and, of course, with their environment. As we get to know more of them, we will see the psychological tasks and traps associated with each.

Unconscious autonomous complexes manifest in the psyche, and at the center of such complexes, Whitmont has noted, we will always find a "god"; astrologically, we would say a "planet." The negative side of the Sun and Moon manifest differently in men and women, but issues of father and mother imagos will obviously be involved. The negative side of Mercury can result in too great an identification with the puer aeternus or the Trickster, or manifest in a person as the compulsion to lie, cheat, or steal. Physically, there can be difficulties with nervous complaints, speech defects, dyslexia, or even schizophrenia. Almost always, in such cases, Mercury will be involved.

The task, then, is to find some compensatory factor which might have been overlooked, which is sometimes, though not always, possible. Generally speaking, "afflictions" taking place in fixed signs (Taurus, Leo, Scorpio, or Aquarius) are more difficult to change and are more apt to show up physically.

One of the healing processes belongs to the next planet, Venus, because her process is *relating*, which differs from

Mercury's connecting and communicating. We suffer mostly through the lack of relationships or through difficulty with them. Venus rules what Jung called "eros," the feminine capacity in both men and women to be affectionate and to reach out to others in a human and loving way, as well as in an erotic manner.

I once did the chart of a nun who was a hermit. She was on the edge of a breakdown. She had been studying Jung, which had apparently constellated much unconscious material which was emerging in dreams. Then suddenly she found herself having emotional outbursts triggered by another sister. She had become frightened at her own atypical and un-Christian behavior.

Her chart revealed an enormous concentration of power, with a great deal of masculine energy. Her persona and demeanor were soft-spoken and gentle. It was not until she settled herself cross-legged on the floor, by choice, that I could see her fierce concentration and self-discipline. She was suddenly transformed into a Zen abbot, a forbidding one at that.

She lived in a hermitage alone, and had been in the order virtually all of her life. Her Venus never had a chance. Now, triggered by reading Jung, it was emerging, but emerging negatively. She had never related to anybody, by choice. So, I congratulated her. Even though they appeared negative, in fact her outbursts were a good sign. Her hatred and annoyance showed that some other person mattered to her. The "abbot" had shut her off in masculine self-denial. After several intense sessions, she went back to her hermitage. She was kind enough to let me know the relationship had eased; the problem was solved. Now a group of sisters were meeting once a week to further their studies of Jung.

We have to distinguish between Venus in a man's and a woman's chart. Venus in a man's chart will show his ideal of the feminine and will be close to what Jung termed the *anima* in a man's psyche. According to sign and aspects received and house position, it will show his capacity for social relationship and his capacity to express the nonrational (not irrational) side of his nature, his moods, and his vulnerability.

137

Venus in a woman's chart will show her capacity to relate to her own femininity and to express it. If you are familiar with Toni Wolff's essay "Structural Forms of the Feminine Psyche," you will readily find the Moon in the Wife-Mother and Venus in what she called the "hetaira." Both need a relationship with a man to define and fulfill themselves, but in very different ways.

The Moon will sit home and read *Good Housekeeping* and envy those women who are free and glamorous like Venus; Venus will cry when her lover leaves her to go home to his wife, and will envy the Moon her home and her children. Then she will curl up with *Glamour* or *Vogue* and try to console herself. (I think there is nothing sadder than an aging hetaira.) Unfortunately, all too often a man will split his anima projections onto two separate women, causing each to feel she has failed. This is especially true in this country.

The goddess Venus or Aphrodite is familiar to almost everybody. She can be a sex kitten like Marilyn Monroe, who carried almost a collective anima projection for men, or she can be the *puella*, the sweet little girl, Daddy's darling.

The positive side of Venus is truly lovely and has to do with youth, beauty, maidenhood, vulnerability, and natural innocence. Psychologically, she rules our aesthetic sense and capacity for artistic creativity and appreciation. Venus must have been the goddess of the Renaissance—one has only to think of the many lovely fresh and childlike madonnas painted during this period, Botticelli's in particular. We think of them trailing flowers in the spring and associate them with rosebuds and baby's breath and all that is dainty and sweet.

Many women today can't stand that much sweetness. That is because they belong to Toni Wolff's other half of the picture: the Amazon or the Medium (priestess)—those women who do not require a man to define them. They can take men or leave them, like Annie Oakley. Yet all women have all four archetypes potentially; a hetaira hides somewhere in every woman's psyche, often too shy to come out and risk rejection.

The glyph for Venus is the circle of Spirit over the Cross of matter.

♀

The glyph of Venus understood in this way is a constant reminder that Spirit is amidst us in the cosmic order, harmony, and beauty of this world and in our aesthetic capacities to appreciate these and to participate in them. "He who does not join the dance, mistakes the occasion," says the Gospel of John. Dance is ruled by Venus.

As mentioned before, Venus rules the signs of Taurus (earth) and Libra (air). Libra is the Sign of the Scales, and rules relationship: in law, marriage, and art. The sequence is not too hard to follow. All laws involve relationships among people and their property. If a law is just, there will be harmony; and where there is harmony, there will be proportion; and where there is just proportion, there will be beauty; and where there is beauty, there can be art. We find this connection even in the double meaning of the word *fair*, which implies both justice and beauty. For the French, *le mot juste* is the perfectly appropriate word.

Libra's connection to marriage as well as to art follows, if you see it as more than just a relationship between a man and a woman. A "marriage" also takes place whenever we look at a painting, read a poem, watch a play, listen to a lecture, or participate receptively in someone else's creation. The artist puts out a work, and we bring ourselves, as we are at that moment, to meet it. But since we are different individuals, there is a different and unique relationship between each of us and that work of art; our "reaction" is the child or result of the *coniunctio*. The marvel is that any work of art becomes unlimited variations of itself in the psyches of others and future generations to come. Such is the power of creativity. Like the flame of fire (Sun) it has the potential to light a million others without itself being diminished.

In the sense of relationship, too, one can say that with every encounter we enter each other, or as Jung put it:

> For two personalities to meet is like mixing two chemical substances: if there is any combination at all, both are transformed.

Thus we are continually being joined to life and drawn and seduced into living more creatively by the art of Venus.

Venus rules love as well as beauty. She is where our heart breaks. Part of the problem, as Anne Tyler says in one of her novels, is that when love turns to hatred, the love doesn't go away.

The Hindus and the Chinese both put a great stress on relationship. The Hindus have no less than five possible relationships to God: 1) son to father; 2) servant to master; 3) mother to child; 4) friend to friend; 5) beloved to beloved. In each of these, the bond of love is the process of Venus. The ancient Chinese (a nation ruled by Libra) stressed the vital importance of harmonious relationships within the individual, the family, society, and government. Jung always wanted his students to remember the Chinese story of "The Rainmaker." Briefly retold, it goes as follows:

> A village was suffering from a terrible drought. It was so bad that at a meeting the villagers decided to pool their resources and call for a famous rainmaker, who lived in the district.
>
> Duly, the rainmaker arrived, an old man of unusual dignity and composure. Deferentially, the villagers asked him if he required anything, to which he replied, "Yes, would you build me a small bamboo hut just outside the village, please." Rapidly the hut was constructed, and the rainmaker sequestered himself therein, and for three days was not seen to come out.
>
> On the fourth day, it poured.
>
> The villagers were astounded and rushed up to thank their benefactor. "But tell us, sir, how were you able to accomplish this?" they cried.
>
> Smiling, the old man bowed and said, "It really was quite simple. The first day I spent putting myself in the Tao. The second day, feeling myself to be in the Tao, I put my hut in the Tao. The third day, perceiving these to be in the Tao, I perceived the village not to be in the Tao. For the village to be in the Tao, it would have to rain. So it rained."
>
> With that, the rainmaker bowed and departed.

The glyph of Venus also reminds us that Spirit is joined to its visible garment of nature (Taurus) through beauty. And the beauty of nature from the cosmic (the word itself means beauty, as in *cosmetic*) to the microcosmic is everywhere.

As you may have gathered, Saturn rules the process of physical structure and manifestation. Saturn is exalted in the sign that Venus rules: Libra. So, hidden behind the apparent "suffering" involved in incarnation, lies the promise that through love we can reach to the ubiquitous beauty linking the smallest universe of an atom to the solar system and the galaxies themselves. I think it was David Bohm who said that the difference between the beauty people create and that of nature lies in the fact that when you enter the microscopic world, beauty continues to take your breath away. "God geometrizes" in every flower, in every snow-flake, and in every dewdrop. We see this in the symmetry and grace of all that is natural, even in the terrifying, as in Blake's "Tiger":

> Tiger! Tiger! burning bright
> In the forests of the night
> What immortal hand or eye
> Dare frame thy fearful symmetry?

or in The Book of Job those majestic chapters (38 and 39) enumerating the beauties of creation, from which comes the question: "Hast thou given the horse his strength? Hast thou clothed his neck with thunder?"; or the words of Agur in Proverbs: "There be three things which are too wonderful for me, yea, four which I know not: the way of an eagle in the air; the way of a serpent upon a rock; the way of a ship in the midst of the sea; and the way of a man with a maid."

This relationship between Venus and Saturn manifests itself also psychologically, in the subtle relationship of beauty to time. As we grow older, time grows precious, and we become more and more aware of the ephemeral nature of human beauty, love, springtime, and youth. Our hearts catch at the sight of the freshness of a child's face, a boy racing on the beach, a young bride bearing a radiance as

141

well as a bouquet. And we older ones find our eyes filling with tears, sometimes not knowing why. Perhaps it overwhelms us to realize that flowers fade and children end up as senior citizens in nursing homes. Perhaps we hear Isaiah:

> The voice said, Cry. And he said, What shall I cry? All flesh is as grass, and all the goodliness thereof is as the flower of the field; the grass withereth, the flower fadeth, because the breath of the Lord bloweth upon it.

Something in us leaps up, as it did in Faust, who felt that he had wasted his youth on a search for wisdom (Saturn) instead of living and enjoying wine, women, and song (Venus). Somehow we can understand his bargain with Mephistopheles to regain his youth, even if it cost him his soul. Poor Faust cried to him, "If ever I should say to a moment, 'Oh, stop, tarry a little longer—this is so beautiful!' then may you lock me in chains."

If ever we beg time to stop so we may hold and savor the joy and beauty of a moment, *that's* when the devil will snatch us! Like Lot's wife, we turn to salt (Saturn). What to do? To look back in longing is to lose, as Orpheus knows.

The message, of course, is that the ego is suffering because it is the part of the psyche conscious of space and time. Animals grow old and die, but they do not appear to worry about it; they simply accept it. They do not anguish the way we do. As human beings, we seem to be in a kind of limbo, because we have been cast out of Eden lest we eat the fruit of that other tree, "The Tree of Life," and become like gods and live forever. Death (Saturn) is the price, it would seem, that we have to pay for living a manifest life.

In Genesis, Adam and Eve have "Gemini" sons: Cain and Abel. Is it not curious that after Cain kills Abel, he carries a mark over his Third Eye? Granted that this might have been a traditional marking of sacrifice. Still we, as children of Cain, cannot "see" the fruit of eternal life; we would only see it with that eye of the Self, since only the Self in us transcends time and space. But we have Venus: it is her process in us which can lead us up to that garden of understanding. It is Beatrice who leads Dante up to

142

Paradiso, not Virgil, and we are reminded by Goethe in *Faust* that "Das ewig Weibliche zieht uns hinan," (the eternal feminine draws us upward). The goddess Shakti's serpent motion is *upward*.

Venus has the circle of spirit above the cross. We tend to forget this because the patriarchal teaching has been one of projecting blame onto Eve, and seeing the seductive nature of Venus as dragging man down to the perdition they called life. Was it Tertullian who asked: *"Habet mulier animam?"* (Does woman have a soul?) To this day, at the famous monastery at Athos in Greece, not even a hen or a cow is permitted. A friend of mine who visited there saw only a magnificent icon of Mary. Mary was weeping. Any wonder?

So the positive process of Venus is her capacity to lead us, through a creative appreciation of intrinsic beauty in nature, to a place of wisdom and trust in God. Having eyes, we can at least see the beauty of creation, given form by the archetypal Mother Goddess. This is the message of Venus in Taurus. In Libra, as mentioned before, she brings us the capacity to love one another.

A wonderful little book has just come into my hands called *The New Story of Science* by Augros and Stanciu. It is a brief summary of where we stand scientifically and philosophically as a result of the new discoveries in astronomy and physics. In it is a chapter on beauty. The authors conclude that though some beauty in nature can be explained in terms of necessity, mostly it is not essential for the physical survival of plants and animals, nor can it be the mere product of chance. It is rather a grace. I was struck by what the authors had to say about music and the human voice, because Venus in Taurus rules the voice:

> The human body also demonstrates that necessity cannot account for beauty. The human voice is more versatile and expressive than any musical instrument. That man has a voice capable of producing beautiful sounds is not demanded by necessity; a dull monotone or a raucous screech would have sufficed to call for help or to communicate physical needs. Darwin himself recognized that necessity cannot explain man's musical endowments: As neither the enjoyment nor the

143

capacity of producing musical notes are faculties of the least use to man in reference to his daily habits of life, they must be ranked amongst the most mysterious with which he is endowed. Necessity might explain why a birdcall is beautiful to another bird, but not why it is beautiful to a man. By the same token, why should a leopard be beautiful to a man? Why a thistle?

I can hear you asking,

"Is there not a negative Venus?"

Indeed yes! All the planets have negative or Shadow sides, and these are richly described in mythology. They are the villains in the story, setting up problems for heroes to run into. They richly personify the variety of complexes the ego has to deal with.

The Shadow side of Aphrodite is Circe—not so much the witch, who is the Shadow of the Moon, as the seductive sorceress who lures men to their doom through temptation. This view of sex and the pleasures of the feminine is not restricted to the Christian era. We find it already in the Sumerian *Epic of Gilgamesh,* the oldest book in the world. The hero Gilgamesh resists the blandishments of the goddess, lest she send him, like others, to perdition. In fact, he tells her off, for which he pays dearly. A little harlot is sent to tempt and destroy the powers of Enkidu, the shaggy beast-man, and after he has fallen for her, he loses his connection with the animals. Then later when Gilgamesh is on his quest to save his friend Enkidu (formerly his enemy), he is almost trapped in the paradisal land of women and leisure, the land of Dilmun. This story is already telling men, before the tale of Adam and Eve, to beware of the threat to manly undertakings posed by the ensnarements of the feminine. Woman's connection to consciousness, symbolized by the little bird so many of them hold, is overlooked. "She" is going to confuse their senses, their rational and purposeful minds, and all their constructive aims to get on with civilization and other noble ideas.

Negative Venus yields the archetypal bitch, the spoiled puella, the gold-digger, the calculating minx, the nymphomaniac, the "doll" who has her hands in the man's pockets

144

for sex and/or money. This is why Venus is said to be in her detriment in Scorpio and in her fall in Capricorn. This does not mean, I must repeat, that all women with these configurations, or men for that matter, will automatically be one of the above. But it does mean that they will be sensitive to such issues, maybe even victims, and need to be alerted to the positive potential of such positions of Venus. The central issue will be the ease or lack of ease in relationships. Such matters may even be fearfully denied, repressed, or projected. And men may find themselves attracting such women.

Some men are attracted by a negative anima projection like moths to a flame, as by Marlene Dietrich in *The Blue Angel*, or they are brought down by their own folly in real life. John Hinckley shot President Reagan to impress a young Venus he had never met. In this case, it was not for the actress at all, but for Hinckley's tragic and destructive projection. The world of literature and drama abounds with variations on this theme.

Well, I wish I could send you one of the snowflakes that are falling outside. Each epitomizes that testament of ephemeral beauty which is the gift of Venus. There are so many ways to love.

Till next time,

20
Mars

Dear friend,

Today is Tuesday, Mars' Day, and so off we go with him. His glyph has changed:

Before   Today

The earlier form is the reverse of the glyph of Venus, and a balance to her process. Too much sweetness needs the process of Mars, and "mucho macho" needs Venus.

The glyph of Mars can be interpreted as a shield and spear, or as the male genitalia, which it rules. Can you see the resemblance of the latter, in terms of process, to a pistol? One shoots life and the other death. Mars rules Scorpio as well as Aries. And Scorpio rules sex, birth, and death.

Mars is an easy planet to grasp because everything about his process is direct and simple masculine energy. If you were to dance it, your gestures would be straight and thrusting, courageous and outgoing: the gestures of almost all sports.

We have to distinguish, archetypally, between the Sun and Mars. Both are creative, but one is the agent of the other. The Sun represents the Solar Hero; Mars, the mortal hero. One is the King, the other the Knight, or Father/son, just as Moon is Queen and Venus Princess, or Mother/daughter. When Jung first defined the anima and animus, it

146

appears to me, these embraced feminine and masculine *in toto*. Later he differentiated them. This has caused some confusion among astrologers and analysts alike. From the astrological point of view, the process of Mars is quite distinct from that of the Sun, and certainly this is true of Moon and Venus. Think only of the solar system, and remember the special functions and positions of Sun and Moon. Astronomically, Venus and Mars flank the Earth and both are active in our daily and practical lives. They facilitate living in a direct and physical way.

Mars has to be seen as functioning differently in the charts of men and women, as does Venus. Mars in a woman's chart will represent her ideal of the masculine and the way she expresses this internally as animus, and how she projects it onto men. Mars in a man's chart will show how he relates to his own masculinity.

A man, for instance, with Venus in Libra rising and Mars in Pisces, to cite an example, could be so gentle a person that he might have great difficulty in asserting himself. He would be more likely to be an artist than a cowboy, shall we say. The world needs artists as well as cowboys. Think of how many young men have suffered because they have felt inadequate and have disappointed their fathers, often turning to their mothers for support, and ended up in therapy with complexes. Had the parents studied the chart of their son, they might have dealt with him more wisely, encouraging him to excel in his own way, and taking pride in his accomplishments.

Often, too, the son may carry the unfulfilled side of the father. I can think of one instance where the father, though he had the Moon in Pisces, was unable to express his depth of feeling. His persona was frozen into a formal and conventional mask, with all the sweetness hidden shyly within. One of his sons was a dreamer, a gifted poet, a pot-smoker, and the despair of his father, who could do nothing with him. And yet the hook was there, the ambivalence, the love. What the father came to realize, after reading Jung, was that he himself was always in a double-bind in his relationship with this child. Unconsciously, he admired and envied

147

the very qualities in his son which he consciously castigated. As the father began to express his own emotions, the son was freed to a certain extent from carrying them for him.

Mars rules Aries and Scorpio; in the body, Mars rules the muscular system, the reproductive and eliminatory systems, the head, nose, and chin. These connections have afforded Europeans much amusement.

Mars, because it is so direct, is an excellent planet to demonstrate the modifications of a process by the elements of the signs. You can see so clearly that the nature of Mars will function easily in the fire signs. In Aries, he will be a hothead, a scrappy, scruffy, feisty boy, always competing, daring, reckless, outspoken. The energy is turned outwards. But Mars in Taurus, a fixed earth sign and the detriment of Mars, reverses this strength and makes it passive. Here it becomes stalwart, protective, stubborn, unchanging, enduring, resisting, conservative. The strength remains but is introverted.

You know enough now to guess what Mars in Gemini (air) would be like. How would such a child fight? Not with his fists, but with words. Such children will argue you to death and become skilled debaters.

Mars is in its fall in the water sign of Cancer, ruled by the Moon. This story is well demonstrated in the Natural Zodiac:

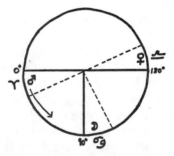

Primordial Conflict (90°) of puer-Mother

Here you can clearly see the mythic and psychological journey of the boy. It is as pronounced as in any board game.

Mars will become a man after he has loved Venus in Libra; until then he will remain a boy, a Son of the Mother. The first square aspect (and all squares will partake of its nature, the nature of friction) comes with the first sign 90 degrees from Aries.

In family life, mothers as a species generally mean well. Their task is to nourish, wash, clothe, and civilize little and much-loved barbarians by transmitting to them the local mores. "Chew with your mouth closed," "Be good," "Say you're sorry." etc. Customs will vary in different cultures and at different times, but the general idea is the same.

The problem comes when the mother is not taught by traditions *when to let go* and let her son join the men. In our country, a Cancer nation, this problem is acute, and probably one of the psychological reasons for gangs. But gangs, unlike sport teams (which serve the same function), do not have coaches. In primitive societies boys are included, after puberty rites, in the male life of the tribe. Older men will be there. In our country there is such a strong drive to make society equal and co-ed, and this is fostering an untenable position for men. The mothers overprotect the sons, and the daughters complain, "Where are the men, there are only boys!" I am all for equal rights and equal pay for men and women, but the psychological distinction between the sexes needs to be appreciated if people are to be happy in relationships. It will be interesting to see fifty years hence what will happen to the male psyche. We need to become more androgynous, which is Aquarian, but not to lose our pleasure in being what we are. As Robert Bly, the poet, says, "We need noble women and gentle men,"—with Mars alive in the women and Venus in the men. The male models on television are often sickening brutes, dependent on substitute phalli: guns, false personas, and cars. Not a day goes by without horrendous fighting and shooting and crime (Mars), and young people acting this out end up, not heroes, but prison inmates.

Going back to the astrological model, if Mars cannot get past the Moon, he will get stuck in Mother. The Mother archetype will turn from a benign figure to a dragon, a

Grendel, a devouring *vagina dentata,* or a castrating institution (job), which may trade security for obedience. If, however, Mars gets past Cancer, he will find the masculine in Leo. All this sheds light on so many fairy tales involving the slaying of dragons for the hand of a fair damsel. It is an archetypal situation, common to all, as in this true story:

On a winter's day in March, a Pisces boy of thirteen is on his way to a school outing. His family is poor, and he has only one pair of leather shoes. (Pisces rules the feet.) Outside there are puddles of melting snow. Mother tells son to put on his galoshes, and son refuses. No other boy will be wearing them. He will not be a sissy. Mother cites "catching cold," and when that doesn't work, the ruining of shoes.

The Pisces son, who is normally tractable and obliging, takes a stand. There is no way he will wear galoshes! There follows a confrontation, and the son goes out, *sans* galoshes, slamming the door. This has never happened before. The boy is as devastated as is his mother, so much so that during recess, he cannot concentrate and collides with another boy so hard that he leaves his two front teeth in the other boy's forehead. He never gets to the outing.

By some strange fortune, the mother has been reading Jung on the wisdom of the East, where mothers in India customarily bring a sacrifice to the temple on the birth of a son, and then again when he is seven. This ritual prepares them psychologically for the eventual sacrifice of control over the son. This mother gets the point, and shortly after goes to church and at the communion rail, moved to tears, offers up her son.

From that day to this, as far as I know, she never ordered her son to obey her, and since he was endowed with a modicum of sense, it really was never necessary to do so.

Another story pertaining to the anguish of mothers and sons also reveals how great a gap exists between what one person means and the other experiences:

A teen-aged Mars is returning by train to boarding school in the city, where a bus will pick him up with other boys. It is Thanksgiving, and his best friend is singing in a cathedral choir presentation. His mother and younger siblings are also on the train because they are going to the cathedral.

The train stops and a fellow student gets on. Quickly, our Mars gets up and joins the other boy. They stand talking at the end of the train. The train pulls into the station, and the boys get off, eventually followed by the mother and children. Mars moves rapidly ahead, never turning to say good-bye, let alone to introduce his family to his friend. At the end of the corridor, he waves his hand surreptitiously behind his back. Mother is crushed and hurt, humiliated, convinced Mars is ashamed of her; she does not merit being introduced. The cathedral concert is ruined for her because of this painful rejection. In fact, she carries the pain for several years. Finally, when Mars is grown up, she asks him if he remembers the incident and how he felt.

"Oh," laughs Mars, "sure I remember that day. I was so grateful to you for not saying anything. I was afraid that guy would think that my mother didn't trust me to travel to the city alone on the train. I was dying with embarrassment the whole time, but you were great!"

Variations on these two tales abound in families. It would help us if we had kept rituals to prepare parents, rituals that mean more than just social parties. In some European countries such as peaceful Switzerland, compulsory military service is required of every male citizen. In the case of the Swiss, beside providing an instant stand-up militia in case of attack, it affords an opportunity for men of all classes and professions to gather together as men. Each is given a rifle to keep, but no ammunition. I remember my oldest daughter going into a Swiss farm house and seeing thirteen rifles in a row: the farmer had twelve sons. And the general at the time was president of a chocolate company! Jung speaks warmly of his service in the army.

Mars in Cancer is in its fall, and it tends to steam in this position. Since Cancer rules the stomach, psychosomatic symptoms of acid indigestion and eventually ulcers may develop unless a positive expression of the Mars energy is discovered. The United States has Mars in Cancer. Collectively, we spend much energy feeding the world.

What is Mars in Libra? Guess. Libra is the sign of Venus and beauty. Here Mars becomes elegant and graceful. He dances with his weapons. Mars in Libra rules fencing, Tai

Chi, sword dancing, and Scottish Royal Tattoos—the martial (Aries) arts (Libra). I knew a man who has Mars in Libra. He was a fencing champion in his youth, and then earned his living engraving (Mars, the burin) wedding (Libra) invitations on copper (Venus) plates! It was one of those metaphoric professions, because with Saturn square Sun, Mercury, Venus, and opposition his Moon, his greatest difficulty was relationships of any kind.

No doubt such a statement might bring up the question, Does such a person have to be that way? As I said before, the answer is that the chart describes the way we are likely to process experience. Through becoming conscious of this, changes are always possible. Painful, yes, but not impossible. As Jung says, a complex has to be drunk to its last dregs, but then it can be dissolved. But the person has to desire it.

Apropos of this, I have always been grateful to Swami Prabhavananda for a marvelous image for cleansing the psyche. He likens this to rinsing an ink bottle. If you keep on pouring in water, eventually it will flush out the very last dregs of ink.

Mars is exalted in Capricorn, and here he becomes *homo faber*; the energy in this cardinal earth sign becomes constructive. He makes things; he becomes a smith, a builder of buildings, and roads, and cities. He becomes industrious and productive, the energy is harnessed to creative and tangible work. Of course, this can occur in a woman, too.

I have two delightful Mars-in-Capricorn stories. One concerns a seventy-year-old woman, white-haired, and diminutive. She had Jupiter and Mars in Capricorn in the Fifth House. I chuckled and told her she had the perfect chart for a carpenter. She grinned at me and said, "But I am a carpenter! Last summer I added a whole porch to my house all by myself. The only thing I needed help with was pouring the cement and putting up the corner posts. But I have to bite my tongue when I see these young fellows starting out. They don't know what they're doing, but it would be humiliating to them for an old grandmother to correct them, so I keep my mouth shut."

The other concerns a businessman. He had come because of marital difficulties. As I drew up the chart, I noticed that he, too, had Jupiter and Mars in Capricorn. I commented that he probably loved playing with dump trucks and cranes when he was a little boy. It turned out he still loved dump trucks and was grieving over having sold a favorite one with a tractor the previous week. His job was in construction and he was head of his own company.

In mythology Vulcan, Loki, and Daedalus are archetypal versions of Mars in Capricorn. Mars in Aquarius is a crusader and fights for principles, and Mars in Pisces is a pacifist who fights only for peace.

I think that you get the picture, and that you can see how the pure essence of Mars will always be there, but modified by the nature of the sign and its element and the house position.

Before closing, since I brought up the matter of the initiation of Mars through passing the square of Cancer, I feel I should mention the equivalent passage for Venus for the young girl on her way to finding Mars. Look again at the zodiac:

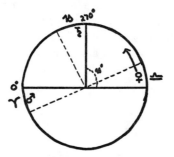

Primordial Conflict (90°) of puella-Old Man

You will see that for Venus the first square will be to Saturn in Capricorn. It is the encounter with the Old Man. He can be either a Wise Old Man or a Dirty Old Man, "an Old Goat." Psychologically speaking, this can mean the introjection of a forbidding authority. Emily Dickinson couldn't make it past her father, but Elizabeth Barrett Browning did.

153

The fairy tale "The Glass Mountain" is a perfect example. In it a young girl is kept prisoner by a cruel dwarf. Other examples are "The Silver Hands" and "Beauty and the Beast." If the rescuer is a prince, read Mars. Venus will remain a puella longing to be rescued by men in outer life. The task, of course, is for her to find Mars, her animus, within her own psyche. The key to the imprisoning tower is in her own apron pocket.

Astrologically, the next sign is Aquarius, sign of liberty and equality. Once Venus reaches it, she can relate positively to Mars in Aries. Again the Natural Zodiac yields a psychological paradigm.

Any woman with a "weak" Mars or an imprisoned one, such as Mars in the Twelfth House, will tend to experience a negative animus. An "animus ridden" woman will have a preternaturally strong Mars. Lucy in the comic strip "Peanuts" is a perfect example of such a strong Mars, and poor Charlie Brown needs to develop his.

Comic strips and television reflect this relationship in ads or situation comedies based on weak little men who act like idiots in the presence of overbearing wives. This is the counterpart to the thug. We are not at present a nation given to hero-worship. A new character, however, is influencing my grandsons. His name is "He-Man." Maybe we can hope!

The placement of Mars in a woman's chart is extremely revealing, especially in the light of Toni Wolff's diagram:

The Amazon, who does not have to define herself through men, is the one most likely to have Mars in Aries, Leo, or Sagittarius, especially the latter. These women challenge men, play with them like brothers, but will not easily be subjugated. You may wonder why I don't put Mars in Scorpio there. The reason is that women with Mars in Scorpio are likely to have strong sexual natures and are more likely to dominate men through sex than through other means. It is the unconscious (or conscious) nature of almost all such women to require every male of any age to acknowledge that they are desirable. It need go no further than that, but the conquest is implied. Their sexuality is like an ever-present fragrance that they are often unaware of.

I have a woman friend, roughly my own age, who is stunningly beautiful. She does not walk, she undulates. Men automatically turn their heads when she passes by. When I first met her, I thought this was put on, but when she invited me for supper, just me, she appeared in a long slinky dress, lovelier than ever, and undulated in and out of the kitchen with the cocktails. Her Mars in Scorpio has not been a boon at all. She has twice been raped and has suffered a great deal through her relationships with men. Like a rich woman who suspects men of wanting her for her money, she suspects men of wanting her for her body and not for herself.

There is a masculine equivalent for Toni Wolff's diagram. I owe this to William Irwin Thompson at Lindisfarne:

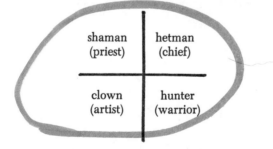

| shaman (priest) | hetman (chief) |
| clown (artist) | hunter (warrior) |

You can see that the hetman or chief would be the Sun, and the warrior Mars. The shaman and clown, or priest and artist, are more likely to be Jupiter and Mercury. It demonstrates that the process of the Sun is quite different from that of Mars. Somebody rules and somebody obeys. In the

New Age this will not change, but we will take turns being a dealer in the game.

As women of our time, we both are privileged to watch these changes in our lives and the lives of other women. "We've come a long way, baby," as the saying goes, don't you agree?

Lovingly,

21
Some problems with Mars

Dear friend,

I think by now you can see why the ancients personified Mars as a warrior and a very masculine energy. Naturally, he also has a Shadow side, which appears in both men and women when that energy is frustrated. Frustration is the one thing Mars can't stand. In fire signs he will get angry and violent; in water signs he will steam and scheme subtle revenge; in air signs he will shout and abuse; and in earth signs he will bang things about.

This, of course, is oversimplification. But negative Mars operates in every criminal, spy, torturer, traitor, and in every sadist, murderer, and rapist. He can be a killer, and we have to remember that at the psychological level there are many ways of killing. ("Hell hath no fury like a woman scorned!") One could almost say that every tragedy in drama depicts the power of a negative Mars, be it an Iago or a Medea. This is what brings the ego to its knees in inevitable pain and suffering. No wonder Mars is the god of war and strife as well as of progress and industry. He destroys and rebuilds and destroys again. "War is the great accelerator."

This aspect of Mars is everywhere in nature, symbolized by two rams butting or any two males fighting over females, territory, or food. This energy strikes, bites, and snarls; it is desirous, wary, suspicious, and can become sarcastic, caustic and, worst of all, cynical. It thrives in narcissism and paranoia and hides in passive aggression. At the root of erotic desire, it can get warped in Don Juanism and many other sexual problems.

How do we recognize negative Mars in a chart? I think most easily by the aspects it forms—difficult aspects, especially squares and conjunctions, which indicate blocks, or triggers, causing the volatile energy to misfire. Being in a difficult element with harmonious aspects will not result in this frustration. But with Mars, being in a favorable element with inharmonious aspects only aggravates the energy.

Mars is not always destructively aggressive; it can also be destructively passive. A weak Mars is the signature of a coward, but one who fears hurting others as much as getting hurt. The masochist is the other side of the sadist. Pisces, Capricorn, and Cancer are the signs most likely to feel hurt rather than angry. Mars in the Twelfth House, especially in air signs, disapproves entirely of physical fighting and believes disagreements should be settled rationally. The positive application of that position is to fight for the underdog, for others.

Fortunately, the civilized sublimation of Mars can be found in competitive sports. It is highly significant that the ancient Greeks stopped their wars during the Olympic games, and we certainly see the projection of collective national rivalries onto the Olympics today.

The therapeutic value of football, baseball, basketball, and tennis is endless and provides a vicarious outlet for Mars energy which is not destructive, though it would be good if more people actually participated in their own games rather than being spectators.

I remember a tradition in my own family in which four generations of mothers and daughters played a card game called Russian Bank. I was duly inducted and passed the practice on to my own children. Grandma King and my mother would not play it in the salons of the hotels, because then they couldn't insult each other. You see, the rule was that during the game you could exchange the vilest accusations and insults. These mock battles were entries into an "as if" reality where generations became equal, and much Mars energy was released in fun. Victories were hailed and

crowed over, scores were kept, sweepstakes run, silly prizes
awarded. I know that all the time the daughters rejoiced in
having a legitimate outlet for being rude and unkind. And
no one ever got hurt, because it was contained in love and
humor. Plays (sic), drama, and games, as Edward Edinger
has suggested, serve as escapes into safer realities, and I
would add that Mars can function well at these levels
without bloody noses. Can you guess what sign my mother's
Mars was in? What element? It was in Gemini, the air sign
of cards and games.

Mercury and Venus are known astronomically as "inferior" planets, which means that their orbits lie between
Earth and the Sun. Mars is the first planet to be dubbed a
"superior" planet, since it is beyond the Earth. Its energy is
extraverted and essential to getting things done. Its process is
that of *making*, a word that, besides practical implications,
carries sexual ones. We "make out" or make love. And the
phallic side of Mars certainly helps make babies, too.

The ideal expression of Mars and of Venus comes when
they are balanced by each other. Then Mars learns to fight
for another instead of against, and Venus becomes strong in
love instead of weak. The result is the splendid dance of
creation.

Mars is different as a lover and husband, and a lot depends on how much the "conquest" means. Mars in Sagittarius loves the chase and is nicknamed "the bachelor" here,
because once the prey is caught, he is on to hunt another.
When Venus marries, her projection will eventually shift
from Mars to the Sun, and when Mars marries, his will end
up with the Moon, though it began with Venus. Thus a relationship matures into a marriage rather than a love affair.
This is the reason why the most soul-searing loves are so
often tragic; love affairs ending in a symbolic if not an actual death. Romeo and Juliet, Tristan and Isolde, Lancelot
and Guinevere, and so many others are always young and
beautiful and somehow doomed for that very reason. Had
Romeo married Juliet, they would become an old married
couple, eating scrambled eggs like anybody else. Don Juan
and the hetaira cannot accept the idea of growing old.

159

Saturn offers old age or death, but if—and this in our culture is a huge if—one can see the other side of Saturn one finds another level of love. Read the beautiful myth of the elderly Philemon and Baucis.

What astrologically is the difference, you may ask, between a love affair and a marriage. A love affair is ruled by the Fifth House and a marriage by the Seventh. In the former, the delight is in giving, risking, and self-expression—one falls in love with love itself. In marriage, it is giving and taking. Nowadays with so many couples living together, which is it astrologically? My rule of thumb is: if giving roses is involved, it's the Fifth, and if someone has to take out the garbage, it's the Seventh! Reality has set in.

As Jung has pointed out, in any marriage four are involved: the husband and the wife, plus his anima and her animus. Difficulties arise over and over between the latter two. As Jung says in his famous quotation:

> No matter how friendly and obliging a woman's Eros may be, no logic on earth can shake her if she is ridden by the animus. Often the man has the feeling—and he is not altogether wrong—that only seduction or a beating or rape would have the necessary power of persuasion. He is unaware that this highly dramatic situation would instantly come to a banal and unexciting end if he were to quit the field and let a second woman carry on the battle. . . . This sound idea seldom or never occurs to him, because no man can converse with an animus for five minutes without becoming the victim of his own anima. Anyone who still had enough sense of humor to listen objectively to the ensuing dialogue would be staggered by the vast number of commonplaces, misapplied truisms, cliches from newspapers and novels, shop-soiled platitudes of every description, interspersed with vulgar abuse and brainsplitting lack of logic. It is a dialogue which, irrespective of its participants, is repeated millions and millions of times in all the languages of the world and always remains essentially the same.

The trap in marriages lies in the tendency of the husband or the wife to split their projections. The wife receives the Moon (Wife/Mother) and the mistress receives Venus (hetaira) as the "other woman"; or the wife chafes under the captivity of the Sun (Husband/Father) and seeks the excitement of a Mars (lover).

The problem is greater for the woman who has children because she is stuck with receiving the projection and often does not have the time or energy to be both Moon and Venus simultaneously. The husband then turns elsewhere, and she feels herself a failure. This scenario is repeated over and over. Today almost two out of every three marriages end in divorce, and more often than not the children suffer.

The therapist has to deal so often with variations on these Sun/Moon and Mars/Venus confrontations, not only in the marital problems of patients, but even in transference and countertransference. Astrology cannot solve this, but it can describe the problem. The planets of one person can be put around the chart of another, which is known as "synastry," and the impact of one person upon another can be foreseen in a marriage or in the consulting room, where sometimes an even more powerful coniunctio can develop "within the vessel." A more recent development in astrology is making a "composite chart" of the relationship itself by using the midpoints of each and every planet in both charts.

The interesting thing about synastry is that in extremely powerful relationships there are so many close aspects. The Sun or Moon or Saturn or Venus of one partner will so often fall on the Ascendant or on the above-mentioned planets of the other. When this occurs, the people involved get a true sense of having been "fated" to meet. Certainly, we can accept this as metaphor. It is "as if" it were true, and the charts will reveal what needs to be worked out. In esoteric astrology, which is not the province of analytical astrology, it would indicate a "karmic relationship."

However, having said this, I could share the experience I had last week of a client who came in asking me to compare her chart with that of her husband. She had far more masculine strength in her chart than he, and he had far more feminine in his. Tactfully, I referred to the relative strengths of her animus and his anima. They seemed almost to outweigh the outer situation. When I was through, she told me that she and her husband had visited a psychic in Europe

161

who told them without any hesitation that they had been married in another life with their roles reversed, he the wife and she the husband. Then the psychic cheerfully looked at the pictures of their children and added that one was new to the family, but the other had been killed in another life by one of the parents! The implication certainly would be: don't hurt anybody if you can help it, or you may end up being related to them next time around. If that is so, the Buddha's counsel for detachment and compassion makes quite good sense. These psychic interpretations may be actually true or they may not; I think it is wise to remain open-minded, yet maintain a certain reserve.

What I can say, with reasonable assurance, is that a child does tend to repeat the Sun, Moon, and Ascendant signs of his or her parents or grandparents, plus other characteristics of their charts. I can say that this is about 95 percent a true fact; it is 100 percent true of my own four children. What the connection might be to heredity and DNA/RNA might make an interesting project for research. I have one grandchild who is the fifth generation to have Saturn in Libra. According to Hermes, this combination refines the process. Nowadays, birthtimes are being regularly recorded, so far more accurate research could be carried out.

The mystery is how do we meet the ones we are fated to meet?

When I was a little girl in Cambridge, I remember going to a friend's birthday party. There was a most magical garden. It was filled with a gigantic white cobweb of strings. From all directions, the strings crisscrossed or wound upon each other, ending tied to trees or bushes. I was transfixed at the sight.

"Later," they told us. "Later!" So we had birthday cake and balloons and ice cream and snappers, and we ran about in our party clothes, and all the time I wondered about the eerie cobweb in the garden. Finally, we trooped out, and each of us was handed the end of a string and a wooden bobbin to wind it on. We were told that at the end of each string was our very own treasure surprise.

Pandemonium ensued. But I remember vividly the brief moments when you had to stop and disentangle your string from another child's, and then, winding furiously, you would cross the whole lawn meeting others on the way. Sometimes the disengaging went rapidly, but there might be a knot which made it more difficult. Finally came the grand moment of coming to your surprise, in my case a book about bears. (No wonder, I call my husband "Polar Bear"!)

I have found this cobweb a helpful simile. Each of us has a string to our own prize, the Self. If we have made the turn and are looking for it, all we have to do is wind our spool and the string will lead us automatically to those we need to meet. If there is a knot, it may take longer to undo (karma!) before we are free to keep winding. This image is also consoling to those in despair of meeting a "someone." If they sit down and cry, it will only delay the process; the secret is to keep on winding.

To conclude, Venus and Mars are processes deeply involved with our emotional lives and how they are acted out in relationships with others. They rule the effective conduct of our everyday lives. Depending on their interaction with the other planets in the chart (aspects), these processes will proceed easily or with difficulties. When they suffer difficult aspects, they will point psychologically to complexes involving the anima or animus, and to possible difficulties of a sexual nature.

With every hope that these letters are proving helpful in one way or another,

Your devoted,

P.S. I hope you are adding to your list of archetypes. Which planetary processes are personified by: Superman? Mata Hari? Hercules? The Artful Dodger? Kanga and Roo?

22
Reflections on karma, synastry and Jupiter

Dear friend,

You are quite right, there are some things that remain total mysteries; they cannot be explained rationally, no matter how hard we try. One of these is "karma." We do seem to attract people and situations which force us to learn and then force us further to apply just what we have, or should have, learned.

There are two myths that might shed light: those of Achilles and Siegfried. Thetis, the mother of Achilles, dipped him in the river Styx to render him invulnerable, but she had to hold him by the heel, leaving him open at that spot. Siegfried bathed in a slain dragon's blood, but a leaf fell on his back, leaving the spot which in the end became a fatal target.

If we are *in potentia* perfect bodies of light, you might say that wherever we are ignorant or wilfully wicked, we leave a chink in our armor. As the winds of life blow over us, wherever we are vulnerable we get snagged and are made conscious of our weakness.

Psychologically, either we take it in or it blows over us. For example, a young mother is confronted by her angry four-year-old who is screaming, "I hate you! I hate you!" Most mothers will not take this personally but ignore the screams and think how cute the baby is, even when having a tantrum. The word-attack sent out by the child glances off an armor of love, and no damage is done. However, the same mother may take a casual remark by her husband personally and interpret it as meaning he does not love her or she has failed. Here she is vulnerable, ready to "process the experience" negatively and turn it against herself. She is needy, and we attract to the area of our need.

When we are young, we tend to exchange needs, so that marriages are held together like molecules, by mutual lacks. This often happens when, for instance, one partner has no planet in one of the elements. Invariably, if it is a first marriage, that person chooses someone with a surplus of the missing element. The need is fulfilled and carried by the other, or there may be an exchange of needs. The couple then is like two halves making a whole; they often divide their psychological tasks. The trap is twofold because each relies on the other to do what he or she cannot or will not do, and growth is arrested. If the purpose of life is moving towards a greater totality, these two are not fulfilling it.

Usually something changes: one of them starts to reach out for a richer life. Often, it will be the wife, who after her children have grown up gets interested in some workshop or seminar or begins to read and think, while the husband continues to work hard and bring home the bacon. She begins to get dissatisfied and wants to be more independent. Soon (if the husband is not growing, too) the marriage becomes a five-legged horse; the husband resents the new directions his wife is taking and feels threatened and unappreciated. Before long the marriage is dissolved, forcing each suddenly to move toward wholeness. This scenario is taking place all over.

The painful truth is that the psyche's unconscious commitment to growth will stop at nothing. However, if both partners can become more conscious of their own needs and learn to help one another and teach one another, the marriage could not only be saved, but would spiral around to meet on another level of richness and love. All too often, however, this proves impossible and growth can be realized only through a new relationship.

As James Hillman has remarked: "All relationship is soul-building." We become different people in different people's presence. Each of us releases something, gives permission or denies it in the other. The greatest good we can feel in a relationship is to be accepted completely, not just partially.

The practice of synastry is possibly a reason more marriages work and are happy in the East than in the West. Synastry means placing the planets of one chart around those in another and evaluating the result. Most marriages in India are planned this way. Believe me, marriage counseling with the help of astrology can be most helpful, because you can point to the mutual needs which are crying out to be met.

When I was in Wales a few years ago, I met a young man called Paddy who had graduated from Oxford. During his time there, he had a best friend, Chandra, who was Indian. This man was reading law, and very handsome and sophisticated; he came from a prominent Indian family.

One day, towards the end of the term, Chandra cheerfully announced he was returning to India to get married. Paddy was flabbergasted. As close as they had been, his friend had never mentioned once that he had a girlfriend. "Oh," said Chandra, "I don't. I've never met her. My parents found her for me and had our horoscopes read. It has all been arranged."

Paddy was shocked that anything so barbaric could be happening to his friend in the twentieth century. The very idea of parents choosing one's wife!

The two parted friends, and were not to meet again for three years when they both were in New York at the same time and agreed to have dinner together. "And I will bring my wife with me," said Chandra.

Naturally, Paddy was curious to see what kind of woman the stars had decreed for his friend. Chandra came accompanied by a young woman dressed in a rose-coloured sari. She was radiantly lovely, charming, and educated. When the men were alone for a minute, Paddy complimented his friend, shaking his head incredulously. "But you see, Paddy," smiled Chandra, "my parents knew just what I wanted."

This certainly is not likely to happen in our freedom-loving country, but it would help many young people to have their charts compared before launching out into marriage.

As Pluto transited Libra in the 1960s, the marital mores changed, and young people in increasing numbers began to live together without benefit of clergy. The idea actually is not a new one. This was practised in the old days in Scotland, and was known as "handfasting." A couple could live together for a year and a day on a trial basis, with no aspersions cast upon the girl if they broke up. The system has merit, and hopefully obviated marriages entered into impulsively for the wrong reasons. Historically speaking, marriages in Europe were often arranged for reasons of property, land, or dowry, and so we see the Scorpio/Taurus axis at work: sex for land.

Our next planets, Jupiter and Saturn, make another pair whose glyphs are reversals of one another, indicating a balance. Both represent loftier and deeper levels of consciousness. The glyph of Jupiter represents the crescent of the Moon over the cross of matter and Saturn's, the opposite.

Jupiter ♃   ♄ Saturn

The process associated with Jupiter is *expansion* and increase. In mythology, he is a powerful and life-giving god with many names in different cultures: Indra, Zeus, Thor and also the father of the day, *dyaus piter*. He is associated with thunder, lightning, rain, and fertility.

When I was in boarding school, I tried making a family tree of the Greek gods. It started out simply enough—until I hit Zeus. No paper was large enough to contain his offspring. The task became more and more time-consuming, and I confess I exaggerated various ailments to get out of gym so I could pursue my research. Each new name would set me off on another genealogical tack. I tracked Zeus through escapades, marveling at his ingenuity in courtship and his many, many disguises. And I certainly had sympathy for his wife Hera who had to put up with it all. I believe I was up to eighty-three children when I got expelled. The chart got lost in the ensuing melee, but years later when I studied astrology, it served me in good stead. I could see that this fertility was a metaphor for the life-giving properties of Jupiter, even in psychological terms.

The lovely word *enthusiasm* comes from the Greek *en theos*, meaning "filled with god." The nature of Jupiter is ebullient, optimistic, generous, and positive. He is full of *élan de vie*—a sort of Olympian John Bull. For us he is none other than Santa Claus, fat, jolly, and generous. I wonder at Clement Moore's Unconscious when he wrote in "The Night Before Christmas", the immortal words "On Donder and Blitzen...." Did he realize, I wonder, the association of thunder and lightning with his archetypal Saint Nick?

Jupiter stands in the role of the "rich uncle," the benefactor, the philanthropist. Psychologically, Jupiter's process is that of compensation and healing; to make strong, and above all, to enable us to be creative through our connection to a philosophical and religious outlook. It is his symbol that appears on every doctor's prescription.

Wherever a person's Jupiter is in the chart, he or she connects to an inner confidence—at least, something is right and we can hope to find a solution. We are almost always blessed in some way by our own Jupiter and by the transits of Jupiter because "God giveth the increase." He is considered benefic.

If the Sun is the life of the one seed, the process of Jupiter makes one seed potentially capable of producing thousands of others. This is the "fertility" of Zeus.

Really, the only vice of Jupiter is excess. Psychologically, inflation and overconfidence which "goeth before a fall" (Saturn!). So, in charts where Jupiter suffers difficult aspects, squares in particular, judgment and restraint may be lacking, as with a person who gives too much.

I once met a man who was almost Jupiter personified, a Sagittarian with Pisces rising, so Jupiter ruled both Sun sign and ascendant and was strongly placed. He was kind, friendly, and overwhelmingly generous. He said yes to everyone and everything.

As we were aboard a ship, when this man would sit down, immediately a dozen people would sit down eagerly beside him, and he would buy everyone a drink. This was fine for the first two or three days, but soon it became evident that people were taking advantage of him. Finally, on one occasion I had lunch with him, and in true Aquarian spirit insisted I would buy *him* a drink. No way! He was so hurt (and European) I had to give in.

As I came to know this wonderful man better, I was puzzled about his Shadow—there seemed no room for any. Then, at his request, I made up his chart, and there sat Jupiter beaming. His fault, if you can call it that, was the inability to receive.

As we became friends, I ventured to tell him of the Hindu tradition that permits *sadhus* (holy men) to beg for food and alms: in so doing, *they give others the opportunity to acquire merit.* This Jupiter could hear: to give away the gift of giving. He had never thought of it that way.

It might be wise to look at the nature of these excesses in terms of therapy. Generally speaking, Jupiter in water signs (Cancer, Scorpio, Pisces) increases emotional activity and can manifest positively in love, compassion, or enthusiasm for wine, women, and song. There is a great capacity for religious devotion, for music and poetry, even for mysticism. Negatively, the above can, through excess, give way to sentimentality, too much self-indulgence, and alcoholism. There may be problems with obesity; even thin ones will have a nice squishy feeling to their flesh.

Jupiter in air signs (Gemini, Libra, and Aquarius) intellectualizes and talks. In committee meetings, he or she will have all the best ideas, concepts, and proposals, but unless there is some strong earth around, nothing will really get done.

It makes you think of "The Road-Song of the Bandar-log" in Kipling's *Jungle Book,* in which the monkeys sing,

Here we sit in a branchy row,
Thinking of beautiful things we know;
Dreaming of deeds that we mean to do,
All complete in a minute or two—
Something noble and grand and good,
Won by merely wishing we could.
 Now we're going to—never mind,
 Brother, thy tail hangs down behind!

A teacher I knew was a Gemini with Jupiter conjunct Mars in Gemini as well. Imagine the effect of these three together: Expansion + aggression + self-identification all in the sign of communication! He was a delightful "puer," a mimic, a balladeer, an imp, a charmer. But he was constantly being fired from work and kicked out of people's houses. He was rapidly becoming paranoid, convinced the world was against him. And in no instance could he see himself at fault.

The chart indicated that he angered quickly and easily and blew his stack. Whenever he was crossed, like a child, he would say anything to anyone. Being a Gemini, his anger was very short-lived and easily forgotten. He bore no grudges. What he needed to learn was that the other person was usually not a Gemini and naturally took umbrage. If this happened to be a superior, he could not be expected to brook such insubordination, and out went poor Gemini on his ear. When the young man caught on to this, it helped. He described the way anger felt as a surge of hot air rushing up into his head and out his mouth. He had a good sense of humor, so with this insight, he began to chuckle at himself and mutter, "Down, boy, down, boy!"

Jupiter in fire signs (Aries, Leo, Sagittarius) rushes into action. Things get done, but sometimes too hastily. These are the ones who run rather than walk. They delight in sports, competing, and achieving; they love to show off, to win, to preach, and to teach. The worst you can say of Jupiter here is that he can become bombastic and boring. Some manifest narcissism because they see themselves as naturally superior. They declaim rather than converse, and exude incredible energy in whatever they do. A well-placed Saturn can help.

You may have noticed that I have not stressed much difference for Jupiter in the charts of men and women, as with the other planets. This is because Jupiter and Saturn function at a different psychological level. A woman can be as talkative as a man, or as active. Both men and women with Jupiter in fire signs will be interested in being the "mostest" in anything. Her headache or her operation will be the worst, her child will suffer the most acute case of whatever, and so forth. They are interested in *The Guinness Book of World Records*. I traveled through Ireland with a student who had Jupiter in Leo, and he was constantly speculating on extremes of every kind: Who was the richest man in the world? Who could hold his breath the longest? Wherever Jupiter is placed, there will be an interest in excellence and the "classical" or universal approach to life.

The process of Jupiter is not as easily expressed through the earth signs (Taurus, Virgo, and Capricorn), and, in fact, Jupiter's detriment and fall are in the latter two signs. You could call it a bulldog effect. The process becomes trapped in the material, so in Taurus, Jupiter becomes interested in "having," in Virgo "collecting," and in Capricorn "conserving." These are the good business people of the world, the farmers, the bankers, the accountants, and the insurers—not just literally, but also symbolically. Jupiter in Virgo loves facts and things that "add up" and make good sense. It increases the sensation function, in Jungian terms. Security, the status quo, enduring, and fear of change are characteristic.

A psychiatrist I know had a patient who was periodically hospitalized for depression. She was a young woman, who had been brought up in Brooklyn by successful immigrant parents. To show their love, they gave her "things" rather than hugs or attention, a common error despite good intention. Perhaps these were the very things they had never had themselves.

With the Sun and Jupiter conjunct Saturn in Taurus, Neptune in Virgo, and the Moon in Capricorn, she was a "poor little rich girl." When depressed, she would go out on shopping sprees and spend thousands of dollars on herself and then lapse into depression because nothing made her happy. She was devoted to her doctor and kept wanting to buy him a gold watch.

The doctor asked for any insight a chart might yield. I looked at it and suggested a rather odd remedy. Instead of a gold watch, I suggested he ask her to buy some nasturtium seeds (they are big) and plant them in a pot and grow him some flowers (Taurus). So he did. A few weeks passed and she came in with her pot. Nothing had grown. The seeds were buried at the bottom of the pot (Saturn). This yielded a fruitful discussion, and the seeds were replanted nearer the surface. The flowers came up and bloomed to her immense delight, and she proudly gave them to the doctor.

A few months passed, and I saw him again and inquired after his patient. The result had been that she had gone out and bought a thousand dollars worth of potted plants! (She lived in the city.)

Ah, but there was a difference. Here the Sun and Jupiter beat out Saturn, since plants are alive and could reverse the process of transforming love into matter to earth and seed yielding life and love, and beauty to boot. This was different from clothes and expensive luxuries and shifted her focus onto participating in a creative process. And it worked! The last I heard of her was that she had bought a property in the country, where she could have a real garden.

This is for me a happy astrological story—it is a practical application of Jupiter's bounty.

I hope that by now you have a good impression of Jupiter and his process of generous and extravagant expansion. In the body, Jupiter rules the liver and the arterial system, and both are sensitive to excess in eating and drinking as well as tension and stress. The tendency is always to overdo, overspend, overact, and overreact. Sometimes it seems as if people with very prominent Jupiters are shouting through megaphones and living a life that is larger than life. This is splendid for dealing with the public; their voices and auras will reach the last row of the opera house. But it is hard to

172

live with on an everyday basis. One actress I know goes on reciting in the diner, on the bus, all the way home, and then more in the living room. Nothing and no one else can exist for her when caught up in the Muse. It is awesome and makes one think of the Dionysian spirit which invaded Dylan Thomas and actually brought about his destruction. This is one example of how an archetype can actually swamp the psyche and bring about a most dangerous inflation. In the case of Thomas, Uranus was conjunct his Jupiter, indicating both his genius and its price.

Jung's unpublished seminar on Nietzsche's *Zarathustra* traces another example of the danger of identifying with an archetype. The Promethean gift to the world is given, though at the terrible price of self-destruction. It is the Jovian inflation that brings one down. Jupiter has to do with unconscious hubris, a lack of restraint, an *élan de vie* which delivers us ineluctably into the hands of the Lord of the Morning-after, one of my names for Saturn.

Almost everybody experiences this at some point in life. A common example is the invasion of Eros: when we fall in love, we can lose all sense and become crazed. We say and do things which shock us later; we appear mad to our family and friends. Yet at such times we feel lifted up into the company of all great lovers. We *know* secretly how they felt: Dante with his Beatrice, or Paolo and Francesca. We become drunk with Eros, and though Neptune is often involved, the excess of emotion will be the inflation associated with Jupiter. Maybe that explains how the god himself got carried away by one amour after another.

You can see that I have Jupiter conjunct Mercury—this letter has turned into a longer one than I intended. I will call Saturn in immediately to end it, since it is growing late.

My love,

23
Saturn

Dear friend,

I am sure you have seen by now that if a planet is conjoined by Jupiter, its process will be intensified and magnified. One can become rapt, carried away by enthusiasm.

Obviously, what is needed is the counterbalance of self-preserving caution, wisdom, and discrimination, and these, fortunately, are provided by the mythological father of Zeus: Kronos or Saturn. His glyph places the cross of matter above the crescent of fluctuation and growth, a direct reversal of Jupiter's.

♄

We should place Saturn next to the Sun, Moon, and Mercury in importance. His process is absolutely fundamental, having to do with three-dimensional manifestation itself. Saturn is that limiting process through which anything becomes embodied. The Moon-Mother gives birth, but the substance of the flesh and the dust to which this returns are ruled by Saturn. He rules the shells which we inhabit and the crystalline structure of all form. As Jung pointed out, the archetypal contents of the psyche are not unlike crystal lattices in their mysterious potential, hiding as they do when *in solutio*. How, we may well ask, do atoms and molecules "know," as they lie in liquid solutions, how to form quartz or salt, let alone the complexities of DNA/RNA? Astrologically, we can only point to Saturn. For the material to become visible, energy has to be slowed down, so that the vibrations lengthen and extenuate into something tangible.

The human shell is ruled by Saturn, and yet it is full of life. It is impossible to say where the "stuff" ends and the life begins; they are intrinsically one. Only those parts which have no nerves at their endings—nails, hair, and in animals hoofs and horns—seem lifeless, and they, along with the skeleton, are more specifically governed by Saturn. The entire mineral kingdom is ruled by Saturn; only when the classification is differentiated into specifics do they come under the subrulership of other planets. And after death (ruled by Saturn) what remains here is also his.

Therefore, the processes of Saturn are in contrast to Jupiter; they are ones of contraction, coagulation, limitation, structure, and boundaries. Without a skeleton and a skin, we would be all over the lot, and it is these that both distinguish and limit us into separate beings. Separate and distinct, both a curse and a glory, but it is the very process of incarnation. The Sun "moves" between the Tropics of Cancer and Capricorn during the course of a year. Symbolically, the Moon and Saturn are the weavers of the life the ego experiences.

Because Saturn says no where Jupiter says yes, his process is associated with ends, pain, suffering, and limitation, and he suffers a very bad press. His figure is that of cruel and devouring time, of the old man with a scythe mowing down the Old Year (Capricorn), the cruel judge, the dirty old man, the miser, the skull of death and corruption, even the Devil himself, with hooves and tail and horns (a caricature of the rejected horned gods, Celtic Cernunnos and Greek Pan).

As I said before, Saturn has a bad reputation. People laugh and shudder at the same time when they see a transit of Saturn coming. What calamity comes next? Let me give you a litany of negative Saturn and the projections that we heap upon him, so that we can get it over with. Then we can try more intelligently to sort things out and redeem the old fellow. Here are just a few, mind you, words the ego may associate with him: cold, dark, old age, pain, grief, poverty, misery, filth, sin, punishment, sickness, suicide, depression, death, decay (sounds like he rules the Bronx!), graves, corpses, fear, ends, suffering, gloom, clocks, tolling bells, starvation, drought, salt, bitterness, winter, ice, snow, misfortune, loss, despair, remorse, anguish, tears, moaning, ashes, rags, ruins, morbidity, apathy, acedia, teeth, hair, bones, dungeons, cellars, prisons, lead, greys, blacks, dark greens and browns, undertakers, mourning, criticizing, complaining, contempt, cynicism, delay, denial, boredom, sullenness, dullness, slowness, lack, and want, plus the fear, guilt, and sense of doom that accompany all the above. By now, I think you get the idea!

When Saturn teams up negatively with Mars, you get action: resentment, anger, jealousy, revenge, hate, murder, pornography, war, torture, wounds, crime, and destruction. This world is full of them. When Saturn pairs up with any other planetary process and furthers its negative expression you will find one of the "seven deadly sins" or, psychologically expressed, one of the repressed or suppressed complexes. See if you can match up the other planets with the classical list of sins: pride, lust, avarice, gluttony, anger, sloth, envy.

Psychologically, it is not that simple. Complexes are not in themselves sins but the results of processes which have been in intense internal conflict, for one reason or another, causing the ego to suffer a lack of harmony and self-acceptance. It is pure hell to hate oneself. I call it "instant abyss." Anytime you want to experience this, begin by defining yourself by what you are not or your lacks, or list your sins of omission. I like to remember what Dorothy L. Sayers said: "The flames of hell are the flames of God's love rejected."

Recently, I did the chart of a woman who had Saturn exactly conjunct Mars in Aries square Sun in Capricorn. She knew she had the potential for both cruelty and hate. What emerged was most interesting. She herself had suffered violent abuse as a child from both her parents—physically from her father, psychologically from her mother—and she had twice been raped. She worked as a therapist dealing especially with victims of abuse. She suffered from terror about confronting her own guilt and suspicion that she herself was capable of inflicting this kind of pain. She associated certain periods of history with torture connected to religious conviction. In a way, her childhood provided a metaphor for what she herself would never do, yet what she suspected she might have done at another time. Understanding that the painful experience of her childhood had a redemptive function in her work of healing others—not just theoretically but out of her own traumatic past—was one step. But seeing the other positive parts of her chart that showed the courageous intention to transform hate and anger into a more healing form of social indignation took her even further. She also had the Moon and Jupiter in Pisces, showing her capacity for compassion and forgiveness, which she needed to give to herself as she could to others.

Let us change elements. Supposing a man had Saturn conjunct Mars in Pisces instead of Aries. Pisces is a water sign and associated with peace and humility. Here the conjunction would evoke a totally different metaphor: the archetype would emerge negatively as a coward and positively as a potential pacifist. The coward fears for himself; the pacifist fears harm will come to others through war. In a woman's chart, this might manifest in her perception of herself as a pitiful victim, a masochist capable of attracting sadism, or more positively a person compassionately interested in helping people "imprisoned," either literally or psychologically. Do you see the difference?

Put Saturn and Mars in Taurus, fixed earth. Here the process becomes one of stubborn refusal to change (fear for personal security), or of loyal endurance and responsibility towards others. You may notice that the word *others* appears in the positive aspect. This is because one of the lessons of Saturn (and why he is exalted in Libra, the sign of the "other") is that we learn more about the Self in us as we serve it in others. "Love thy neighbor as thy Self" works both ways. Also, we keep only what we give away.

This paradox, by the way, is most beautifully explained in

Jung's *Transformation Symbolism in the Mass*. In it he shows that the reason for religious sacrifice (Saturn) is that we can give away only something we truly have in the first place. Thus by "sacrificing" it, we sanctify its presence *ab origine* within us.

The client mentioned above who was working with other victims was also healing herself and discovering the Self's capacity to heal her ego as well as to help others. One can suggest to clients who are overgenerous with others and hard on themselves that life is like a gin rummy game. If you give all the cards at the outset to your partner, there can be no game. You lose, yet you get angry. You have to start out dealing: one for you, and one for me. Saturn is fair.

Saturn is also at work in a negative inflation, the earmark of hidden pride. We tend to experience Saturn, whoever we are, as a cruel inner judge and critic, a voice telling us why we cannot do something, a real party-pooper if ever there was one. We do not see that it is our pride that makes us so hard on ourselves.

To my clients, and to myself, I suggest the following remedies:

1) Ask yourself if you would judge others as harshly as you judge yourself. Invariably the answer is no. Well, then, set Saturn to judging his own judgment. (That'll keep him busy for hours!).

2) Use the judgment mantra. This mantra was the gift of a young woman I met several years ago. She suffered from one of the worst self-images I ever came across. She thought herself fat, ugly, and stupid, but was actually pleasingly plump, radiantly alive, and a theology major. It finally occurred to me that humor might work for her. So I told her she needed a magical mantra. She leaned forward so earnestly that I could almost hear her devout resolution to apply it. Looking every bit as solemn as she did, I whispered the mantra, "Heah come de JEDGE!"

It works. You catch "de jedge" every time you become conscious of him. Then you begin to wonder who's catching him. Ha!

3) Does this inner voice tell you why you can't do something? Is it because it wouldn't be good enough, perfect enough, so it's no use? If a child of yours proudly showed you a drawing or a poem, would you reject it with so little compassion? Had you ever thought of confronting Saturn and saying, "I know perfectly well why I can't do this, but could you tell me *how I could?*"

This latter transforms because it enlists the cruel judge to help instead of hinder, and it finally gives Saturn permission to unmask himself as the Wise Old Man. He's probably been hanging around moping in the psyche for years waiting to be invited! It comes as such a surprise to find out that one's worst enemy can also become one's best friend.

I must sign off and fix lunch before I judge myself as delinquent.

Love,

24
The balance of Jupiter and Saturn

Dear friend,

Here is a beautiful quotation from Rowley's *Principles of Chinese Painting*. It expresses perfectly the relationship between Jupiter and Saturn:

> When you expand *(k'ai)* you should think of gathering up *(ho)* and then there will be structure; when you gather up *(ho)* you should think of expanding *(k'ai)* and then you will have inexpressible effortlessness and an air of inexhaustible spirit.

Close your eyes and feel this perfect tension between the two, and see how Saturn relates to art and to beauty. That delicate restraint is present every time you fill a glass with water to the brim and it hovers there not spilling over. I intuit that when we intone the sound *OM*, its nature is to curve back on itself like the edge of a flower petal tenderly separating from the space around. This quality of restraint is peculiar to ancient China, which is now ruled by Libra, and expressed so wisely by Lao Tzu, Chuang Tzu, and later by Confucius. It shows the importance and relevance of space, silence, and time in art and in relationships. This is something alien to the West. Yet, curiously, following the rule that any nation conquered will eventually conquer its conqueror *culturally*, we are getting a taste of this in the influx of goods and design from Japan, and now even from

China. This sense of restraint is something we sorely need to know more about.

I remember two years ago being a captive participant in a day's tour of Rome and the Vatican Museum. It felt like being forcibly stuffed with ten tons of golden scrambled eggs. Masterpiece after masterpiece, encrusted with curlicues of gold, mile on mile. One cried out for space—for just one wall with one painting and the time to sit and experience it. In oriental art, the importance of a bamboo shoot or a mountain is magnified by the emptiness around it, framing it with significance.

There is one tale of Chuang Tzu that I particularly treasure because it has a practical application in life. In it, he observes that if two men are out fishing and their boats collide and their lines entangle, an argument will very likely ensue. On the other hand, should one of them be alone and run into another boat, he will simply quietly disengage himself and move on his way.

This wisdom helps on early mornings when you look out the window and see that raccoons have gotten into your garbage can and strewn everything all over the driveway. This can be infuriating, unless you have a good friend like Chuang Tzu. I somehow think of him fondly, as I silently pick up the empty sardine cans and orange peels. This is a homely lesson of Saturn's. Deal calmly with life's little annoyances, and you will learn to cope with the bigger ones.

Barbara Hannah tells a story about Jung when he was visiting Ceylon (now Sri Lanka). She writes:

> Two things happened to him in Ceylon which made an especially strong impression on him and of which he often spoke later. Two peasants collided and got stuck with their carts in a narrow street. Jung waited for the furious mutual accusations that would certainly follow such a mishap in Europe, but to his amazement, "they bowed to each other and said: 'Passing disturbance, no soul!' That is to say, the disturbance takes place only outwardly in the realm of Maya and not in the realm of true reality, where it neither happened nor left a mark. One might think this almost unbelievable in such simple people. One stands amazed."

Many years before Jung was in Ceylon, I had been enormously struck by a similar incident. On my second visit to Bollingen in 1930, Jung hit the doorpost with the fender of his car while backing out of the garage. I expected him to be very much annoyed and upset (as most people are by such things), but not at all. It did not seem to touch him in any way. Evidently it was just "a passing disturbance, no soul," and left no mark at all in the world of reality!

On that Chi-ops tour in India I mentioned earlier, this story came in handy. We arrived in Delhi quite confused by the screaming and gesticulating crowds at the airport. Getting the luggage and going through customs, at 2:00 a.m. in humid heat was a test of patience. As we racketed out on the bus towards the hotel, I got up and, hanging on for dear life, shared this story about "no soul." It really paid off because in subsequent weeks we were often sorely tried. To my delight, I would hear laughter and the words, "No soul, no soul!" float up. Today I marvel at the gift those two peasants gave us through Jung and Hannah, and on and on. They haven't a clue that their lives changed ours, but that's just the point. We really never know.

Of all the planets, the process of Saturn seems the most important; his is the "bottom line," where we are forced to confront our own Shadow, own it, be responsible for it, and learn to accept and to love it, too. This has immeasurable importance to the world, for by working on our "Saturns" we take just that much darkness out of the Collective Shadow and replace it with a widow's mite of consciousness. It is a holy task.

By now you must realize the interaction between the Moon as ruler of Cancer and Saturn in the opposite sign, as ruler of Capricorn. Both of these are involved with the process of ego building and ego sacrifice. Both are symbolically present at Easter. The story of the Crucifixion acted out in history the paradigm of that sacrifice necessary before our rebirth into a larger dimension of psychic reality.

The ego falls easily out of sync, out of the Tao, and when it does nothing seems right. Strangely enough, the cosmos doesn't fall like that. I think of the French poet Francis

Jammes, who said: "Tout est vain, qui n'a pas le grand calme de Dieu." (Nothing matters which has not the vast calm of God.)

The psychic menu common to us all seems to call first for our incarnating, then developing consciousness, then developing an ego, then identifying with the ego, then sacrificing that identification and moving on to a glorious and deserved dessert: awakening to the reality of a Self which was there all along. It is like the birthday cake mandala, hidden in the kitchen until the candles are lit and the celebration is at hand. It is this rebirthday that Earth celebrates as it enters Aries every Easter/Passover/spring.

To compare the passion of Christ to a birthday party is a bit much, even for me, but the promise hidden in both is of a great and joyous surprise. The place where we are collectively stuck is in sacrificing ego-identification, and here Saturn holds the key.

The task of the Age of Gemini was the development of consciousness. The collective task of the Age of Taurus was developing a sense of personal identity through psychic investment. The task of the Age of Aries was the development of the ego. The task of the Age of Pisces was its sacrifice.

The task of the new Age of Aquarius is the discovery of the Self, the Second Coming within the individual, and also the loving fellowship of mankind and the return of the feminine.

Saturn has to be the guide here, because psychologically Saturn rules both the pride of Lucifer and the humility necessary before the Unknown God and Source of our Being. "The great offense" which we pray to be kept from is hubris, the fatal inflation of the Tragic Hero, who represents the human ego trying to deny the power of the Self. Edinger points out that the irony of classical tragedy lies in that, at a certain level, each of us knows the outcome of the plot. The ego is doomed to agonize in the amphitheatre of life, to fall from heaven, to suffer crucifixion, and to die. But the Piscean Age shows us that the key lies in our willingness to be a "full and living sacrifice." We can take the prideful arrogance of the Age of Aries, which knows it all and mocks anything greater than ourselves, and offer it up in loving and faithful humility, which is Saturn's other side. Then the ego is reborn and finds its rightful place, knowing its potential and its limits at the same time.

The lesson of Saturn teaches us to turn to the source of light within *(metanoia)*, to empty ourselves, become concave *(kenosis)* that we may become chalices filled with spiritual energy (Aquarius). When the ego becomes to the Self what the Moon is to the Sun, then the individual incarnates and discovers a spirituous Earth. Thus we discover the intangible within the tangible and the Reality of the real.

As Ramana Maharshi said, "When a man thrashes his robe on the stone in the river and wrings it, it is not because he wants to hurt it, but because he wants it clean for the feast day. In the same way, when God strikes a man and washes him in tears, it is because He wants to be clad in him."

If you look at the litany of Saturn in my last letter, you will see that most of the words describe negative conditions experienced by the ego. The ego process is to gather experience and to apply this as consciously as possible, sorting input from both the outer world and from the inner world of the Unconscious. In the chart, this task falls to the Moon and to Saturn. For a therapist, knowing about timing (Saturn) can be of tremendous help, and the model of the chart also describes various cycles of time:

1) Every twenty-four hours every point of the 360 degree zodiac makes a full turn clockwise through the circle of houses.

2) Every month the Moon makes a complete tour counter-clockwise through every sign in every house. Usually you get thirteen of these in a year. With every lunation, full moon and quarter moons thus take place and subtly emphasize various aspects of our daily lives, our ordinary garden-variety ego life, which is the scene of the potential epiphany of the Self at any given moment.

3) The Sun does its royal progress in one year with Mercury and Venus dancing rings around him; Mars does this in

184

two years; Jupiter in twelve; and Saturn in twenty-nine, give or take a bit.

It is vital to realize that *by progression* (counting a day for each year after the person's birth) it will take the Moon about twenty-eight years to come back to its own place, and Saturn *by transit* about the same amount of time. So whatever the Moon is about, Saturn seems to be keeping a watch over it, so to speak.

The application of this can be extremely significant in psychotherapy. To know the position of the progressed Moon and the aspects formed by transiting Saturn will point to what the "opus" of the present moment is. The Moon will show the focus, like a spotlight highlighting an issue, and Saturn and the other planets will describe the psychological "weather conditions." Knowing where a patient's Saturn is in the natal chart, and where the transiting one is can be one of the most helpful things of all.

Saturn is often called "the Lord of Karma," which is to say that his process is associated with consequences, results of previous actions. Unfortunately, we often project a vengeful Yahweh-like archetype onto him, as if he were out there scheming how to fling us to damnation. It is we ourselves, and our Saturn within us, who lack mercy and understanding. Karma is the law of action and reaction, and Saturn is the process through which the ego wakes up to its responsibility for consciously creating its own reality.

As an aside, I cannot help wishing the concept of karma were more prevalent in this country. If kids falling into lives of crime and drug-abuse could only see that whatever they do to others, they are doing to themselves! Whoever lies ends up trusting nobody. Whoever steals ends up fearing loss. Yet "cast your bread upon the waters" (Virgo on Pisces?) and it will come back again after many days.

The words of Paul to the effect that "unless the seed die" refer to this Saturnian process of a death preceding a far greater life. When the ego lets go of its insistence, the identification dies, and the greater life can begin. One could paraphrase Paul into psychological language: "The first man

[ego] is of the earth, earthy: the second man is the Lord [Self] from heaven." These, most poignantly, are the words on Jung's gravestone.

Alchemy begins with Saturn, the task being to make gold out of lead, or wisdom out of suffering and experience, or individuation out of a life that appears to be merely "one damn thing after another." The interesting thing is that both salt (Saturn) and gold (Sun) have cubic crystals. The Sun is hidden in Saturn and Saturn is contained in the Sun.

The key to positive Saturn is wisdom, personified by the Wise Old Man or the Wise Old Woman. In ancient times, older people were not expected to become senile but to become wise. In Rome men became senators (*senatus*, senior = old); in China they became sages; in India, they became holy men and women; among the Celts, the women also became the Wise Ones, as in Greece. In modern times, we are told to rush to the mirror and fight every wrinkle and dye every gray hair, lest Saturn creep up on us.

I have done many a chart of women panicking because of approaching old-age. It should be, and can be, a time of shining, a time of fullness and deeper growing, a building of the body of light we will use to step out of the shell we leave behind, a time to practice "flying out of the nest" of this body. As Dadaji says, "Do not deprive old people of their death; they have deserved its comfort." If the ego has "died" in the life, the greater life will already be familiar, and the attitude will change. Take for example this lovely old Egyptian poem from about 3000 B.C.

DEATH IS BEFORE ME TODAY
Death is before me today
Like the recovery of a sick man,
Like going forth into a garden after a sickness.

Death is before me today
Like the odor of myrrh,
Like sitting under the sail on a windy day.

186

Death is before me today
Like the course of the freshet
Like the return of a man from the war-
   galley to his home.

Death is before me today
As a man longs to see his home
When he has spent years in captivity.

                  Blessings!

25
Uranus

Dear friend,

For millennia, the solar system appeared to consist of seven bodies, with Saturn representing the outer limit, literally and symbolically. In the last two centuries, we have added three more planets (four, if we count the planetoid Chiron). The impact of this is quite significant.

Uranus, Neptune, and Pluto have emerged on the scene synchronistically with powerful historical events. The implication is that we discover a new planet only when we are ready to take the next collective step in consciousness. All three have such slow orbits they would seem to apply to the collective; yet each has the potential to affect individual consciousness, if it is listened to with spiritual ears.

Uranus is now the ruler of the sign Aquarius, and therefore of "The New Age," an age deeply concerned with the emergence of the common man. It holds the promise of the Second Coming within the individual psyche. It could be the age in which, having survived the sacrifice of the collective ego in the Age of Pisces, we may be ready to discover the Divine Guest, the Self within, and at the same time learn to love and respect it in each other.

It seems highly appropriate, therefore, that Uranus, the new planet, should have been discovered by a "common man," William Herschel, who was not a professional astronomer at all. He was a most remarkable individual, a musician, a true amateur of mathematics, and a tinkerer with parabolic lenses. He was born in Germany and moved to Bath, England, where he continued his studies. Here is his own account of the discovery taken from a letter published in 1784.

Among other mathematical Subjects optics and Astronomy came in turn & when I read of the many charming discoveries that had been made by means of a telescope I was so delighted with the subject that I wished to see the heavens & Planets with my own eyes thro' one of these instruments. Accordingly, I hired a 2 ft. gregorian Reflector. The satisfaction I received determined me to furnish myself with a capital telescope.... the price tho' moderate appeared to me so extravagant that I formed the resolution to make myself one.

In the pursuit of this laborious, but to me delightful undertaking I persisted for some years till to my infinite satisfaction I saw Saturn in the year 1774 thro' a 5 feet Newton reflector of my own making. I proceeded to larger instruments.... I soon made a 7 ft., a 10 ft & a 20 feet reflector. I persisted with such obstinacy in compleating the parabolocal [sic] figure of a 7 ft telescope that I made above 200 object specula, till at length I obtained one that would bear any power I could apply to it.

All this while I continued with my astronomical observations & nothing seemed now wanting to compleat my felicity than sufficient time to enjoy my telescopes to which I was so much attached that I used frequently to run from the Harpsichord at the Theatre to look at the stars during the time of an act & return to the next music. To this perseverance at length I was owing the Discovery of the Georgium Sidus [the first name given to Uranus by him in honor of King George III] which happened on the 13 of March 1781. It has generally been supposed that it was a lucky accident that brought this star to my view. This is an evident mistake. In the regular manner that I examined every star of the heavens not only of that magnitude but many far inferior it was that night its turn to be discovered. I had gradually perused the great Volume of the Author of Nature & was now come to the page which contained a seventh Planet. Had business prevented me that evening, I must have found it the next, and the goodness of my telescope was such that I perceived its visible planetary disk as soon as I looked at it. And by the application of my Micrometer determined its motion in a few hours.

The discovery was reported to the royal astronomers and confirmed. Unlike Galileo, Herschel was congratulated, and the new planet renamed after him, and it is still often called "Herschel" in Europe. However, the great Roman deities Mars, Jupiter, Saturn being followed by Herschel must have been too much of a shock to classical ears, so the new planet ended up being called Uranus. The psychological process, however, does not truly fit the myth of the Titan Ouranos as much as it does Prometheus, as has been beautifully demonstrated by astrologer John Tarnas of Esalen.

The nature of the new planet was soon discovered to be revolutionary and iconoclastic. Even its satellites orbit in an opposite direction from those of Jupiter and Saturn. The rigidity of Saturn was suddenly subtly transcended.

In my opinion, the dawning of the New Age began with this momentous discovery, and, indeed, it coincided with three great revolutions made on behalf of the "common man." Two of these are the American and French Revolutions. What can be more Aquarian than a slogan calling for "Liberty, Equality, Fraternity"? The third revolution was eventually to transform every life on earth, either directly or indirectly. This was the Industrial Revolution. Thanks to it, machinery and appliances have freed men and women from much physical slavery, and nowadays women are catching up on all fronts, questing for their own liberty, equality, and sisterhood. It touches me greatly to see a direct connection between my writing to you on my computer and the amiable figure of Herschel peering into his homemade telescope sitting in his garden in Bath!

The collective nature of Uranus shows itself in the cry to burst the bonds of Saturn and usher in a new spirit of freedom and change, two watchwords belonging to its process. One of its most powerful expressions comes in the final movement of Beethoven's Ninth Symphony when the chorus breaks into the "Ode to Joy," with words by Friedrich von Schiller. Originally, Schiller had written "Freiheit, Freiheit, Tochter des Elysium," (Freedom, freedom, daughter of

Elysium) but this was changed to Freude [joy] for political reasons. Yet the Aquarian nature of the Ode and its music are implicit in the rest of the text:

Joy, beauteous spark of God
Daughter of Elysium
Drunk with fires,
Goddess, to thy shrine we come!
Your magic heals and binds
That which culture's torn apart
All mankind is turning brothers
Neath your gentle spread of wings.

If you substitute the word *freedom* for *joy,* you can see what was coming. Schiller himself had Uranus in Aquarius, and so was a child of his time and of the age to come.

The process of Uranus also has to do with invisible energy and its transmission. It is the higher octave of Mercury and works at another level of communication, an almost instantaneous one. Electricity, prana, auras, X-rays, radio, telegraphy, television transmission, cosmic rays, outer space, computers, space travel, science fiction, telepathy, kinesiology, astrology(!), astrophysics all come under this planet's jurisdiction, to say nothing of the endless number of mechanical inventions which have changed the face of the Earth and the scope of humanity in the cosmos. Its glyph is held high unwittingly on rooftops all over the world.

The process of Uranus is electric and is balanced by Neptune's, which is magnetic. The personifying archetypes are the Magician and/or the Inventor. The occultist "zaps": legendary lightning comes directly out of his fingers. Indirectly it comes out of the modern global technology invented by contemporary industrial "magicians"; one might add, some white and some "black magicians." The process itself has always been available, but are we ready for it?

It is Uranus who overthrows our Saturnian concepts of time and space. If the President sneezes in the White House, it can be heard simultaneously on any other spot on Earth or in outer space. But it is the three trans-Saturnian planets, Uranus, Neptune, and Pluto, that are forcing us towards universal brotherhood—or extinction. Our global interdependence is a fact. We may need to change the words "Love thy neighbor as thyself" to "Love thy neighbor, s/he *is* thyself."

Not all people respond to Uranus, except at the collective level, but an ever-increasing number of individuals are responding. In the natal chart, the position and aspects of Uranus will point to anything from eccentricity to genius, from rebelliousness to spirituality. Uranus questions every status quo. Its cry is, "Why not?" Its prominence in a chart marks a person who feels "different" or even exiled. In children this can be very trying, especially for the parents and teachers.

My mother used to say, "If you want to take a pig to Dublin, pull him by the ear to Cork." Her way of getting me to do something was simply to tell me flat out that she did not consider me capable of doing it. Naturally, my Uranus would rise to the bait every time to prove her wrong.

Uranus concerns intuition and higher consciousness, but when it is not able to express itself on this level, the person may feel driven by sudden erratic compulsions. The result can be highly scattered behavior which often appears, and well may be, irrational.

I remember a young man who had the Sun conjunct Uranus in the Eleventh House square Mars. He wanted to become a doctor. His intensity was such that his entire body vibrated and quivered like a fox terrier. His great agitation would surely make any patient sicker, so I counseled him to channel his energies into the computers he was so interested in.

On the other hand, some people who are hospitalized as schizophrenics might actually have problems related to Kundalini awakening or the breaking into consciousness of alternate realities, which medicine still has difficulty comprehending. Nowadays there are efforts to prevent this misdiagnosis and to provide a network of professionals who can distinguish the difference. Kundalini energy has to do with Uranus and often with its transits. This is something that should be known.

One positive effect of the drug generation has been more general acceptance of alternate realities and the idea that the level to which collective humanity is generally tuned in is not necessarily the only one. It is as if there are parameters to "normal (ego) consciousness." Occasionally people fall below or rise above these and experience "hell" or "heaven," or another level of experience. In the case of St. Anthony or Gautama Buddha when he experienced the Temptations of Mara, the world of the lower astral seems to have opened up. We may consider these as "religious" nightmares, but such confrontations are not limited to saints and saviors; they are experienced by many under the influence of extreme stress or when artificially induced by drugs. One can compare the drawings of people under LSD and the weird paintings of Hieronymous Bosch. Actually, such negative and scary confrontations are less the product of Uranian consciousness than Plutonian, but the process of Kundalini is related to Uranus. The awakening of the chakras and the acceptance of these realities will be part of the development of the Aquarian Age.

From the therapist's point of view, it is extremely important to observe the transits of Uranus over planets in a patient's chart. Uranus is the Great Awakener, and the potential is there to raise the process of whichever planet is in question to a higher dimension of understanding and expression. The general effect is one of restlessness and excitement, and such transits can mark a time of change, chaos, and yet ultimate growth and insight. Breakthroughs and synchronicities can occur, new insights emerge. The intuition flowers, and people find themselves "knowing" and not knowing how they know. But if people are not ready for this, the impact can be as chaotic as the upheaval of an earthquake.

One could make a long list of "geniuses" with Uranus powerfully aspected. Among them would be Jung himself, a

Leo with Uranus in Leo squared by the Moon in Taurus. When by his own account he "woke up" that day as a boy, his progressed Sun had reached his Uranus. Yeats had the Sun conjunct Uranus in Gemini; his writing opened a whole new dimension of poetic expression.

If you will take your own chart and look into the transits of Uranus, you may be surprised. The cycle of Uranus is eighty-four years. Roughly, Uranus will square its own place when one is twenty-one and oppose its own place by the age of forty-two. Its trines (120 degrees) are always creative times.

It may sound as if Uranus were a disruptive process. It is whenever it is not functioning at its proper level. If one wakes up at the right time, then exciting things begin to open up in the psyche, and new awareness develops.

You might guess that astrology comes under the rulership of Uranus, whose process gives intuitive capacity to recognize extraordinary connections on many levels of reality. Uranus represents another way of thinking, another way of perceiving, and a spontaneous approach to symbolism. It connects us directly to the transpersonal Unconscious.

Do you remember those puzzles where the task is to find the hidden faces in a tree or hidden animals in a scene? This is what Uranus takes for granted: it perceives things within other things. Nature becomes a gigantic Rorschach Test.

Uranus and Neptune provide a bridge into other dimensions of being. It is as if the Third Eye is beginning to open and one sees the tree half in leaf and half in flame. For example, Van Gogh's paintings fairly leap to life off the canvas—they convey such a powerful reality hidden within what to others was merely everyday Arles. I hope you "intuit" what I am trying to say. Uranus goes faster than words, by far. If you read poetry, you will be forced to another level of perception within yourself; reading a chart is like that, because the images surface spontaneously.

Uranus's process is never dangerous if it can be grounded and integrated into everyday life. Then it is at its best, bringing new solutions to problems or to lives, which like mine, were stuck. Jung's essay "On the Transcendent Function" is an example of how the process works in the psyche: a seemingly hopeless situation, a deadlock of opposites, is forced by its very nature to triangulate and find a solution at another level. All the more reason to carry the opposites as consciously, even if painfully, as possible.

It is always fascinating to watch the way the spirit of the times changes. When these larger planets change signs, shifts in culture, custom, and taste occur. When I taught classes of children year in and year out, I discovered the classes were like vintages of wine, each with its own bouquet. The students would all share the larger planets, from Jupiter on out, and you could see the focus of enthusiasms and dislikes vary from year to year, just as clearly as do the songs on the hit-parade. Whenever Uranus enters a new sign, the effects of the sign will show a change. When in Libra, art and marriage customs changed; when in Scorpio, sexual mores changed; when in Sagittarius, religious outlooks; and so forth. Neptune ushers in trends, but Uranus brings abrupt changes.

I haven't mentioned the houses much as we have not discussed them in any detail, but needless to say the transits of Uranus through the various houses coincide with opposite ways of looking at the affairs of a given house. Thus it's safe to say that when Uranus transits the cusp of the Seventh House, issues pertaining to relationships are likely to be occupying the consciousness of the person. A need for a change is desired, and if not forthcoming, a sudden separation might become an issue. The important thing to remember is that one will have to see things from a different level or take the consequences.

In the body, Uranus would seem to rule the etheric body or the aura or field of energy surrounding all living things. I would speculate a connection to the *chi* meridians associated with acupuncture. We are only beginning, in the West, to accept these matters, and there is a long way to go—2,000 years, at least.

Well, my Uranian microwave is waiting to "zap" supper, so I will sign off my Uranian computer. The love, however, is real, no matter what the transits.

26
Neptune

Dear friend,

If you are familiar with *Winnie-the-Pooh*, you will recognize Uranus immediately in Tigger. Tigger, bouncy and irrepressible, who with his cheerful and unpredictable nature turns everything upside down. There is a quality of the harlequin, the kook, the coat of many colors, the Fool. Uranus is always the archetype to bring in some new way of looking at things. He is a sort of cosmic Jester, yet always detached.

This Uranian detachment reminds me of the toll machines on the turnpike which flash a green light saying "Thank you." Or a well-known New Age teacher who would write letters to his flock and sign them "with a divine radiance of love," even though they were mimeographed. That's transpersonal, all right!

We can see this detachment at work politically. Never before has the world been so concerned for the welfare of the common man. The various forms of government in the last two hundred years are all experiments in this direction: communism, socialism, and democracy. Even fascism started out that way. The trap, of course, is that of Leo, the opposite sign that rules monarchy. "Le Roi Soleil," the Royal Sun, becomes the Shadow, and no matter how hard the idealistic Uranus tries, an elite group rises to the top and spoils the whole idea. "Men were created equal, but some were created more equal than others." We take this literally and forget that the possibility for the process of individuation is what makes us equal: we all really do have an equal chance to become ourselves, as infinite variations of the One.

The traps of Uranus are many, but the worst is brilliance without feeling. It shows in technology the world over, which knows how to build slicker machines for life and for death, but all too often remains unguided by wisdom, reverence, or compassion. Machines print welfare checks and send them out by Social Security numbers; no love or *caritas* is enclosed. Then we wonder why people languish, loot in times of trouble, and resort to crime. What is missing is the human touch, the personal expression of transpersonal love, *through people*, not equipment. Mother Teresa summed up the task for the New Age in one sentence, when she said, "I believe in person to person [Leo] and that God is in everyone" [Aquarius]. It is for this very reason I find it necessary to write these letters to *you*, a real, live, and wonderful individual, a friend. As you so wisely remarked, this is the feminine way of relating.

I mention this by way of introducing our next transSaturnian planet, Neptune. It provides the yin, the feminine balancing process to Uranus. Uranus is electric, Neptune, magnetic.

Neptune's process dissolves boundaries, just as Uranus breaks them, and so it, too, goes beyond Saturn's limitations. In the initial stages of our experience with this process, we may easily find ourselves lost in an unmarked wilderness. Let me give you a list of things both positive and negative that Neptune is said to rule and see if you can find the essence of its functioning: clouds, perfumes, incense, drugs, alchohol, photography, television, movies, plastics, rubber, chemicals, fumes, gases, ether, music, poetry, inspiration, illusion, delusion, swamps, the Unconscious, dreams, visions, memories, martyrdom, musing, wishing, yearning, iridescence, oceans, foam, echoes, chanting, prayer, swaying, intoxication, hypnosis, spells, lassitude, laziness, impressions, smells, smoke, sacrifice, masochism, immolation, sorcery, veils, mysteries, pastels, oils, images, clowns, pathos, self-pity, paintings, addictions, fanaticisms, sleep, bliss, mysticism, meditation, dissolutions, absolutions, erasures; in music, Indian ragas, Debussy's "La Mer," or Ralph Vaughn Williams; in art, Leonardo Da Vinci, French impressionism, Turner, the drawings of Kahlil Gibran.

The process is the subtle changing and shifting of consciousness. Negatively, it is the attraction of lapsing back into narcoleptic unconsciousness. Today's drug addict or alcoholic is often a mystic manqué who confuses tuning in, tuning out, and dropping out with the real thing—the bliss of *samadhi*. Here Neptune in the chart can be a potent danger. Psychologically, the lack of realism, the passivity, and the desire to escape, dissolve, or die all come under the afflictions of negative Neptune.

Let me give an example. I will mention only those planets dealing with the complex:

This young man appeared to embody the neat, quiet Virgo of his ascendant. Yet the Sun in Sagittarius in the Fourth House indicated that much of who he really was remained purposefully hidden. When I said this, he smiled enigmatically. Then we got to the extraordinary T-square involving the Moon conjunct Uranus in Cancer opposed to Venus in Capricorn in the Fifth and squared by Neptune exactly conjunct Saturn in Libra. The image arising from the chart was that of a man fascinated by unusual and Circe-like women. Such a one would be passive, half-drowsing, lying back while they put him under exotic sexual spells. This turned out to be precisely the case. My client had been involved with a number of powerful and seductive women, and felt helpless in dealing with them. He was working at a small occult book store, actually a center of attraction for witchcraft. He was both attracted to and repelled by this. Only the previous week a man had come in and whispered, "Do you have any candles made of human fat?"

He pleaded for help. Something, I confess, gave me the courage to roar at him in no uncertain terms. I told him this was a case of life and death; it was as if he were drugged and needed to wake up before spiraling down into destruction. I warned him that if he did not leave the bookstore immediately, and if he did not assert himself and address this complex, he would be doomed. This shook us both up. Finally, I mentioned a novel Jung often referred to, one which described this man's psychological situation, but that, alas, he was probably too young ever to have heard of. "What book is that?" he asked. "*She* by Rider Haggard," I replied.

There was a stunned silence. And then the young man said, "Not only do I know the book, I illustrated it a year ago when I was working for a pulp magazine." (He later sent me a copy.)

This synchronicity affected him deeply. He held open his hands and asked me what he should do. I suggested that he go into a Jungian analysis as quickly as possible. With whom? How to go about this?

It so happened that, quite by chance, that a gifted woman analyst was waiting for me in the next room. I asked if he would like to meet her. He nodded, and so I fetched her and introduced them. He asked for an appointment, and they made the earliest one possible—on Hallowe'en!

The story has a very happy ending. The young man quit the job, broke up the relationship, went back to his university and majored in psychology. He kept up the analysis, paying more for it, at his own request, as he gradually could afford it. Today he is married and well into a new and constructive life.

The keys here are the powerful aspects of Neptune, Uranus, and Saturn, and the overwhelming impact on the "feminine," the Moon and Venus. For such a young person, it would have been almost impossible to hear all that with "spiritual" ears. Remember, a chart describes the way one is likely to process experience. His life was the unconscious way he was suffering his chart. What enabled him to reverse the situation was becoming conscious and taking charge, rather than perceiving himself a passive victim of "She." Also helpful was the discriminating Virgo and Jupiter in Taurus, which when undrugged could give him common-sense and stability. I have the most profound respect for this young man and for the analyst, to say nothing of the unfathomable mystery which brought him to an astrological analysis and to her in the first place.

It is as important for the therapist to understand Neptune's process as to understand that of Uranus. Negative Neptune can distort and delude; reality can seem as weird as the reflections of crazy mirrors in a fun house. The person is often hazy, woolly-minded, ungrounded, and unfocused. There can be a starry-eyed gentleness and sweetness—Hamlet's Ophelia or the lovers in Bergman's "Elvira Madigan." The sacrificial pathos of a Camille or poor Mimi in *La Bohème* would be other examples.

In fact, coincidental with the discovery of Neptune came the flowering of the romantic period in art, literature, and music. It plumbed the tragic sacrificial nature of romantic love, with images of lovers entwined in death, and gave us the searing melodious beauty poured into music by Beethoven, Brahms, Schubert, and others. The whole period moved into a minor key. All this is intensely Neptunian.

In science, ether was discovered, photography invented, and Freud turned his eye to the inner images of dreams. The mechanical Newtonian universe gave way to fields of energy; the world shimmered and swayed in its release from the corsets of rationalism. Or look at impressionist art, or listen to Satie and Debussy, and feel how Neptune seeps through Saturnian measures and rigid structures into a suffusion of color and feeling.

Neptune also brought changes in philosophy, as Eastern philosophy finally reached Europe, and later America with the Transcendentalists.

The transits of Neptune aspecting a planet are the equivalent of a "fog attack." One simply cannot fold up a cloud and put it in a drawer. This is very threatening to people with a lot of common sense. When Mercury is affected, one becomes absent-minded, misplaces things, and forgets. This is downright humiliating. I can see now my client who was an older woman suffering a transit of Neptune over her Sun and Mercury. She was afraid she was becoming senile because she couldn't remember anything. Indeed, she couldn't pay me, she had forgotten her checkbook, and to her horror she recalled that she was to meet a friend at a restaurant, but couldn't remember which one! I was able to reassure her that this would pass—slowly, to be sure.

When Neptune transits Venus, one is apt to fall hopelessly in love with someone unobtainable. The love has to be spiritualized, like St. Francis and St. Clare. If it transits Saturn, there is a real chance to dissolve old patterns and rigidities. If Saturn, on the other hand, transits Neptune, it is time to manifest and materialize one's ideals. Do you get the distinction?

Wherever Neptune is, there will be a yearning and a potential for fanatic attachment. There is now a whole generation of middle-aged people with Neptune in Virgo: the "Granola generation." They are the ones who have blown the whistle on food additives and pollution, and have become so diet conscious sometimes they make themselves sick worrying about what they eat and drink.

When Neptune moved into Sagittarius in the late 1960s and 1970s, new interest in religions and meditation sprang up, and we also began to see joggers (Sagittarius rules the thighs and running). With Neptune there, running became almost a religious experience. People spoke of "highs" and altered states of consciousness. The entire hippie generation, the flower children, psychedelic art, the Beatles, the drug culture, passive TV watching, and the peace movement with its stress on nonviolence and universal love are all expressions of Neptunian process.

The period when Neptune was in Libra brought new approaches to relationships and sexual mores, dissolving previous conventions of marriage. When Neptune entered Scorpio, issues of abortion and gay rights emerged, requiring the dissolution of centuries of public opinion.

I hope you can see the collective effect of Uranus and Neptune. It really is extraordinary how the shift is already taking place. In this age, hopefully, we will continue to do things voluntarily, not because we are forced to by fear or greed. Nobody forced people to show up at Woodstock, nor at subsequent peace demonstrations, nor to open hundreds of self-realization centers and conferences. No one is forcing us to individuate. This is real progress.

I am reminded of the story of Rabia, the Sufi. One day, she ran through the streets with a candle in one hand and a bowl of water in the other. When asked why she was doing it, she replied, "I want to burn up heaven with my candle, and quench the fires of hell with this water. Then, perhaps, people will love God for Himself alone!"

Neptune now enters the sign of Capricorn, and we will see another shift, one that should last till the end of this century. It should come in our approach to nature. We will need to acknowledge the presence of consciousness in nature. Maybe, at long last, we will see our earth as holy, and come to love and cherish the imminence of the goddess who is the personification of nature. I certainly hope so.

Not long ago I had a dream that seemed possibly prophetic. I dreamt of a church with a lovely conventional spire. I saw it from a distance. It was placed in the center of a huge crystalline astral cathedral which encompassed the whole world. What was so breathtaking was that the delicate geometric lattice work was alive and "breathing." Can man let God out of the Church and into the world?

Neptune is the higher octave of Venus, and so it offers a new capacity for transpersonal love. Its archetype is the Mystic, the Sage. The coniunctio in the psyche of both Uranus and Neptune could result in the true Guru. The great savior figures in history and especially the sacrificial figure of Jesus, are obvious examples.

Merlin of the Arthurian tales is a mythic example, as is Gandalf in Tolkien's saga. Perhaps, we should add the extraterrestial Seth, of the "Seth Material." Jung encountered him and personified him as Philemon. The difference between "the Wise Old Man" of Saturn and that of Neptune is that Neptune is a guide in the spiritual dimension, a psychopomp. Neptune speaks to us of transpersonal love, of agape. It shines out of the faces of saints. It points archetypically to the trinity of power guided by love and wisdom. Jung's encounter with Philemon has that quality.

Nor are there only masculine examples. The returning goddess carries it, too—Tara, Kuan Yin, and the Virgin Mary.

All those who live out Buddha's injunction to have unending compassion for all sentient beings, those who show understanding and mercy as well as wisdom and strength—they are the ones expressing the process of Neptune in its fullest and most spiritual sense. A Mother Teresa, for instance, grounds this and connects it to relentless service to others. "We can do no great things," she says, "only little things with great love." That's Neptune.

Here we find the combining of the higher consciousness that Uranus represents with that tender compassion of unconditional love. When these can be connected to and grounded in the individual—body, mind, and soul—then we will have found heaven on earth.

Love,

27
More on Neptune, and we meet Pluto

Dear friend,

The glyph of Neptune is appropriately that of the triton.

$$\Psi$$

You can see that here the crescent is pierced by the cross, a symbol of sacrifice.

The trans-Saturnian planets appear to rule the subtle bodies and perhaps have connections to the pineal and pituitary glands. When I was in Ganeshpuri in India, at the ashram of Swami Muktananda, I learned the purpose of the endless chanting that went on there and all over India. I was told that the repetition of certain sounds has an effect upon the pituitary gland, causing it to release a "nectar" that affects consciousness, as well as the energy of the bodies, subtle and physical.

Only recently in *Brain/Mind Bulletin* there was an article concerning Gregorian chanting and its effects on the energy of the monks. In one abbey, they cut down on the chanting to save time and found that this had a deleterious effect. R.I.L.K.O. has found that during the Middle Ages the architecture of certain churches and cathedrals was specifically designed to coincide with Gregorian chants in certain keys, so that a physical and harmonic resonance could raise the level of consciousness of the people participating in the rituals. Certainly, the work of Hans Jenny in "cymatics" would seem to bear this out. The implication is that there is a relationship between physical containers and their contents. This kind of thinking is at the same time new and yet old. It is forcing science to another level.

We now come to Pluto. Neptune takes approximately 164 years to orbit the Sun, and Pluto takes 247.7 years. You can see why these planets function more at the collective than the personal level. They don't move much in an individual's chart. Neptune was discovered in 1846, and Pluto in 1930. We have not yet been able to observe a whole orbit for either of them, though we certainly saw the historical synchronicities retroactively with Uranus and Neptune.

You may wonder how astrologers decide on the nature of the process of a newly discovered planet. It seems to me that it is a slow and gradual determination arising from careful observation. In the case of Uranus and Neptune, the synchronicity with historic events makes their natures quite clear (by hindsight). Pluto's nature is, in my opinion, not fully understood. So far, much of what has been revealed has been negative and downright fearsome. Yet we must remember that this planet, too, is part of the solar family and, therefore, has an important role to play.

Pluto was discovered in 1930 and its symbol named for Percival Lowell. Its glyph is variously given as:

In America, we favor the first, though symbolically the second shows the mandala of spirit in the chalice of sacrifice. In my opinion, it may be too soon to assess Pluto as a process in the individual psyche. So far, we seem to have experienced much of the dark side and little of the positive, which means our "spiritual ears" are not yet attuned. But there are hints.

Hades, the Greek equivalent of Pluto, also means *wealth*. In mythology both gods rule the underworld. Hell, in the Middle Ages, was literally pictured underground, which may account for the distaste people projected onto matter— an unfortunate idea, to say the least!

Psychologically, though, we know that we must go down

into the Unconscious to find the "wealth" hidden there. Though Freud discovered the personal unconscious, he had difficulty in accepting Jung's theory of the Collective Unconscious. Jung felt that we have to go through and confront our own Shadow and repressed demons (complexes) in our personal unconscious, but that at the same time we are being helped and healed by the archetypal contents of the Collective Unconscious. For him here is the accumulated "wealth" of wisdom of all life from the beginning. Its language is stored in the mythologies and religions of the world and speaks to us through archetypal figures and symbols. Ira Progoff's simile of the Collective Unconscious cannot be surpassed: it is like the water table which feeds each of our individual wells. Our psyches are fed by a common wellspring.

It is possible that Pluto rules the "personal unconscious" of the collective, and that we have to deal with and integrate the cumulative crimes of hate, fear, anger, greed, and the abuse of power, of nature and of sexuality perpetrated throughout history. These are our collective complexes and, like an international debt, each of us carries a share. Pluto's process is severe. It teaches that there is a difference between nature's laws and the ego's moral laws. Cosmic law is absolute, and nature stronger than we are. But we forget. As Jung has pointed out, our greatest enemy is ourselves. The retribution is implacable. We must learn or suffer the consequences.

This could be why we have such negative associations with Pluto's process. Collectively, we have witnessed the unspeakable atrocities of the Holocaust, a global war ending with the explosion of two atom bombs made of "plutonium," and now we face the increasing threats of nuclear war, transpersonal death through terrorism, and the potential plague of AIDS. Each of the above is associated with negative Pluto, and each could have been avoided if humanity as a whole had continued to hold nature sacred and holy, and if we had seen and respected the presence of Spirit in each other, as our "Teachers" over the centuries have enjoined us to do. Our most distinguishing and precious gift, as human beings, is consciousness, and yet more and more of us are throwing it away with drugs and alcohol. The puzzle is, Why? Is it a need to escape the crushing banality, as Jung mentioned, of a meaningless life?

When an individual is neurotic, usually the personal unconscious sends up a warning in the form of nightmares. Too many nightmares will eventually drive a person to seek help in analysis, and the Pandora's box of the personal unconscious is carefully opened. (The butterfly of hope, I presume, is still there.)

I think Pluto's process has surfaced, now that we are ready to be more conscious and willing, with the help of Uranus and Neptune, to deal with the collective. He rules the collective nightmare we are seeing acted out: the "Hades" around us wherever there is rejection and desecration of the gifts given us with life itself. Pluto will insist that we integrate our collective Shadow and our international complexes. We have no other choice. Nuclear accidents like the one in Russia at Chernobyl in 1986 are warnings that *all* life is affected. Our neighbor is ourself.

Pluto in the individual chart points to transformation and where it will come from. His process is that of *enantiodromia*, that sudden flip of polarity which is the result of excess in one direction. An example is the Inquisition where, in seeking the devil in others, the devil walked into the inquisitors. Our fortunes can change in the twinkling of an eye.

The conversion of St. Paul is Plutonian in its suddenness. You will remember that Saul was a consistent persecutor of the followers of Jesus Christ. Then he witnessed the heroic death of Stephen, who was accused of blasphemy and stoned to death. Yet Stephen prayed for the very ones who were killing him. The incident haunted Saul. But he continued on his way to Damascus to get permission to imprison any followers of Jesus. And the well-known story goes on:

> As he journeyed, he came near Damascus: and suddenly there shined round about him a light from heaven: and he fell to the earth, and heard a voice saying unto him, "Saul, Saul, why persecutest thou me?"

Saul was blinded for three days afterwards. Ananias, a follower of Jesus, restored his sight by the laying-on of hands, as instructed by the voice of the Lord.

> And immediately there fell from his eyes as it had been scales: and he received sight forthwith, and arose and was baptized.

This kind of transformation by Pluto is very alchemical, because it shows that the "gold" of the Self can precipitate only after it has made the descent into the *nigredo,* the dark mixture of ash, muck and feces which is the garbage of centuries. It is our collective *prima materia,* in which the "wealth" is hidden. How can this opus be performed? Jung has suggested that it will come through each of us working on our own Shadow. In so doing, we bless the world with a bit more released light of consciousness.

Pluto rules mistletoe, and it was in Norse mythology that this parasitical plant was considered so harmless that Odin did not exact a promise from it not to hurt his son, the Solar Hero Baldur. Baldur was killed by the blind Hoder with an arrow made of mistletoe, guided by the Plutonian Loki. Yet today we kiss under mistletoe at Yuletide.

This myth was prophetic because so much of the evil done to the Self and to that of others through history has been done blindly, often in the very name of religion, as I have mentioned before. Yet the religions have at their heart the commandments not to kill, but to love one another. Pah!

How do we handle this? One way is to remember that Pluto, too, reflects the Sun. Collectively, we have a Self to whom we have given the name God. This *deus absconditus,* the Hidden God, remains the Unknown Ground of our being. We are like atoms making up His/Her body of light. It passes understanding, but, at least, we can remember to lead a "symbolic life."

For some, this could involve "the circulation of the light," a yogic process by which energy is spiraled through the glands, descending from the highest to the lowest in the body, making them one. (Pluto rules the gonads [Scorpio].)

This is described for us in the Chinese masterpiece *The Secret of the Golden Flower,* to which Jung wrote an introduction. For most of us, the process is hidden in our own charts. To work on one's own shortcomings, honestly and with humility and perseverance, is the opus, the Work. If we take one step, help already appears. Look at the position of Pluto by house and by aspect—a whole generation will share the sign—to see where and how individual transformation could take place. When Pluto is afflicted or "afflicts," redemption may be a harrowing experience rather than a sweet one. Whichever way, it will mean integrating our dark side, making a pet of the wolf at the door, and letting our black sheep graze with the white ones. The witch gets to come to the birthday party along with the good fairies, and we stop denying those parts of us that otherwise continually betray us. Our job is not to deny them, but just keep them in sight.

The myths of the underworld, of Hades, of the kingdoms of Set in Egypt and of Arawn in Wales are all expressions of Pluto's process. The message is clear: we have to go down before we go up. Dante's Inferno came before his Paradiso.

Pluto is now in its own sign, Scorpio, and with ever-increasing intensity, we seem to be confronting matters of desecration: the effects of death-dealing chemicals, pesticides, pollution of the earth; child abuse, molestation, and sexual promiscuity without love. Controversial issues such as abortion and genetic mutation also belong here.

Psychologically, some women may seem to have "Plutonian" animuses, as did the dread goddess of the Sumerian underworld, Ereshkigal. This manifests itself also in the archetype of the Ice Queen, the implacably cold-hearted bitch, or the would-be murderer of Snow White. These are the castrating mothers or women guards in concentration camps and some prisons—and even boarding-schools. In turn, some men have "Plutonian" animas, like Erishkegal. The depiction of this process is powerfully illustrated in the book *Descent to the Goddess* by Sylvia Perera!

We have to be able to distinguish between Saturn's process and that of Pluto. Saturn is passive; it is a yin planet. Pluto is active. What we have yet to learn is how to render this process positive. It will be a fateful struggle in years to come. We have to recognize fully and responsibly that we have an enemy, and "the enemy is us." Jung has warned that the future of the entire world hangs on the slender thread of the individual psyche.

I would like to end this letter with a dream about Jungian analyst Edward J. Edinger, which I am quoting with permission from the dreamer. It seems relevant:

> I come to Dr. Edinger's office in New York. When I enter the door, I find the curtains drawn and the room darkened, except for one point of light on his desk, which is more brilliant than any light I have ever seen in real life. Slowly I approach the desk, where he is seated. As my eyes become accustomed, I see that the light is a fire that is burning freely inside a glass vessel of water. An impossibility!
>
> I gasp, and Dr. Edinger smiles and looks quite pleased. "The energy here is the strongest force on earth. It is a secret weapon that could make any country the most powerful on earth. In fact," he adds, "some people from the Pentagon are about to arrive to look at it."
>
> No sooner does he say this than a knock comes on the door. A group of about ten men in military uniform enter. They are from the various Armed Forces. As a group, they too gasp and exclaim at the brilliant point of light burning in the water.
>
> Very solemnly, Dr. Edinger repeats what he had told me. The men crowd around to get a better look. They cannot bear to get too close. Finally, a general asks, "What do you call it?"
>
> Dr. Edinger stands very straight and looks at each man in turn. In a low voice he answers the question. "I call it Love."
>
> There is a stunned silence. Then the men burst out, "But we can't call it that at the *Pentagon!!!*"
>
> True.
>
> Dr. Edinger turns to them again and quietly says, "In that case, gentlemen, good day."

Surely, one of our privileges is that we can find and use this "secret weapon." I think Pluto will force us, hopefully before it is too late, to find it in the alembic of our hearts. In the end, this process of Pluto may yet turn out to be our benefactor. And, at long last, under the bitter dregs of pain in the chalice, we will find precipitated the reborn Self, that great triune pearl of love, wisdom, and true power.

Love again,

28
Envoi

Well, dearest friend, I want to thank you for this whole rich experience and the opportunity of sharing in these letters. This is but a primer on astrology, a touching of the hem, which you with your greater knowledge of Jung, and with your clinical experience, can take so much further as the years go by. It has been my intention throughout to show how helpful astrology can be not only to therapists, but to anyone interested in thinking symbolically.

I close this correspondence with my favorite prayer, whose source is unknown to me:

> O, Master, let me touch
> as many lives as possible
> for thee,
> and every life I touch
> do thou by thy Holy Spirit
> quicken
> whether through
>   the words I speak
>   the words I write
>   the prayer I breathe
>   or the life I lead.
> I ask this in thy name.
>
>   Amen
>
>   Ever yours,

Bibliography

Addey, John M. 1976. *Harmonics in astrology*. Green Bay, WI: Cambridge Circle, Ltd.

Albertson, Charles, ed. 1932. *Lyra mystica: an anthology of mystical verse*. New York: Macmillan.

Ardalan, Nader, and Laleh Bakhtiar. 1973. *The sense of unity: the Sufi tradition in Persian architecture*. Chicago: University of Chicago Press.

Arroyo, Stephen. 1976. *Astrology, psychology, and the four elements*. Davis, CA: CRCS Publications.

_____. 1978. *Astrology, karma, and transformation*. Davis, CA: CRCS Publications.

Assagioli, Roberto. 1976. *Psychosynthesis: a manual of principles and technology*. New York: Penguin Books.

Augros, Robert M., and G.N. Stanciu. 1984. *The new story of science*. Lake Bluff, IL: Regnery Gateway.

Augustine, Saint. 1943. *Confessions*. New York: Sheed and Ward.

Blair, Lawrence. 1976. *Rhythms of vision*. New York: Schocken.

Blake, William. 1936. *Poems*. W.B. Yeats, ed. New York: The Modern Library.

Bohm, David. 1957. *Causality and chance in modern physics*. Philadelphia: University of Pennsylvania Press.

The book of common prayer. 1892. Oxford: Oxford University Press.

Boswell, Winthrop Palmer. *Roots of Irish monasticism*, Ph.D. Dissertation. Ann Arbor: University of Michigan.

Bord, Janet and Colin. 1973. *Mysterious Britain*. New York: Granada.

Buber, Martin. 1970. *I and thou*. New York: Scribners.

Bunyan, John. 1965. *Pilgrim's progress*. New York: Viking.

Campbell, Joseph. 1959. *The masks of god, vol. I: primitive mythology.* New York: Viking

———. 1962. *The masks of god, vol. II: oriental mythology.* New York: Viking

———. 1964. *The masks of god, vol. III: occidental mythology.* New York: Viking

———. 1968. *The masks of god, vol. IV: creative mythology.* New York: Viking

———. 1974. *The mythic image.* Princeton: Princeton University Press. Bollingen Series C.

Capra, Fritjof. 1975. *The tao of physics.* Boulder, CO: Shambala.

Carpenter, Edward. 1883. *Towards democracy.* Folcroft, PA: Folcroft.

Charpentier, Louis. 1966. *The mysteries of Chartres cathedral.* London: Research into Lost Knowledge Organization.

Chaucer, Geoffrey. 1952. *The Canterbury tales.* Nevill Coghill, tr. Baltimore: Penguin.

Chevalier, Jean, and Alain Gheerbrant, eds. 1973. *Dictionnaire des symboles.* Paris: Seghers.

Corbin, Henri. 1977. *Spiritual body and celestial earth.* Princeton: Princeton University Press.

Critchlow, Keith. 1977. *Earth mysteries.* London: R.I.L.K.O.

Dante Alighieri. 1962. *The divine comedy,* vols. I-III. Dorothy Sayers, tr. New York: Viking.

Edinger, Edward F. 1972. *Ego and archetype: individuation and the religious function of the psyche.* New York: G.P. Putnam.

———. 1985. *Anatomy of the psyche.* La Salle, IL: Open Court.

Eliade, Mircea. 1958. *Rites and symbols of initiation: the mysteries of birth and rebirth.* New York: Harper & Row.

Eliot, T.S. 1971. *The complete poems and plays 1909-1950.* New York: Harcourt, Brace & World.

The epic of Gilgamesh. 1960. English version by N.K. Sandars. Baltimore: Penguin.

Fox, Matthew. 1980. *Breakthrough: Meister Eckhart's creation spirituality in new translation.* Garden City, NJ: Doubleday.

———. 1983. *Meditations with Meister Eckhart.* Santa Fe, NM: Sun Bear & Co.

Freeman, Katherine. 1971. *Ancilla to the pre-Socratic philosophers.* Oxford: Basil Blackwell.

Goethe, Wolfgang von. 1962. *Faust.* Walter Kaufmann, tr. Garden City, NJ: Anchor Books, Doubleday.

The gospel according to Thomas. 1959. Guillamont et al., tr. New York: Harper & Brothers.

Greene, Liz. 1976. *Saturn: a new look at an old devil.* New York: Samuel Weiser.

Grof, Stanislav. 1975. *Realms of the human unconscious*. New York: Viking.

Guggenbuhl-Craig, Adolf. 1976. *Power in the helping professions*. Zurich: Spring Publications.

Haggard, Rider. 1976. *She*. St. Louis: River City Publ.

Hall, Manly P. 1945. *The secret teachings of all ages: an encyclo-pedic outline of masonic, hermetic, qabbalistic, and rosicrucian symbolical philosophy*. Los Angeles: Philosophical Research Society Press.

Hall, Nor. 1980. *The moon and the virgin*. New York: Harper & Row.

Hand, Robert. 1976. *Planets in transit*. Rockport, MA: Para Research.

Hannah, Barbara. 1976. *Jung: his life and work*. New York: G.P. Putnam.

Harding, M. Esther. 1971. *Women's mysteries, ancient and modern*. New York: G.P. Putnam.

Hartmann, Franz. 1932. *The life and doctrines of Paracelsus*. New York: Macoy Publ. Co.

Hitching, Francis. 1977. *Earth magic*. New York: Simon & Schuster.

The holy Bible: King James version. 1928. Oxford: Oxford University Press.

I ching—book of changes. 1961. Richard Wilhelm and Cary Baynes, tr. Bollingen series XIX. Princeton: Princeton University Press.

Jaffe, Aniela. 1984. *Jung's last years and other essays*. Dallas: Spring Publications.

Jaynes, Julian. 1976. *The origin of consciousness in the breakdown of the bicameral mind*. Boston: Houghton Mifflin.

Jenny, Hans. 1967. *Kymatik/cymatics*. Basel: Basilius Presse.

_____. 1974. *Cymatics Vol. II*. Basel: Basilius Presse.

Jobes, Gertrude. 1962. *Dictionary of mythology, folklore, and sym-bols*. New York: The Scarecrow Press, Inc.

Jones, Marc Edmund. 1960. *The essentials of astrological analysis*. Stanwood: Sabian Publ.

_____. 1972. *The guide to horoscope interpretation*. Wheaton, IL: Theosophical Publishing House.

Joy, Brugh. 1978. *Joy's way*. Los Angeles: J.P. Tarcher.

Jung, Carl Gustav. 1953-1979. *The collected works*. R.F.C. Hull, tr. Bollingen Series, 20 vols. Princeton: Princeton University Press.

_____. 1963. *Memories, dreams, reflections*. New York: Pan-theon Books.

215

_____. 1973. Letters, vols I, II: 1906-1981. R.F.C. Hull, tr. Gerhard Adler and Aniela Jaffe, eds. Bollingen series XCV:1. Princeton: Princeton University Press.

Kant, Immanuel. 1951. *Ausgewahlte schriften*. Sigbert Mohn Verlag.

Kingsford, Anna Bonus. 1924. *The perfect way or the finding of Christ*. New York: Masonic Publishing Co.

Kipling, Rudyard. 1929. *The jungle book*. London: Macmillan.

Koestler, Arthur. 1972. *The roots of coincidence*. New York: Random House.

Kramcr, Noah. 1959. *History begins at Sumer*. Garden City, NJ: Doubleday Anchor Books.

Krishna, Gopi. 1967. *Kundalini: the evolutionary energy in man*. Boulder, CO: Shambala Press.

Michell, John. 1983. *The new view over Atlantis*. London: Thames & Hudson.

Milne, A.A. 1949. *Winnie-the-pooh*. New York: E.P. Dutton.

_____. 1950. *The house at pooh corner*. New York: E.P. Dutton.

Neumann, Erich. 1954. *Origins and history of consciousness*. Bollingen series XLII. Princeton: Princeton University Press.

_____. 1955. *The great mother: an analysis of the archetype*. Bollingen series XLVII. Princeton: Princeton University Press.

_____. 1973. "On the moon and matriarchal consciousness," *Fathers and mothers*. Pat Berry, ed. Hildegard Nagel, tr. Zurich: Spring Publ.

Origen. 1956. *The song of songs, commentary and homilies*. R.P. Lawson, tr. Ancient christian writers. vol.26. New York: Newman Press.

Pagels, Elaine. 1978. *The gnostic gospels*. New York: Random House.

Paracelsus. 1969. *Selected writings*. Jolande Jacobi, ed. Bollingen series XXVIII. Princeton: Princeton University Press.

Perera, Sylvia Brinton. 1981. *Descent to the goddess: a way of initiation for women*. Toronto: Inner City Books.

Rama, Swami and Rudolf Ballantine. 1976. *Yoga and psychotherapy*. Honesdale, PA: Himalayan Institute.

Robinson, James M., gen. ed. 1977. *The Nag Hammadi library in English*. New York: Harper & Row.

Rosenblum, Bernard. 1982. *Astrologer's guide to counseling: astrology's role in the helping professions*. Reno, NV: CRCS.

Rowley, George. 1959. *Principles of Chinese painting*. Princeton: Princeton University Press.

Rudhyar, Dane. 1970. *The astrology of personality*. Garden City, NJ: Doubleday.

Schiller, Friedrich von. Undated. *Schiller's werke*. Ludwig Bellermann, ed. Leipzig: Bibliographisches Institut.

The secret of the golden flower. 1931. Richard Wilhelm, tr. New York: Harcourt Brace.

Shakespeare, William. Undated. *The complete works*. London: Collins.

Sheldrake, Rupert. 1981. *A new science of life: the hypothesis of formative causation*. London: Blond & Briggs.

Stevenson, Ian. 1974. *Twenty cases suggestive of reincarnation*. Charlottesville, VA: University Press of Virginia.

Teilhard de Chardin, Pierre. 1955. *The phenomenon of man*. New York: Harper & Row.

_____. 1968. *The divine milieu*. New York: Harper & Row.

Thom, Alexander. 1967. *Megalithic sites in Britain*. London: Oxford University Press.

The Upanishads. 1949. Swami Nikhilananda, tr. New York: Harper & Row.

Van Doren, Mark, ed. 1928. *An anthology of world poetry*. New York: Literary Guild of America.

Van Waaveren, Erlo. 1978. *Pilgrimage to rebirth*. York Beach, ME: Weiser.

Von Franz, Marie Louise. 1980. *Projection and re-collection in Jungian psychology: reflections of the soul*. La Salle, IL: Open Court.

_____. 1981. *Puer aeternus*. Santa Monica, CA: Sigo Press.

Warner, Marina. 1976. *Alone of all her sex: the myth and cult of the virgin Mary*. New York: Viking.

Watson, Lyall. 1973. *Super nature*. New York: Bantam Books.

West, John Anthony, and Jan Gerhard Toonder. 1973. *The case for astrology*. Middlesex: Penguin.

Whitmont, Edward C. 1978. *The symbolic quest*. Princeton: Princeton University Press.

_____. 1980. *The return of the goddess*. New York: Crossroads.

Willcocks, David, and John Rutter, eds. *Carols for choirs*. 1970. London: Oxford University Press.

Wolff, Toni. 1956. *Structural forms of the feminine psyche*. Zurich: Privately printed for the students of the C.G. Jung Institut.

Yeats, William Butler. 1956. *The collected poems*. New York: Macmillan.

About the Author

Alice O. Howell has been a pioneer in linking psychology and astrology. She is an analytical astrologer and has counseled clients in that area for over forty years. A former faculty member of the C. G. Jung Foundation of New York and the C. G. Jung Institutes of Los Angeles and Chicago, she has lectured widely. She has given keynote addresses to the International Transpersonal Psychology Association and the Association for Transpersonal Psychology. Several universities and Jungian institutes have invited her to speak, and she has lectured to physicians and psychiatrists at Grand Rounds, both in this country and in London. She has conducted numerous seminars and workshops.

By the age of eighteen, the author had lived in or traveled to thirty-seven countries on four continents and undertaken the study of comparative religion, mythology, and literature. She earned the Deutsch Diplom at the Buser Institut in Switzerland and for many years taught English and world history. She has published a book of poetry, *The Song of Magdalen*, and has won several awards for her poetry. Now a grandmother, she lives with her husband in the Berkshires.

QUEST BOOKS
are published by
The Theosophical Society in America,
Wheaton, Illinois 60189-0270,
a branch of a world organization
dedicated to the promotion of brotherhood and
the encouragement of the study of religion,
philosophy, and science, to the end that man may
better understand himself and his place in
the universe. The Society stands for complete
freedom of individual search and belief.
In the Classics Series well-known
theosophical works are made
available in popular editions.

Quest publishes books on Healing, Health and Diet, Occultism and Mysticism, Philosophy, Transpersonal Psychology,, Reincarnation, Religion, The Theosophical Philosophy, Yoga and Meditation. Our other books on Astrology include:

Astrology: A New Age Guide *By Ed Perrone*
The evolution of the soul from an astrological point of view.

Astrology of Transformation *By Dane Rudhyar*
The distinguished occult-philosopher, composer, painter, offers a four-step approach to psychology through astrology.

Guide to Horoscope Interpretation *By Marc Edmund Jones*
The "dean of American astrologers" presents the "whole view" of a horoscope using planetary patterns.

Principals of Astrology *By C.E.O. Carter*
An astrological classic that provides many basic and essential facts on charts and signs.

Twelve Doors to the Soul *By Jane Evans*
An astrology of the inner self. Incorporates the concept of a reincarnating ego.

Available from:
The Theosophical Publishing House
306 West Geneva Road, Wheaton, Illinois 60187

Sat
✓ Finish menu   ✓— Call
- fix Biz card   Mark
                              Hughes
- fix map
- go to printers   ✓— Call Diane
                              B.

✓ mt Bill Robtson   ✓Kathleen Cont[
✓ Paint stationary
✓ Finish reading june
      singer chapter

Sun
✓ Finish whitmont reading
✓ Fax info

Mon   — 2hrs
- Printers for brochure
+ Paint biz cards — 4hrs
      + brochure
        work
- Submission for unit 2

Tues
- Finish tarp info
- Caroline Casey
-

Wed am
- Tie up loose ends on tapes + first 2 of ITP

when

pers. — Asc
~~star~~
Self — sun — p.73 , p.75 better
Ego — Everything ~~tha~~ of } p.106
p.74 which we're
p.99 conscious

perhaps an intermediate
step — whole chart is
Jung's Self, but maybe
the Sun is ..... something
b'tron the 2

☉ ☿ ♂ — inf - reclaiming power;
the power of my ☉ in ♑ — which
is also intercepted